sifted

DIARY OF A GRIEVING MOTHER

KAREN HARMENING

LITTLE CRICKET
BOOKS

Sifted: Diary of a Grieving Mother
Copyright © 2024 by Karen Harmening
www.karenharmening.com

Published by Little Cricket Books
Huntsville, Alabama
www.littlecricketbooks.com

All rights reserved. No part of this book may be reproduced in any form or by any electronic or mechanical means, including information storage and retrieval systems, without written permission from the author, except for the use of brief quotations in a book review.

This work is a diary and depicts the author's perceptions of actual life events as truthfully as recollection permits and/or can be verified by research.

Unless otherwise noted, scripture quotations are taken from the (NASB®) New American Standard Bible®, Copyright © 1960, 1971, 1977, 1995, by The Lockman Foundation. Used by permission. All rights reserved. lockman.org

Scripture quotations marked ESV are from The ESV® Bible (The Holy Bible, English Standard Version®), © 2001 by Crossway, a publishing ministry of Good News Publishers. Used by permission. All rights reserved.

Scripture quotations marked NIV are taken from the Holy Bible, New International Version®, NIV®. Copyright © 1973, 1978, 1984, 2011 by Biblica, Inc.™ Used by permission of Zondervan. All rights reserved worldwide. zondervan.com The "NIV" and "New International Version" are trademarks registered in the United States Patent and Trademark Office by Biblica, Inc.™

Scripture quotations marked KJV from The Authorized (King James) Version. Rights in the Authorized Version in the United Kingdom are vested in the Crown. Reproduced by permission of the Crown's patentee, Cambridge University Press

Cover Design: Katherine Motta
Interior Artwork: Sarah Harmening

Library of Congress Control Number: 2024909263
ISBN 979-8-9905515-0-3 (casebound)
ISBN 979-8-9905515-1-0 (paperback)
ISBN 979-8-9905515-2-7 (ebook)

*To Scott, Katelyn, Kristen, and Sophie,
My steadfast valley companions.
You are deeply and indescribably loved.*

*Eagerly awaiting our reunion day with
Sarah Lauren Harmening,
Our "little cricket."*

CONTENTS

Foreword — xi
Preface — xv
Introduction — xvii

1. SUFFERING, ANGUISH AND REDEMPTION — 1
2. SORROWS LIKE SEA BILLOWS — 7
3. WHAT IF? — 10
4. WAVES OF AGONY AND GRACE — 15
5. THE HEZEKIAH YEARS — 19
6. LAYERS OF GRIEF AND LOVE — 23
7. "RESTORE TO ME" — 26
8. SWALLOWED UP BY LIFE — 29
9. ANOTHER MISSION TRIP — 32
10. WHY SARAH? WHY US? — 35
11. DEATH IS NOT GOOD — 40
12. NEW MERCY FOR TODAY — 43
13. WAITING IN THE PIT — 46
14. HEALING OR ADAPTING? — 48
15. INTERMINGLED JOY AND SUFFERING — 52
16. "HOW AWESOME IS THAT?" — 56
17. THE "LITTLE CRICKET" MARTYR — 60
18. SOWING IN TEARS — 65
19. LEARNING TO WALK — 68
20. SHELTER IN THE STORM — 72
21. ALL TO JESUS, I SURRENDER — 76
22. HEART, SOUL, AND MIND — 79
23. BROKEN HALLELUJAH — 82
24. THE SANITIZING OF GRIEF — 86
25. WAITING IN SOLITUDE — 90
26. SORROWFUL YET ALWAYS REJOICING — 96
27. THE STEWARDSHIP OF PAIN — 98
28. MY CHILD DIED. GOD IS GOOD? — 102
29. LONGING TO DIE — 105
30. NOT SO MERRY CHRISTMAS — 110
31. A MOTHER'S PAIN — 115

32. EXTRACTING THE PRECIOUS	118
33. MOMENT BY MOMENT	122
34. LAUGHTER IN THE VALLEY	126
35. RAINS OF REFRESHING	131
36. MORNING IS COMING	134
37. REDEEM MY PAIN, O GOD.	137
38. "FAKING FINE" IN THE MIDST OF GRIEF?	141
39. ALONE, YET NOT ALONE	145
40. THIS THORN OF MINE	148
41. THE GOD OF THE VALLEYS	152
42. TAKING HOLD OF HOPE	155
43. WHEN DELIVERANCE DOESN'T COME	158
44. WHEN GOD IS SILENT	162
45. DEATH'S STING IS RIGHT HERE, RIGHT NOW	165
46. I'M SUPPOSED TO BE STOIC?	169
47. "A STRANGER WITH THEE"	173
48. THE SECOND YEAR IS HARDER?	177
49. SOUL MELTING SORROW	182
50. REMEMBER MY CHAINS	189
51. HOPE FIXED COMPLETELY	194
52. WHY I WON'T SAY "CHOOSE JOY"	199
53. THE HYPOCRISY OF GRIEF	205
54. WALKING IN DARKNESS	210
55. THE VOICE OF THE LORD IN THE STORM	216
56. ABANDONMENT IN GRIEF	221
57. BE OF GOOD COURAGE	229
58. DO I REALLY BELIEVE?	234
59. STEADFAST	237
60. THE LINES HAVE FALLEN FOR ME	242
61. LONELY AND AFFLICTED	245
62. SERVE LIKE _____	252
63. EASTER IN THE SHADOW	256
64. SUNSHINE CHRISTIANITY & FORBIDDEN LAMENT	259
65. CHILD LOSS: THE SECOND YEAR	262
66. RESPONDING TO ABANDONMENT	273
67. FELLOW PARTAKERS	277
68. JUST KEEP TRYING	283
69. IN JUST A LITTLE WHILE	287
70. A STRANGER WITH A FRIEND'S FACE	290
71. SORROW LOOKS BACK	293

72. KEEP CRYING OUT AND TESTIFYING	297
73. A SWORD PIERCED SOUL	303
74. NOT A HAPPY BIRTHDAY	306
75. FLEEING FOR REFUGE	309
76. COMFORTED AND COMFORTING	313
77. PRAY BELIEVING	316
78. GRIEVING TOO LONG	320
79. WORSHIP IN AFFLICTION	325
80. GOOD FRIDAY AND SIBLINGS DAY	328
81. EAGERLY WAITING	331
82. HOPE AGAINST HOPE	335
83. THREE YEARS AGO TODAY	339
84. JOY INEXPRESSIBLE	345
85. PEACE BE WITH YOU	348
86. FACING DEATH	355
87. BLESSED MOURNER	360
88. HOPE GRIEVES	363
89. GRACE UPON GRACE	367
90. NESTLESS	369
91. A NEW SONG	373
92. HER FIFTH BIRTHDAY	376
93. FIVE YEARS: BEAUTY FOR ASHES	379
94. SUICIDE PREVENTION OR AWARENESS?	384
95. LONG AND NEW SORROW	387
96. THE CUP OF SALVATION	390
97. MISSING YOU TODAY ESPECIALLY	394
98. HER PRESENT ABSENCE	397
99. STILL TALKING ABOUT IT	400
100. SEVENTH YEAR SABBATH	405
Sarah Lauren Harmening	409
TOPICAL INDEX	413
Understanding & Navigating Grief	413
Hard Questions & Decisions	414
Loneliness & Abandonment	414
Spiritual Warfare & Perseverance	414
Hope	415
Redemption	415
Understanding & Finding Joy	416
Hard Days & Dates	416

FOREWORD

KEVIN J. MOORE

The Lord is My Shepherd…

"The Lord is my Shepherd…." These precious words have captivated the hearts and minds of believers around the world and have become one of the most beloved descriptions of God in all of Scripture. The promises of Psalm 23 have comforted and encouraged countless sojourners for thousands of years. What wonderful truths; that God will guide you, care for you, and provide for you all the days of your life. What a blessed thought that your Shepherd will lead you to green pastures and beside quiet waters.

It's easy enough to delight in God, our Good Shepherd, when times are good. But what if the unthinkable happens? What if tragedy strikes you at your core and leaves your heart shattered? What if your family is devastated by death and lives in excruciating emotional pain? Is there still hope in the Good Shepherd?

For some of you opening the pages of this book, these are not hypothetical questions but daily realities that leave you gasping for breath and desperate for hope.

On June 8, 2017, Sarah Harmening, a sweet, Jesus-loving seventeen-year-old, went to be with the Lord following a bus crash just

FOREWORD

outside of Atlanta. Her shocking and tragic death dealt a life-altering, crushing blow to her family, her close friends, and our beloved church. The horror and the sorrow of that day have been forever etched on my heart.

I remember hearing the news of Sarah's death while I was still pastoring in Arlington, Texas. I was in the process of transitioning to assume my new role as the Senior Pastor of Mount Zion Baptist Church in Huntsville, Alabama when I received the call.

I flew to Atlanta and met with Scott, Karen, Katelyn, Kristen, and Sophie in the hotel where they were staying only hours after the crash. What I recall from that night is that, even during the immediate aftermath of this horrible tragedy, the Harmening family was clinging to their Good Shepherd. Amidst the tears and the overwhelming sorrow, there was a palpable sense of an unshakeable faith in the God of Psalm 23. In their desperation, God gave them a faith larger and stronger than the horror of what had happened to Sarah. In the epicenter of the darkest moment in their entire lives, they were trusting in the Good Shepherd to lead them through the "valley of the shadow of death."

As they have followed the Good Shepherd over the last seven years, I have seen the Lord bless them. As you will read in the pages of this book, God has been faithful to comfort, strengthen, and even redeem the horrible tragedy for good. I have seen the Good Shepherd sustain their hope, their witness, and their joy. I have seen the Lord be a firm and secure anchor for their souls (Heb. 6:19). I have witnessed the Good Shepherd give them strength when the waves of grief crashed relentlessly over them. I have observed the wonderful promise of Romans 8:28 in their lives. Indeed, the Lord has redeemed Sarah's death for good "according to His purpose." People have come to faith in the Lord Jesus Christ. Others felt prompted to grow deeper in their walk with Jesus Christ. I have even seen God mobilize people and resources for international missions. One of the surprising things about my friendship with the Harmenings is how frequently our interactions are filled with laughter and even joy. Even amidst the profound sorrow, our Good Shepherd has been faithful to fill them with "inexpressible and glorious joy" (1 Pet. 1:8 NIV).

Karen's book is an exquisite articulation of just how glorious our Good Shepherd is. Written in journal form and presented in chronological order, you will encounter in this wonderful book how the Lord, step by step, revealed Himself to Karen and the Harmening Family.

If you have experienced an unthinkable loss, read and digest the pages of this book. Learn about the God who is stronger than death and mightier than the grave. Explore the strength, peace, and hope that your Good Shepherd stands ready to provide for you. You can trust the Good Shepherd in your journey through grief. If you are plagued by a specific aspect of grief, please find the helpful index at the back of the book.

After you have read every page of this book, as I have, I pray that you will take a copy and place it gently into the hands of someone who has suffered unconscionable loss. My prayer is that God will use this book to draw you and others near to the Good Shepherd. May the Good Shepherd pursue you with His Goodness and Mercy all the days of your life.

In this life, I do not foresee a day when the Harmenings' pain will cease. But I hold fast to the promise that the afflictions of this life will one day give way to the eternal weight of glory in heaven (2 Cor. 4:17). With faith, I look forward to the day when our Good Shepherd will "wipe every tear" from their eyes. When that Great Day comes, I know that the Harmenings will be reunited with Jesus and their Sarah, where *together* they will "dwell in the house of the Lord forever."

Come, Lord Jesus.

Kevin J. Moore Ph.D.
Senior Pastor
Mount Zion Baptist Church

PREFACE

Dear Reader,

I have prayed for you as I have prayed for each person who comes to read these pages, that even in the midst of great suffering and sorrow you will be overwhelmingly encouraged to embrace and hold fast to the hope found in Jesus Christ.

This book is an intimate account of my painfully wrestling through the devastating loss and excruciating questions, experiences, and emotions that accompanied the death of my daughter, Sarah. It is my diary of reconciling inexpressible sorrow with faith.

It is shared with the understanding that everyone's grief journey is different. Each journey is shaped by the griever's personality, previous life experiences, type of loss, circumstances surrounding the loss, and countless other factors. This book is not shared to teach how to grieve, but is instead humbly offered as a testimony of hope: Hope that it is possible to bear up under seemingly unbearable grief—even the death of your child.

After Sarah died, my husband and I were desperate for testimonies of parents surviving the loss of their children; we needed to know it was possible. I am grateful to join the ranks of those having gone

PREFACE

before us in testifying that it is not only possible to survive but, through the grace and strength of God, to amazingly thrive amid the ongoing pain of missing our child.

Sifted testifies to these truths through individual entries written across a span of seven years and shared in diary format. Read each entry and seize the rare opportunity to intimately journey alongside a grieving mother through the first seven years of grief.

Sifted can be read chronologically as presented, or topically by using the topical index located in the back of the book to quickly and easily find entries on specific grief-related issues. Both ways allow you to uniquely confront many questions, emotions, and struggles of grief, and to experience through successive entries the progressive unfolding of greater understanding.

As you read this diary of grief and faith, I pray you will discover you are not alone in your suffering, and that you will be encouraged there is hope, peace, and comfort sufficient to meet every sorrow already encountered, and each yet to come.

The handwritten notes and artwork scattered throughout this book were collected from Sarah's journals, notebooks, and sketchbooks. I hope you enjoy getting a glimpse of her tender heart through them as you journey alongside me into the shadowed valley of her absence.

Much love in Christ,
Karen

Hand Lettering by
Sarah

INTRODUCTION

June 23, 2017- "God spoke clearly and firmly to me almost immediately after the crash that Satan was attempting to sift us, but that He, God, would take what Satan had intended for evil and use it for good if we will remain faithful."

In 2017 my husband, Scott, and I had been married for twenty-three years. We were enjoying a wonderful season of raising our four daughters, ages fifteen, seventeen, nineteen, and twenty-one years. Our home was peaceful and joyful, and life was bustling with exciting activities and milestones.

On June 8, 2017, in an instant everything abruptly, unexpectedly, radically, and excruciatingly changed for our family. Our third daughter, seventeen-year-old Sarah, was tragically killed in a bus crash while traveling to Botswana on a church mission trip.

In the moments after learning Sarah had been killed, I clearly heard God speak to my heart that Satan had asked to sift us, but that if we would hold firmly to Him, He would carry us through. The following week I searched the Bible for accounts of sifting and was reminded of Christ forewarning Peter of his impending sifting in Luke 22.

INTRODUCTION

> Simon, Simon, behold, Satan has demanded [permission] to sift you like wheat; but I have prayed for you, that your faith may not fail; and you, when once you have turned again, strengthen your brothers. (vv. 31-32)

Through Sarah's death I, like Peter, was sifted like wheat—abruptly and violently shaken. In the days, weeks, months, and years that followed her death, everything I held dear was painfully sifted and forever altered: my family, my beliefs, my faith, my worldview, and every relationship.

But just as God was faithful to sustain and teach Peter through his sifting, He has faithfully sustained and taught me through mine. He has redemptively used Satan's sifting to incrementally shake away chaff in my heart and life, purposefully continuing His ongoing sanctifying and transforming work in me.

The pages that follow are the diary of my sifting and His faithfulness. Peter was given the precious opportunity to turn and strengthen his brothers after his sifting. Likewise, I pray my transparent testimony will be used to strengthen my brothers and sisters journeying this and other painful paths.

We have an adversary who delights in his evil schemes to steal, kill, and destroy. His sifting can be indescribably painful. But we also have a sovereign, omnipotent, loving, ever-present, merciful, and compassionate God who graciously offers to take that which is intended for evil and use it for good.

I pray as you read this diary of His proven faithfulness, you will be emboldened to entrust your painful circumstances to Him. He alone is God, and He stands ready and willing to strengthen you *"with all power, according to His glorious might,"* to enable you to victoriously persevere through whatever sifting the adversary may craft for you (Col. 1:9-12).

> "But the Lord is faithful, and He will strengthen and protect you from the evil [one.]" 2 Thessalonians 3:3

SUFFERING, ANGUISH AND REDEMPTION

JUNE 18, 2017

At 2:48 p.m. on June 8, 2017, a twenty-two-second phone call revealed that our lives as a family had been forever altered. Scott, who was driving behind the bus that crashed with our precious Sarah and thirty-seven other members of our church on board, called and said, "Karen, there's been a horrible wreck, the bus has flipped and Sarah is pinned under it, but if you will pray there is still hope."

God in His grace had all three of our other girls home, extremely unusual at that time of day. We immediately dropped to our knees and faces and cried out together to God to spare our precious Sarah, to preserve her life, to supernaturally prevent her from being scared or in pain, and to wrap His arms around her and Scott.

My parents, who live next door, immediately came over and we all left together. I drove; we went 90 miles per hour most of the way. I suppose it took three to four hours to get there, but I'm certain it will forever be the longest drive of my life. The entire time I sang the song "Even If" by MercyMe, over and over again; initially silently in my head and eventually out loud as, in the absence of updates from Scott, I began to assume what had happened.

After a couple of hours of driving we hoped Sarah was safely at a hospital, so Katelyn, our oldest daughter, called Scott to get the name of it. He was evasive and said he would send us the address, which he eventually did. When we finally reached the vicinity of the address it was a low-rise industrial park with no hospital in sight. Katelyn called to tell him he must have given us the wrong address, he responded: "It's not a hospital."

I knew then.

We eventually found the address he had given us, it was an EMS office he had been taken to. As we walked in, everyone who worked there looked away or down. No one spoke it, but I already knew. I finally found Scott in a small office in the back of the building, alone. My heart breaks for him every time I think of him alone there for hours. The look in his eyes required no words, but he spoke them anyway, "she didn't make it."

We as a family wept together for a time, and then turned to the Lord in prayer, begging Him to redeem it in some way. At the time we had no idea what redemption might be or look like, we just knew we were desperate for it, and would continue to be desperate for it in the days ahead. We also prayed for the other students and leaders on the bus, that there would be no more deaths. After we prayed, I told the EMS office workers that we needed Sarah's backpack from the crash. I knew she had her journal with her and I had an urgency to get it; I was so hopeful God would have something encouraging for us in it.

I have no concept of time for the day, but after what I assume was a couple of hours they loaded our family in the back of two ambulances to sneak us away from the media frenzy at the EMS office to a church that would be the center for reuniting the other families with their children. We were placed in an upstairs conference room at the church, away from the reuniting families in the sanctuary below. Eventually, we got word that the bags from the crash site had been delivered to the church, so Katelyn and Sophie went downstairs to search for Sarah's backpack. When they brought it back, with heavy anticipation I hurriedly found her journal and immediately flipped to the last entry which we quickly discovered was written on the bus that day—moments before the crash.

God is so gracious. Sarah's gentle, tender heart was so in tune with Him that I have no doubt she wrote exactly what He gave her as a message of hope for us to hang onto for the remainder of our separation from her. Hope that she was absolutely confident that she was called to this, and hope that God will indeed redeem it and "do incredible things."

SARAH'S LAST JOURNAL ENTRY:

Botswana Day 1 - June 8, 17

I was just sitting here in the bus feeling a little sad. I guess because I am going to be gone so long and I was feeling a little uncomfortable. Then I decided to read my Bible. I prayed and opened up to 1 Peter 5 and 2 Peter 1. Pretty much everything I read applied to me now. It talked about watching over the flock entrusted to you, which would be my little buddies in Botswana, humbling yourself which I will need to do (and that also means being a little uncomfortable), it talked about the devil prowling about like a lion seeking whom he may devour, which he will especially be doing on this mission trip, and how we need to be alert and of sober mind, and lastly how we get to participate in His divine nature! I mean, how awesome is that? So mostly I was just reminded of why I'm here and that God has called me here and He's done so for a reason. So I know He's going to do incredible things.

We were all immediately overwhelmed by the journal, what a precious gift. We shared it with the mayor, Red Cross workers, and various other people assisting us. After a short time, I told my family I thought we should share her journal with the media, and Scott agreed. We asked each of the girls if they were okay with that and each wholeheartedly agreed we had to do it. In addition, Katelyn said she felt led to share one of the last text messages Sarah had sent to their cousin, Ariel (forwarded by Ariel after the crash).

> SARAH'S TEXT:
> "For you have been born again, not of perishable seed, but of imperishable, through the living and enduring word of God. For, 'All people are like grass, and all their glory is like the flowers of the field; the grass withers and the flowers fall, but the word of the Lord endures forever.'" 1 Peter 1:23- 25 NIV
>
> This is such a great reminder! We are like a wisp of smoke. We are only here a moment. And this is not about us. Life is not about us. It's about God who is eternal. So I want to dedicate the one moment I'm here completely and entirely to him.

The media crews were still stationed outside the building we were in, so I asked the mayor to let them know we would like to speak with them. We prayed together asking God to go before us and speak through us that His name may be lifted high through Sarah's life and testimony—her greatest desire. In so doing, only hours after our precious Sarah's departure, God began to redeem our suffering and anguish.

> But we have this treasure in earthen vessels, so that the surpassing greatness of the power will be of God and not from ourselves; we are afflicted in every way, but not crushed; perplexed, but not despairing; persecuted, but not forsaken; struck down, but not destroyed; (2 Cor. 4:7-9)

Among other things, Merriam-Webster defines "redeem" as to "offset the bad effect of" or "to make worthwhile."[1] As Christians when we cried out to God to redeem Sarah's leaving us, we were asking God to be true to His Word, as He always is, in working even this for our good and His glory. Initially one might hope redemption would somehow remove or at least diminish the pain, but I can testify that is not the case. The suffering and anguish persist, but redemption provides a purpose in the pain that enables us to persevere. We can boldly proclaim the truth of His Word together as we so clearly see His hand at work. Each life impacted by Christ through Sarah's and our testimony serves as redemption.

As we receive testimonies of people coming to Christ through the sharing of Sarah's testimony we rejoice greatly; there is no greater redemption. Equally impactful, though, are the stories of complacent believers challenged in their faith to pursue Christ as Sarah did, more blessed redemption.

> In the same way the Spirit also helps our weakness; for we do not know how to pray as we should, but the Spirit Himself intercedes for us with groanings too deep for words; and He who searches the hearts knows what the mind of the Spirit is, because He intercedes for the saints according to the will of God. And we know that God causes all things to work together for good to those who love God, to those who are called according to His purpose. (Rom. 8:26-28)

In sharing this I must interject that I do not believe God caused the bus to crash. I am fully convinced Satan was the author of the crash, that he intended to sift us and perhaps others on the bus as he did Job in the Book of Job, and Peter in Luke 22. As in both of those situations, I believe our sovereign God allowed it to happen. But I take courage that my precious Jesus, our Great High Priest who lives to intercede for us, was praying for us in advance just as He did for Peter: that our faith would not fail and that our brothers and sisters would be strengthened through Sarah's and our testimonies.

For over a year our family has been praying for a holy revival to sweep through our church, community, state, nation, and the ends of the earth. In retrospect, I believe that desire was set in our hearts by God to make the redemption He is providing for the absence of our sweet Sarah all the sweeter. Granting us the desire He set in our hearts beforehand; enabling us to persevere, praise, and worship Him through the suffering and anguish of the valley of the shadow of death.

If you do not know Sarah's Jesus, our Jesus, as your personal Savior and Lord, we implore you to seek Him today

> And there is salvation in no one else; for there is no other name under heaven that has been given among men by which we must be saved. (Acts 4:12)

> Botswana day 1   DATE June 8, 17
> I was just sitting here in the bus, feeling a little sad. I guess because I'm going to be gone so long and I was a little uncomfortable. Then I decided to read my Bible. I prayed and opened up to 1 Peter 5 and 2 Peter 1. Pretty much everything I read apply applies to me now. It talked about watching over the flock entrusted to you, which would be my little buddies in Botswana, humbling yourself which I will need to do (and that also means being a little uncomfortable), it talked about the devil prowling about like a lion seeking whom he may devour, which he will especially be doing on this mission trip, and how we need to be alert and of sober mind, and lastly, how we get to participate in his divine nature! I mean, how awesome is that? So mostly, I was just reminded of why I'm here and that God has called me here and he's done so for a reason. So I know he's going to do incredible things.

---

1. "Redeem, V. (6b)." *Merriam-Webster Dictionary*, merriam-webster.com/dictionary/redeem. Accessed 18 June 2017.

SORROWS LIKE SEA BILLOWS

JUNE 19, 2017

Horatio Spafford and his wife Anna have been on my mind today. The inspiration for his penning the lyrics of "It Is Well With My Soul" is heartbreakingly unfathomable. On the heels of financial disaster from the Great Chicago fire, he and Anna tragically lost all four of their young daughters in a shipwreck. He is said to have penned the words while looking over the location where the ship went down.

> When peace like a river attendeth my way,
> When sorrows like sea billows roll,
> Whatever my lot, Thou hast taught me to say,
> It is well, it is well with my soul.
>
> —Horatio Spafford

Having four daughters, and now having had to part with one for a time, I'm unwilling to entertain the thought of the agony of parting with all four. Though I know their pain only in part, the truth of the lyrics of his song still resonates deeply within me. We have learned over the past eleven days the painful truth that sorrows do indeed roll like sea billows. Like Horatio and Anna, we entrust all to God, and whatever He chooses to allow "is well with our souls." Our faith is sure and certain, anchored securely on the unshakable Rock. That being said, having our foundation as the Rock does not prevent the waves from crashing down upon us. But, praise be to God it does prevent us from being swept away.

> By awesome deeds You answer us in righteousness, O God of our salvation, You who are the trust of all the ends of the earth and of the farthest sea; Who establishes the mountains by His strength, Being girded with might; Who stills the roaring of the seas, The roaring of their waves, And the tumult of the peoples. (Ps. 65:5-7)

Dr. Jimmy Jackson, "Brother Jimmy" to those who know and love him, is our former pastor who lost his son in a crash as well. He spoke at Sarah's funeral service and described the waves of grief in great detail. He shared how just as the waves of the ocean roll in, so will the grief. Sometimes you look up and see them coming so you can keep your balance a little better, but other times they come from behind and knock you down. Today is one of the latter days. A tidal wave of sorrow hit me as soon as my eyes opened this morning. Thoughts of the many ways I am already missing her flooded my mind along with the staunch realization that I am going to continue to be bombarded daily by new ways I miss her. Each agonizing new realization is another wave and a challenge to stand or fall.

> I will lift up my eyes to the mountains; From where shall my help come? My help comes from the LORD, Who made heaven and earth. He will not allow your foot to slip; He who keeps you will not slumber. (Ps. 121:1-3)

> Now to Him who is able to keep you from stumbling, and to make you stand in the presence of His glory blameless with great joy, to the only God our Savior, through Jesus Christ our Lord, be glory, majesty,

dominion and authority, before all time and now and forever. Amen. (Jude 1:24-25)

So today I cling to His many rich promises that He will keep us from slipping, stumbling, falling, or being swept away. Brother Jimmy said the waves will gradually spread further and further apart over time, I will trust him on that and look forward to longer reprieves between them in the future. In between the waves I can testify to sensing His peace like a river, and I look forward to the time when those times are greater and the waves are less. In the meantime we will stand together as a family, securely anchored to the Rock that is higher than us.

> From the end of the earth I call to You when my heart is faint; Lead me to the rock that is higher than I. (Ps. 61:2)

WHAT IF?

JUNE 23, 2017

With a great deal of trepidation, I am going to allow access to the darkest crevice of my mind. It's an area I have vigilantly tried to avoid since June 8, 2017, to no avail. What if? What if we had not allowed Sarah to sign up for the mission trip to Botswana? What if we had not allowed her to get on that bus that day? What if Sarah had not been killed in that horrible crash? *What if?*

I didn't want Sarah to go to Botswana. She is the most childlike and innocent of my four girls and the thought of her being that far away was almost unbearable. I was shocked when she told me she wanted to go. How can this seventeen-year-old who is afraid to walk our dog out in our backyard at night by herself want to go to Botswana without her family? I still remember the moment she told me. She was standing in the living room right next to the sofa, she said she had been praying about it and was certain she was supposed to go.

On more than one occasion after that, she reaffirmed that she was confident she was supposed to go because she had peace about it. I told her she would have to earn all the money herself to go, and then I secretly hoped she would just give up. The more she prayed and the harder she worked to earn all that money, the more confident and excited she became. The week before the trip she said once again that she knew she was called to go, but this time she added with striking confidence, "So whatever happens is within God's will."

So, what if we had refused to allow her to go? What if I told her she couldn't go because in my gut I was afraid something was going to happen to her? *What if?*

My entire adult life I have been scared to ride in buses, they terrify me, and that fear is compounded when my children are in them. For the past few years, Scott has driven the forty-four-passenger bus ("the big bus," as most of us refer to it) for many if not most of our student ministry trips. Some of my fears are alleviated with him driving because he takes the responsibility so very seriously that his prayerfulness and intense focus are visible and palpable. When he agreed to drive the students to Atlanta we assumed he was driving the big bus with the students in it. I planned to ride along with him so I could eat lunch with Sarah that day before seeing her off in Atlanta, and then keep him company on the way home.

A couple of days before they were to leave he received an email informing him he would not be driving the big bus with the students, but would instead drive the smaller bus full of luggage, by himself, following behind the big bus. We were both very disappointed. That night I gave vent to my fears. I can see and hear the conversation Scott and I had that night as if it were ten minutes ago. I spoke these words, "We have never ridden with him, I have no idea how he drives. What if something happens? We would be right behind them and see it all, that is my worst nightmare." After a lengthy conversation, Scott told me I should not go and I reluctantly agreed.

So, what if Scott had disagreed with the email and had requested or demanded that he drive the big bus instead? What if I had heeded my fears and refused to allow her to get on that bus? What if I had told her she had to ride in the smaller bus with her dad instead? *What if?*

What if Sarah had not been killed in that crash that day? What if God had not preserved her journal and put it in our hands that very night? What if God did not clearly speak to us moving us to share her journal and text message with the world? What if God had not created in our hearts a longing for revival the year before? What if God had not moved in the hearts of multiple reporters and news channels to not only listen to us urging people through Sarah's journal and text to come to Christ, but to air it in its entirety on national television? What if James Spann had not shared that very press conference and 1.2 million people had not seen it? What if CNN had not shared nationally in writing the parts of the transcript that overtly pointed to Christ? What if the countless people who have contacted us to say they have been complacent in their faith, but are now on fire for the Lord because of Sarah, were instead left in their complacency? What if those individuals so impacted by Sarah's testimony that they have surrendered their own lives to Christ, were never impacted? What if Sarah was not where she longed to be, worshipping at the feet of Jesus?

God is so very gracious and merciful. For the year leading up to Sarah's death, He had my family and me going through an intensive period of preparation. Through a pastoral search process, He was nailing down vital truths my family and I already held, battening down the hatches for the hurricane coming our way. He put me in a position where my ability to hear Him was painfully challenged. Out of that anguish, He graciously spoke and led me clearly, powerfully, and miraculously. He trained my ear to hear His voice even when it is only a gentle whisper, and He gave me confidence in His faithfulness to speak and answer when I cry out to Him. I did not learn those lessons alone, though. We learned and shared every lesson during that time as a family. He is a gracious and merciful God who prepared us in advance to walk through this deep dark valley.

We praise Him that, because He trained us to listen for and to hear Him, His voice now rises above the cries and accusations of the enemy who longs to cripple us with his *"What-ifs."* We let Sarah leave to go to Botswana, we let her get on that bus, and she was killed in that crash. But amid those truths, our precious child, who told each of her sisters separately and on multiple occasions that she "can not wait to go to heaven," and she is "so excited about heaven," is there now.

She has heard her Lord and Savior say, "Well done, my good and faithful servant." Sarah loved the Lord with all her heart, soul, and mind; she is basking in His presence at this very moment, worshipping Him and adoring Him. She truly is rejoicing evermore, and as Scott has said on multiple occasions, even if she could come back, she wouldn't want to.

God spoke clearly and firmly to me almost immediately after the crash that Satan was attempting to sift us, but that He, God, would take what Satan had intended for evil and use it for good if we remained faithful. So, we trust Him that He is working all things out for our good and His glory. It is good that Sarah is with Him, though our hearts ache so deeply with longing for her presence. It is powerfully good that He has used His united body in a multitude of churches and denominations across the state and nation to continue to carry us through this valley in prayer. It is exceedingly good that the number of people who have shared they have been shaken from complacency in their faith is so great that we have now lost count. It is indescribably good that God is stirring at Mount Zion Baptist Church and beyond, answering Sarah's and our prayers for a holy revival.

So, What if?

What if you don't believe God is God alone, and He is good? What if you don't believe God can or will speak to you? What if you doubt He loves you enough to answer you when you cry? What if you think your sin is too deep and too wide for Him to look your way? *What if?*

If you hear any of those things, you have heard the voice of the enemy who comes to steal, kill, and destroy. Take those lies captive and cling to the truth of His Word. He alone is God, and He is good. He longs to speak to you personally and intimately through His Word and prayer. He is a long-suffering God of compassion and is faithful to answer us as we cry out to Him. And praise God, there is nothing that can separate us from the love of God which is in Christ Jesus.

From Sarah's Journal:

3/3/17

 Lord, I want to thank You that I found You when I sought You with all my heart. I'm again in fellowship with You and I want to thank You for showing me that in You I find the peace that surpasses all understanding. I tried to find it before, but I just tried to do what was right without fellowship with You. But I have found the peace and for that I greatly rejoice! Whatever comes my way, I will never lose you and therefore will never lose the peace. Thank You, Lord for continually teaching me new things. And thank You for continually showing me new aspects of Yourself and new mercies! I love You, Lord. In your precious name I pray, amen.

— SARAH HARMENING

The LORD is near to all who call upon Him, To all who call upon Him in truth. He will fulfill the desire of those who fear Him; He will also hear their cry and will save them. (Ps. 145:18-19)

Who will separate us from the love of Christ? Will tribulation, or distress, or persecution, or famine, or nakedness, or peril, or sword? Just as it is written, "FOR YOUR SAKE WE ARE BEING PUT TO DEATH ALL DAY LONG; WE WERE CONSIDERED AS SHEEP TO BE SLAUGHTERED." But in all these things we overwhelmingly conquer through Him who loved us. For I am convinced that neither death, nor life, nor angels, nor principalities, nor things present, nor things to come, nor powers, nor height, nor depth, nor any other created thing, will be able to separate us from the love of God, which is in Christ Jesus our Lord. (Rom. 8:35-39)

WAVES OF AGONY AND GRACE

JUNE 25, 2017

Waves of agony have become our new reality over the past seventeen days. The waves vary in size, intensity, and duration, but they continually come. Thankfully from the very beginning, intermingled within the waves of agony have been waves of grace. Grace to enable us to breathe when we were certain we could not. Grace to do unthinkable tasks. Grace to continue to parent our other three daughters as we grieve the absence of Sarah. Grace to still see good in the midst of the terrible.

Today was an exceptionally difficult day. For me, on some level, it rivaled the intensity of the pain in those first couple of days after she left. So I'm sitting here now, more for myself than anyone else, remembering some of the grace that has served to help us keep our balance amid the staggering waves of agony. A testimony to myself and my children, and anyone else who needs it, that though He allows the agony to continue to flow, He is faithful to send grace in the midst of the agony.

Seventeen days ago the tsunami hit as Sarah abruptly left us to go home to our Lord. That same night a wave of grace rushed in as we read her last journal entry and her text message to her cousin, and we realized they were God's grace-filled gifts to us. More grace rushed in through precious friends who drove and flew to be with us and minister to us that night.

Sixteen days ago a wave of agony crashed down upon us as we prepared to leave Atlanta without Sarah, and then struggled unnecessarily with the powers that be to have her released to Huntsville. Then grace washed in through precious friends and family who rallied around us again. Some drove over an hour to the hotel just to drive us twenty minutes in our own vehicle to the airport, because we just couldn't do it. Another flew us home in his personal jet so we didn't have to endure the four-hour drive. Another joined us on the flight just to be there for us despite his fear of flying. Another agreed to drive our vehicle home from Atlanta. Two more picked us up at the airport in Meridianville and delivered us home, then sat in our kitchen alone praying for us as we took some time to grieve together as a family.

Another wave of agony washed over us that day as we walked into our home for the first time without Sarah, knowing she would never be there with us again. My heart was shattered as I longed to hear her singing and laughing again. She was constantly singing; she sang loudly and joyously all the time. How can I endure never hearing her sing again? It was a crushing feeling sitting in the living room and glancing at the door to her room, longing for it all to be a big mistake, and for her to come around the corner singing once again.

Yet another wave of agony hit on that same day when Scott told me we needed to write an obituary for Sarah. I was paralyzed at the thought. How does one write a synopsis of their child? Where do you begin? How can anything less than a book suffice? But then a wave of grace followed in the middle of the night as I was lying there unable to sleep. I felt the words coming to me, so I got up at 4:00 a.m. and started typing. God in His graciousness poured the words out of me that I believe appropriately honored our precious Sarah.

Fifteen days ago another tidal wave of agony hit as we as a family went to the funeral home to make all the arrangements for Sarah. We had agreed that Sarah needed a white coffin representing her innocence and purity. A secondary wave of agony hit as we stood in the middle of a coffin showroom and learned a white coffin might not be available. We huddled together as a family between the coffins and prayed that God would provide a white coffin. It still takes my breath away to say it: "We prayed for a coffin for our daughter." We waited for the funeral director to come back for what felt like a very long time, though I don't know if it really was. She finally returned and brought with her a wave of grace as she told us they were paying to overnight a white coffin to us for Sarah. I'm pretty sure she had tears in her eyes as she told us, her empathy received as more grace. We rejoiced over a coffin for our child that day, proof, as if any was needed, that our lives had been turned completely upside down.

Fourteen days ago a huge wave of grace rolled in as we discovered Sarah had recorded herself singing on her iPod; we got to hear our little girl sing again—a tidal wave of grace. But then as sure as the rising and setting of the sun, that night another wave of agony washed in. This time in the form of someone sharing details of the crash that I did not want to know and that Scott had worked vigilantly to keep from the girls and me. The words created an image in my mind that still painfully lingers. As I tucked one of my sweet daughters in that night I prayed with her that God would guard our minds against the enemy during the night. Nighttime had been unbearable to this point, so we prayed we would not see those terrible images but would instead be flooded with sweet memories of Sarah. A ripple of grace came in that night as our thoughts stayed on sweet memories of Sarah rather than images of those terrible last moments.

Thirteen days ago a wave of agony rushed in as we prepared for the funeral, it was compounded by a now gripping fear that the girls and I would be bombarded with details about the crash that we did not want to know. But then another wave of grace washed in as I felt the Lord providing words to share in a post on social media to address it. Once again I felt as though God poured the words out of me that would serve to protect our girls and me, but it turns out they also encouraged many others. Countless people shared how much the words helped them as they prepared to come to the funeral that day, freeing them from worry about what to say to us. Person after person spoke the words I asked to hear in that post, telling us they loved us, were hurting with us, and praying for us, a gentle wave of grace.

The days between then and now have been a steady and constant flow of waves. In and out they roll, grace followed by agony, and agony followed by grace. Today was a larger-than-anticipated wave of agony as we prepared to go to church for the first time since Sarah's departure. We knew it would be hard, but our imaginations failed to prepare us for how excruciating it actually was. The wave washed over all five of us simultaneously, taking us to our knees. We huddled together and prayed again, and then went to church without Sarah. Our hearts ached the entire time, but a wave of grace came in the form of sweet friends to walk beside us physically and spiritually. Together they prayed fervently for us before and during church and walked beside us at church distracting and encouraging us through the daunting wave still bearing down on us.

I'm told the waves of grief will gradually slow, I certainly hope that is true. In the meantime we press on, choosing to rejoice that despite the relentless battering of the waves of agony crashing over us, the waves of grace continue to roll in as well.

No matter how deep the pit, His love is deeper still.
—Betsie Ten Boom

THE HEZEKIAH YEARS

JUNE 27, 2017

The night of the crash the Lord clearly spoke to my heart, He reminded me of something long forgotten to make me appreciate an outpouring of grace that might have otherwise gone unnoticed.

That night He impressed upon my heart that He had extended the days of Sarah just as He had the days of Hezekiah. It was such a clear and strong impression that I was compelled to share it with several others that very night and in the immediate days that followed. I initially refrained from sharing it publicly because I recognized it pushes the bounds spiritually for some, undoubtedly me included had He not impressed it so undeniably on my heart.

I remember the first time I was overcome with the thought that Sarah was only going to be with us temporarily. She was sitting in her blue car seat, an adorable little blue-eyed infant with a headful of tousled dark brown hair. We were at my parents' house, the thought was so strong as it washed over me that it made me feel physically ill. I immediately attempted to squelch it as paranoia, but I never forgot it.

Over the next couple of years, it would periodically wash over me again out of nowhere with the same crippling impact. I had no logical reason for thinking it; I have four children but only wrestled with this regarding Sarah, which made it all the more unsettling. Each time it would strike, my reaction would fluctuate between either attempting to disregard it as fear or fervently interceding for God to spare her life. When I interceded, I would cry out to Him begging if He intended to take her home, that He would instead pour out His mercy on us and extend her days here just as He had Hezekiah's.

Each time I would strive to relinquish the fear but often found myself gripped by it and pleading for more time with her. It climaxed in 2004 when I finally came to the place where I surrendered both the fear and her to Him, trusting Him to sustain us no matter our plight. In the following years, those thoughts and concerns faded from daily life, only rarely coming to mind, and even then only as a concern of the past. On the rare occasion that it came to mind, it was generally in the form of questioning what had happened in those days: Was it simply release from an irrational fear, or was it indeed a reality and answered prayer?

The account of the extension of Hezekiah's days, which was the foundation of my prayers during that time, is recorded in Isaiah 38.

> In those days Hezekiah became mortally ill. And Isaiah the prophet the son of Amoz came to him and said to him, "Thus says the LORD, 'Set your house in order, for you shall die and not live.'" Then Hezekiah turned his face to the wall and prayed to the LORD, and said, "Remember now, O LORD, I beseech You, how I have walked before You in truth and with a whole heart, and have done what is good in Your sight." And Hezekiah wept bitterly. Then the word of the LORD came to Isaiah, saying, "Go and say to Hezekiah, 'Thus says the LORD, the God of your father David, "I have heard your prayer, I have seen your tears; behold, I will add fifteen years to your life. (vv. 1-5)

Though I have journaled intermittently for many years, I did not expect to have a record of the struggle of that season. I frequently avoid journaling fears out of recognition that writing thoughts often reinforces them. Instead of journaling the negative thoughts, I will usually journal the truths that combat the negative thoughts or fears.

Frequently I journal passages of Scripture followed by my understanding of how the Scripture applies to strengthen or refine my heart and attitudes, without overtly recording the specific fear or concern.

Yesterday morning I finally pulled out my old journals to see if there was any record of that time of intercession. True to what I expected I did not find a record of the fear or my wrestling in prayer for the extension of Sarah's days, but I did find a record of the day I surrendered both to Him.

From My Journal:

August 17, 2004

Philippians 4:4-7 – "Rejoice in the Lord always. I will say it again: Rejoice! Let your gentleness be evident to all. The Lord is near. Do not be anxious about anything, but in every situation, by prayer and petition, with thanksgiving, present your requests to God. And the peace of God, which transcends all understanding, will guard your hearts and your minds in Christ Jesus."

This morning I woke up at about 3:45 a.m. overwhelmed with the weight of longing to meet the needs of each of our children and Scott. In addition, I am frequently plagued with the feeling that Sarah is a temporary gift. I always immediately suppress the thought as foolishness, but this morning I was unable to. With the words "while it was yet dark He arose and went out" in my mind, I too arose while it was yet dark and sought my Lord. He is good and faithful and met me there. I opened the living Word and He spoke to me. I don't know how many days I will enjoy the blessing of each child but I will rejoice for the moments I have already enjoyed. I choose to rejoice for His mercy and grace are abundant and He will sustain me. I choose to rejoice because no matter what our plight I know He will reunite us in glory. I pray now that God will pour His wisdom into me that my flesh will be silenced, that I will hear only His quiet leading. I pray that He in me will meet the needs of each of my children in abundance. I pray that they will know how very much they are loved, that they will know His love as well as mine. Let me point to Him in everything I do, let me not be a stumbling block for them but rather a mason helping them to build upon The Rock. I dedicate this day to You Lord, inhabit me that it may be to Your glory.

To reinforce the reality of the answered prayer, about an hour after I found the journal entry a friend from Tennessee arrived for a visit. I couldn't wait to tell her what I had found and began to explain to her how years ago I had a season of interceding for added days with Sarah, she interrupted and said she remembered me sharing that burden with her at that time. She was reminded of it the night of the crash before the name of the fatality had been released; she said as my words from all those years ago came back to her mind she knew in her heart that it was Sarah.

I praise God for "the Hezekiah years" of Sarah's life. So many rich memories were added during that time, and so many were blessed by and through her. My heart still deeply grieves her absence but I am overwhelmed by God's grace in the revelation of answered prayers of old. So today I pray the same prayer of surrender offered up so many years ago, entrusting her and our entire family to Him. Though the depth of our aching is beyond words, I choose to rejoice today for the moments we enjoyed with Sarah, with an added sweetness in the Hezekiah years. I choose to rejoice that His grace and mercy are abundant, and He is sustaining us. And above all else, to His praise, I choose to rejoice because He absolutely will beyond any shadow of doubt "reunite us in glory."

LAYERS OF GRIEF AND LOVE

JUNE 29, 2017

Our pastor, Kevin Moore, came to visit yesterday and asked a question I failed to answer completely. He asked what we have learned about grief that we thought might be helpful to others.

Scott quickly answered well for both of us as he described the waves of grief that repeatedly roll in, and referred to Horatio Spafford's painfully accurate line "when sorrows like sea billows roll," from the song "It is Well With My Soul." But there is another significant lesson I have learned as well: When we lose someone we deeply love, we have layers of grief.

My heart as Sarah's mother is broken, she is my precious child whom I love with an everlasting love. I carried her and nurtured her through infancy and childhood. I prayed over her and discipled her for seventeen years. I richly celebrated and savored every milestone along the path of her life and faith. I deeply grieve her absence, painfully longing to hold my child, rub her back, hear her laugh, listen to her sing, and see what amazing things God would have done through her if she were still here.

In addition to my own grief, I have another layer of grief as Scott's wife. I love him deeply as well. He is brokenhearted, sending me a text yesterday saying he has never identified more with Romans 9:2, *"that I have great sorrow and unceasing grief in my heart."* He is burdened with the additional agony of seeing the crash and its aftermath and bearing the scars of those images in his mind. He nurtured and loved Sarah exceedingly well as her father. He sacrificially laid down his life for her daily. They enjoyed regularly quoting funny movie lines to each other, she challenged him each time he left the house to "have fun storming the castle!"[1] And he would tease back saying, "I hope you find your dad!"[2] My heart breaks for the agony my husband is enduring in Sarah's absence.

There are three more excruciating layers of grief, one for each of my other three precious daughters, Sarah's sisters. They each have unique relationships with Sarah, and I grieve for each of them individually as I watch them endure the agony of missing their sister.

Additional layers are heaped on as I grieve for each of the grandparents who are missing Sarah so very deeply. More layers are added for each aunt, uncle, and cousin, all longing for her presence. I also grieve for Sarah's close friends as I see the hurt in their eyes, as well as her Sunday School teachers. I grieve for the little children Sarah loved so well at church, I am so saddened that they already know the sting of death at such an early age.

The day Sarah left, and in the days immediately following, I was acutely aware of each layer as it was added, each one another heavy weight draped across my heart. At times the weight of the layers was so great I questioned my ability to breathe. But somewhere along the path, I began to recognize the beauty and blessing of the layers. Each of the layers is a layer of love for Sarah and one another. We hurt deeply together, but that shared hurt increases our deep love for one another. As we, in each of the layers, grieve with and for one another, we are carrying one another's burdens, both through personal experience and prayer. I've come to wonder if perhaps we may even be lightening one another's individual loads through the shared lifting and carrying of the crushing weight of our grief.

I've also come to appreciate that there is an outer layer beyond the inner layers I've just described. I neither carry the weight of this layer nor bear any burden for it in grieving Sarah's absence. However, it is a vital protective outer layer that shields and seeks to hold together the fragile inner layers I am a part of. This outer layer is the love of the body of Christ at our local church and abroad, friends and strangers included.

What a blessing this outer layer is. They are grieving with us and carrying us before the throne of the Father daily in prayer. Hundreds of cards, texts, and messages testify to their love, grief, and prayers for us. While I thankfully feel the impact of their prayers in carrying us through this dark valley, I'm certain I will never grasp the entirety of its magnitude. Words can never express my gratitude for this layer.

If Jesus Christ is your Savior and Lord but you are not actively involved in a local body of believers, I challenge you to get involved today. Christ has called us to be members of the body, to carry one another's burdens, to weep, mourn, and rejoice together. We do all of those things best when we are intimately acquainted with one another in a local church. If you are in our area we would love for you to visit our church, but I encourage you to prayerfully find the church home He has for you. He has a position for you to fill, He has uniquely gifted you to serve and minister there. I am so thankful for those who have accepted their positions in our local body and as a result, know and love us deeply so they are able to vitally minister to us through this valley, faithfully lifting us up to the Father and weeping with us.

> Let us hold fast the confession of our hope without wavering, for He who promised is faithful; and let us consider how to stimulate one another to love and good deeds, not forsaking our own assembling together, as is the habit of some, but encouraging one another; and all the more as you see the day drawing near. (Heb. 10:22-25)

---

1. *The Princess Bride*. Directed by Rob Reiner, Twentieth Century Fox, 1987.
2. *Elf*. Directed by Jon Favreau, New Line Cinema, 2003.

"RESTORE TO ME"

JULY 8, 2017

The song "Restore to Me" by Mac Powell has been a bit of a theme song for me for the past two to three weeks.[1] It's a simple but profound song based on Psalm 51:12 that resonates deeply within my heart right now:

> Deliver me from this hour of darkness
> Through the pain and brokenness and
> I will sing of your loving kindness
> And of your righteousness
>
> Restore to me the joy of your salvation
> Restore to me the wonders of your love
> Restore to me the joy of your salvation
> Restore to me, Restore to me

Joy was one of the first thoughts I had after Sarah left us, questioning if perhaps she took it with her and we would never find it again. But that very night as I looked into her sisters' eyes and saw the brokenness of loss, I knew Scott and I as their parents would have to lead them back to joy. We would have to help liberate them from the crippling bonds of grief to embrace joy. To do so we as parents would have to make a conscious decision to not be enslaved by our own grief.

We committed to Katelyn, Kristen, and Sophie that very night to be fully present in their lives, to strive daily for joy, and to celebrate every milestone with them as if Sarah was still here celebrating with us. We assured them that just as our home had always been a place of joy, rich with hope and laughter, through God's grace and power it would be restored in His time, despite the persisting pain.

Since immediately after the crash, 1 Peter 1:6-8 has regularly echoed in my mind.

> In this you greatly rejoice, even though now for a little while, if necessary, you have been distressed by various trials, so that the proof of your faith, being more precious than gold which is perishable, even though tested by fire, may be found to result in praise and glory and honor at the revelation of Jesus Christ; and though you have not seen Him, you love Him, and though you do not see Him now, but believe in Him, you greatly rejoice with joy inexpressible and full of glory...

I long to *"greatly rejoice with joy inexpressible and full of glory,"* but in the darkness of this valley, the light of joy can seem so elusive. Through this valley, I have been reminded that the source of our joy is the presence of the Lord (Ps. 16:11). All superficial, temporal pleasures of this world quickly become irrelevant and impotent in the presence of deep grief.

The only joy capable of withstanding the tides of grief is that which is rooted in the eternal, in God Himself. His Word tells us His testimonies are the joy of our hearts (Ps. 119:111). We can affirm this as truth as His promises alone bring us joy right now. The promises regarding the security of Sarah's salvation, her presence with Him, and our eventual presence with Him and her are particularly sweet to us. Our hope in Christ and the peace that passes understanding are expressions of our joy in this valley.

I find myself pondering if our joy is found in the presence of the

Lord, and He is near to the brokenhearted, then perhaps His joy should be more authentically experienced in this valley (Ps. 34:18). Perhaps our deep grief uniquely positions us to recognize and more profoundly know the joy found only in Him.

I'm reminded of times when we've escaped the lights of the city, driven far away, and gazed into the night sky. The stars shine so much brighter in the dark night sky unpolluted by all the manmade lights. So it is with our joy in this deep dark valley: As all the manmade lights of superficial happiness fade away, the unquenchable light of His joy shines brighter. Every outpouring of grace, every promise of His Word meditated on, each a bright light in the darkness. Every bright joy that remains is directly linked to Him.

Initially, I was concerned joy would only be found on the other side of this valley, but thankfully I was mistaken. Our joy came in the depths of the valley and intermingled with mourning. Glimmers of joy initially shone through in the very early days and continue now as we see God beginning to redeem the pain of Sarah's absence by using her life and testimony to point others to Him.

Joy also shines through as He consistently ministers to us through His Word and His people. Day by day, little by little He is restoring our joy. It will be a long journey, but praise God we do not have to complete our journey through the valley before we once again find joy. It is available now, and it coexists with the pain and agony.

I'm praying that as the storm clouds clear in the months and years ahead, more and more of His joy will be visibly restored to us. I pray that we as a family, and Scott and I as a couple will choose to rejoice always, pray continually, and give thanks in all circumstances knowing that this is God's will for us in Christ Jesus (1 Thess. 5:16-18). By His grace, may we consistently be characterized as a family by *"joy inexpressible and full of glory,"* even in our pain.

---

1. Powell, Mac. "Restore to Me." *Glory Revealed*. Glory Revealed/ Provident Label Group LLC, 2007. CD.

SWALLOWED UP BY LIFE

JULY 15, 2017

"For we know that if the tent that is our earthly home is destroyed, we have a building from God, a house not made with hands, eternal in the heavens. For in this tent we groan, longing to put on our heavenly dwelling, if indeed by putting it on we may not be found naked. For while we are still in this tent, we groan, being burdened–not that we would be unclothed, but that we would be further clothed, so that what is mortal may be swallowed up by life. He who has prepared us for this very thing is God, who has given us the Spirit as a guarantee. So we are always of good courage. We know that while we are at home in the body we are away from the Lord, for we walk by faith, not by sight. Yes, we are of good courage, and we would rather be away from the body and at home with the Lord." 2 Corinthians 5:1-8 ESV

Since Sarah left I've learned that she talked a lot about heaven with family and friends. She talked about heaven with me but stopped short of saying she "can't wait to go." The same can't be said for her friends and sisters, though. She readily made it known to them that she was ready and excited. Initially, when her sisters told me she had been telling them she was excited about heaven I thought it was just a desire to be away from a fallen world and in heaven for all the obvious reasons. After all, we all look forward to unimaginable beauty, the presence of the Lord, and freedom from the pain and suffering of this world.

However, as I've spent the past weeks reading her journals I've learned I underestimated her heart and desires. Over and over again in her journals, she wrote about her frustration with her fallenness. Her tender heart grieved over moments of impatience or sometimes struggling to love someone well.

She commiserated with Paul in Romans 7, she longed to walk in obedience to Christ but regularly found herself repenting at the end of the day for failure to obey despite her best intentions. Her precious tender heart poured out words of brokenness into her journals each time she fell short of the standard of Christ.

> For I do not understand my own actions. For I do not do what I want, but I do the very thing I hate. ... For I delight in the law of God, in my inner being, but I see in my members another law waging war against the law of my mind and making me captive to the law of sin that dwells in my members. Wretched man that I am! Who will deliver me from this body of death? (Rom. 7:15, 22-24 ESV)

Today as I was spending time in 2 Corinthians 5 it suddenly hit me. I underestimated my child. She understood and embraced something I had failed to fully appreciate. Her desire for heaven was not fueled by wanting to avoid pain and looking forward to the beauty of heaven, it was fueled by her longing for righteousness. She understood life on this earth would be continually about sanctification, but she longed for glorification. She longed for death to be stripped away and to be *"swallowed up by life."* She longed to be with her Savior in the unimaginable beauty of heaven, but she also longed for deliverance from her flesh and its constant inclination toward sin.

> For we know that the whole creation has been groaning together in the pains of childbirth until now. And not only the creation, but we ourselves, who have the firstfruits of the Spirit, groan inwardly as we

wait eagerly for adoption as sons, the redemption of our bodies. (Rom. 8:22-23 ESV)

Sarah longed to be swallowed up by life, and in so doing she had greater maturity than her mother. I've loved the Lord since I was five years old, but I also love this world. I love good and wonderful things in this world. I love being a wife and mother, I love investing in college students and high schoolers, and I love spending time with family. I am convicted now that I have loved those things more than righteousness; I have never truly groaned to put on my heavenly dwelling. I have always longed to stay here in this world; heaven is for later, I have too much to look forward to here first.

Sarah told Katelyn she couldn't wait to go to heaven. Katelyn told her not to say that because she had lots of wonderful things to do here first, that she needed to get married and have a family. Sarah said that would be great but heaven would be better. I never would have said that at her age. She understood so much more than me, she got it and I did not, she was burdened and groaning for her mortal being to be swallowed up by life.

I have a longing for heaven now, and I will be quick to admit it is significantly impacted by a longing to be with my precious Sarah again. But I also get it now, Sarah showed me something I failed to appreciate and I am thankful for it. I am joining her by longing to be liberated from this body of death, to be swallowed up by life. I have accepted the challenge of Sarah's testimony and have set my heart on using every part of my "moment" to point others to Him as I eagerly await abiding with my Savior and her—groaning with longing to be free of death and swallowed up by life.

> We are like a wisp of smoke. We are only here a moment. And this is not about us. Life is not about us. It's about God who is eternal. So I want to dedicate the one moment I'm here completely and entirely to Him.
>
> — SARAH HARMENING

ANOTHER MISSION TRIP

JULY 17, 2017

"Therefore, those also who suffer according to the will of God shall entrust their souls to a faithful Creator in doing what is right."
1 Peter 4:19

The verse above is so perfect for today. Scott and I with heavy, raw, grieving hearts delivered Sarah's younger sister, Sophie, to church this morning and watched her get in the back of a vehicle and leave on a mission trip. There was a part of this mother's heart that wanted to refuse to let her go; it's certainly reasonable to say it's too soon for that, right? I can justify it, I'm certain I can.

But the Holy Spirit will not allow me. He is convicting me daily to trust my God with what is most precious to me. I am called to entrust to Him that which is much more precious to me than my own life—my children.

As He has called me to entrust my very soul to Him, in like manner I am convicted He also calls me to entrust my precious children to Him. I'm particularly drawn to the Psalms these days, in them He implores me over and over again to trust Him, to fear not, and to be faithful. In great detail, He repeatedly shows me throughout His Word why He alone is worthy to be trusted.

Most impactful to me right now in this regard is the account of His speaking to Job in chapters 38-41. He alone is God, the God who laid the foundation of the earth, the God who directs the lightning, the God who alone can do all things. The God who sets all things in motion and maintains them by the power of His Word deserves and demands my trust.

Another passage also comes to mind, a passage that I cling to for a variety of reasons but is appropriate for me today as well, Jeremiah 9:23-24:

> Thus says the LORD, "Let not a wise man boast of his wisdom, and let not the mighty man boast of his might, let not a rich man boast of his riches; but let him who boasts boast of this, that he understands and knows Me, that I am the LORD who exercises lovingkindness, justice and righteousness on earth; for I delight in these things," declares the LORD.

I love this passage because it so clearly reveals that He allows us to know Him personally. Not that we can comprehend all there is to know about Him, He is infinite and we are finite, but we can intimately understand and know Him. Through knowledge of His Word, we have a clear portrait of who He is because He has chosen to reveal Himself to us there.

What blessed assurance and comfort to confidently know that He exercises lovingkindness, justice, and righteousness, and that He delights in those attributes. The culmination of a nurtured intimate relationship with Him through the power of His Word is our ability to trust Him fully. We are able to trust Him with that which is most precious to us because He alone is worthy to be entrusted with them.

He has repeatedly graciously and mercifully shown Scott and me He is worthy to be trusted. He has confirmed in the depths of the valley He alone is worthy to be trusted because He alone is willingly able to carry us through. May we be strengthened to continually and fully entrust our souls and our children to Him, though our hearts are grieved.

May we continue to find rest, peace, and comfort in our knowledge and understanding of Him, our faithful Creator. May we be ever reminded that He will never leave us nor forsake us, that we can always find refuge in the shadow of His wings, and that He will sing over us and quiet us in His love (Ps. 64:7; Zeph. 3:17). And may we always boldly and confidently say, *"The Lord is my helper, I will not be afraid"* (Heb. 13:6).

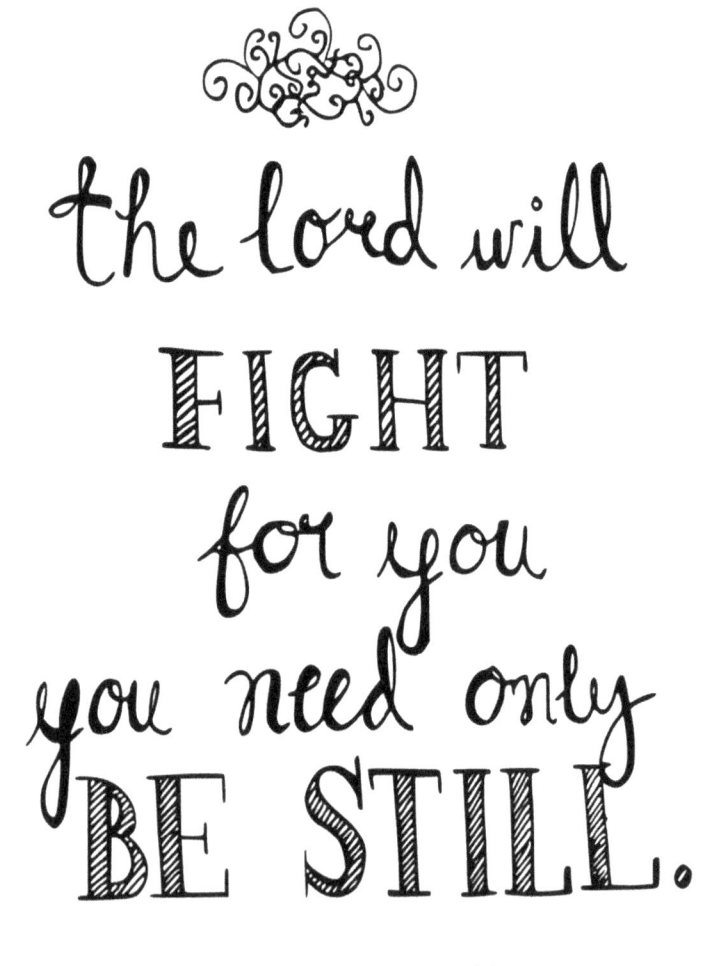

the Lord will FIGHT for you you need only BE STILL.

Exodus 14:14

WHY SARAH? WHY US?

JULY 19, 2017

When Scott and I wake each morning it still seems incomprehensible that Sarah is gone. Also incomprehensible is that thirty-seven other students and adults on the very same bus have already made or will make full recoveries. I have avoided seeing the crash footage for the most part and don't want to know any more details than what I already know, but based on what I do know it is safe to say that the hand of God delivered those thirty-seven other people on the bus from physical death.

Not only did He deliver those thirty-seven people from physical death, but He also miraculously delivered each of them from severe injury (severe injury meaning life-altering spinal cord or traumatic brain injuries). It is undeniable that the hand of God protected those other thirty-seven people, so why not Sarah? Why are we left grieving the absence of our daughter when the hand of God was very clearly delivering others at that exact moment? Did He abandon her and ultimately us as her family?

I suppose one could be tempted to think perhaps Scott and I had not prayed adequately for her safety, perhaps failure to pray on our part or hers is the reason she alone did not survive.

Thankfully, I can confidently report that is not the case at all. Her journals testify she had prayed over this trip for months. In addition to Scott's and my prayers in the days and weeks preceding the trip, I was so fearful and burdened about Scott not driving the bus that I spent a particularly prolonged period in prayer the afternoon before the crash. The Lord led me to Psalm 91 and I prayed it at length over my precious Sarah. As I prayed through that Psalm as well as other Scripture that afternoon, evening, and the next morning before they left, I walked through the process of entrusting her to Him once again.

I cried out to God that afternoon, praying verses 9-12 specifically. I reminded the Lord that we as a family love Him with all of our hearts and that we have made Him our refuge. I pled with Him to honor the prayer of this Psalm in our lives, to protect Sarah as she traveled: to set His angels guard around her, to have them bear her up in their hands, and to protect her from harm.

> For you have made the LORD, my refuge, Even the Most High, your dwelling place. No evil will befall you, Nor will any plague come near your tent. For He will give His angels charge concerning you, To guard you in all your ways. They will bear you up in their hands, That you do not strike your foot against a stone. (Ps. 91:9-12)

I thought about that prayer after the crash, at first it broke my heart that He apparently had chosen to disregard the very prayer I felt He led me to lift to Him. I had believed as I prayed Psalm 91 that He had specifically led me to it, that He led me to pray that prayer for my child, to entrust her to Him as I put her on that bus. I obeyed in prayer but it appeared He had disregarded the very requests I felt He had led me to bring before Him.

In the days following the crash, I prayerfully went back to Psalm 91 and reread it once again. God opened my eyes and spoke to my heart to show me how in His faithfulness He had inspired, heard, and graciously answered the cry of Psalm 91 in the life of Sarah that day, though painfully not at all in the temporal way I had intended.

God did indeed set His angels to guard Sarah on the day of the crash, just as I had petitioned through Psalm 91. I believe that, though

Satan was allowed to sift us by taking Sarah's physical life, God Himself set limits on what was inflicted on her; He spared her physical pain and suffering, and for that, we are all deeply grateful. He has consoled me that He honored my prayer that His angels be set guard around her and that she was no less held and protected than any other person on that bus. He commanded them to bear her up in their hands, and I am confident they obediently did just that as they ushered her directly into His presence.

The day before she left, as I prayed Psalm 91 over her, verse 14 struck me, *"Because he has loved Me, therefore I will deliver him; I will set him securely on high, because he has known My name."* I remember requesting of the Lord as I prayed that day, "You know how much Sarah loves you, so please deliver her, keep her safe as only you can."

However, as I look back I am struck by His promise there, that He *"will set him securely on high,"* which of course reminds me of the verse Sarah chose for this mission trip, *"Lead me to the rock that is higher than I"* (Ps. 61:2). Sarah was already crying out to Him and trusting Him to set her securely on high, safely upon the Rock that is higher than us. When His angels ushered her into His presence He fulfilled that promise, she was swiftly and safely led on high to *"the Rock that is higher than I."*

As I prayed Psalm 91 for Sarah the day before the crash, I prayed for His provision and abiding presence to be with her through the words of verse 15, *"He will call upon Me, and I will answer him; I will be with him in trouble; I will rescue him and honor him."* How precious it is that even as sweet Sarah was on that bus she was doing exactly what this verse said. She recorded in her journal that she was nervous and she called upon Him, seeking Him through His Word. She even testified in her journal that He answered her in her trouble at that moment. He kept His promise in the Psalm prayed over her the day before, and He quickly answered her on that bus setting her at ease.

This mother's heart agonizes that her child was not rescued physically as every other mother's child was on the bus that day. Even so, I can testify without a doubt that He did "rescue" her from death, delivering her to life everlasting through the blood of Jesus.

And He has most definitely honored her. The testimony of a quiet little girl few knew has been propelled around the globe by His faithfulness and for His glory. She set her heart in the preceding days and weeks to be on a mission to be used by Him, saying she knew He would do "something incredible." Indeed, He has been faithful to do something incredible, and as He has brought glory to Himself through it, He has also graciously and mercifully honored our precious Sarah.

The final verse of Psalm 91 that I had prayed over Sarah before she left is verse 16, *"With a long life I will satisfy him And let him see My salvation."* Of course, my heart as I lifted this prayer to God was for Sarah's physical life to be long, but I acknowledge that was a finite perspective.

Despite being painfully grieved at her absence, we rejoice that, like Sarah, we all know that this physical life is like a "wisp of smoke," and the greatest is yet to come. Praise God that His Word is clear that when we are in Christ Jesus we live even though we die (John 11:25-26). Sarah is enjoying eternal life, the epitome of "long life." She is no longer constrained by impending death, it is powerless over her.

Lastly and most importantly, God has allowed Sarah to see His salvation. As she has seen her Savior and God face to face, her faith has become sight (Matt. 5:8; 1 Cor. 13:12).

So, Why Sarah? Why us? I guess I don't really have a good answer to those questions, except to answer with opposing questions: Why not Sarah? Why not us?

God through His Word has prepared us, He has forewarned us that we live in a fallen world far from the perfection of His original design for us. He told us in Genesis of the entry of sin and death into the world and He warns us throughout His Word that we will face trials and tribulations as a result. He warns us—as Sarah pointed out in her last journal entry—that we have an adversary, the devil, who prowls around longing to devour, scheming and devising ways to steal, kill, and destroy (1 Pet. 5:8; Eph. 6:11; John 10:10).

In the midst of all that bad news, though, God offers a sea of rich promises for us, all available through the blood of Jesus Christ. I've shared before but I will share again, that in the moments after learning of Sarah's departure, God undeniably impressed on my heart that Satan had asked to sift us but that if we would cling to Him, He would carry us through. And He profoundly impressed it not only on my heart but ultimately on the heart of each member of our family.

We don't know why Satan requested to sift us specifically, and we don't know exactly why God said yes, but we accept and trust His decision. Now we, like Peter, long to persevere through this excruciatingly fiery trial, through this sifting, to allow Him to not only use it to refine and sanctify us but also to strengthen our brothers and sisters in Christ as well (Luke 22:31-32).

So, we share and I write, knowing that He will redeem it in His time. He will eventually exchange our ashes and mourning for gladness and praise. May He enable us to stand as mighty oaks for Him, that He may be glorified.

> To grant those who mourn in Zion, Giving them a garland instead of ashes, The oil of gladness instead of mourning, The mantle of praise instead of a spirit of fainting. So they will be called oaks of righteousness, The planting of the LORD, that He may be glorified. (Isa. 61:3)

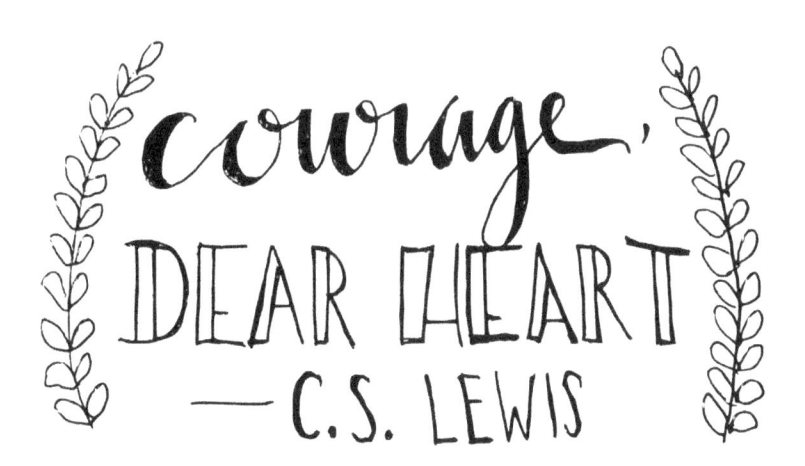

courage, DEAR HEART — C.S. LEWIS

DEATH IS NOT GOOD

~~~

JULY 21, 2017

"And we know that God causes all things to work together for good to those who love God, to those who are called according to His purpose."
Romans 8:28

Sharing our focus on looking for redemption for the anguish of Sarah's departure has become a bit of a double-edged sword. We want to consistently point to the hope and redemption that God so faithfully brings in fulfillment of His promise to work all things together for the good of those who love Him (Rom. 8:28).

However, in focusing so much on redemption we have learned there is a risk of some misconstruing that the redemption might somehow make Sarah's death *"worth it,"* or even *"good."* It can lead to such excitement in some about what God is doing that sensitivity is lost to the indescribably deep loss that precipitated the need for redemption to begin with. Statements about Sarah's death being worth it or good are like daggers in the hearts of those grieving her absence.

Almost immediately after the crash, our prayer as a family was for God to allow us to see redemption for the unimaginable pain we were experiencing. We knew redemption would in no way eliminate the pain or make the pain worth it or good. We would never willingly choose this painful journey, but we knew redemption could fuel our perseverance through it.

Redemption does not answer the question *"Why?"* It answers the question *"How?"* When we look for and see redemption, it does not indicate that is *why* God allowed Sarah's death, instead, it shows us *how* God is faithfully fulfilling His promise to use all things for our good, even the worst thing—death.

God has been so faithful to answer those prayers for redemption. We have received countless emails, texts, cards, and letters all testifying to the impact of Sarah's life and testimony. What a tremendous blessing every single testimony has been to us, each poured over us like a soothing balm.

God is indeed mightily redeeming the taking of Sarah's life and He is turning the evil intended for harm to use it for good. God is using the devastation of Sarah's death for good, but that does not make Sarah's death good.

Death is not good.

Parents having to bury their child is not good. Sisters grieving the absence of their sister is not good. Grandparents mourning the death of their grandchild is not good.

Sarah's death is not good.

When God proclaimed creation "good" and "very good" there was no death in it. God's perfect creation did not include death, death is an enemy introduced through the fall. While we as Christians have the glorious hope of eternity, that does not remove the pain and anguish death inflicts through the void left in the earthly lives of grieving families.

We do not grieve Sarah's future, we grieve ours here without her. We grieve because there is a massive void in our home where Sarah once was. Our entire family dynamic is forever altered by that wretched thief called death.

God did not create us to die. Death is worthy of grieving: deep, broken grieving. Jesus wept at the death of Lazarus, knowing He would raise him, so it is certainly acceptable for us as believers to weep at the death of our loved ones.

Praise God, though, that as we grieve we do not grieve without hope (1 Thess. 4:13-14). Though this temporary separation takes our breath away, we know eternity is looming and with it a glorious reunion.

We are so very blessed to have so many faithfully walking alongside us simultaneously grieving our unimaginable loss and rejoicing over stories of redemption with us. Some days grief prevails and they weep with us, and other days stories of redemption prevail and they rejoice with us (Rom. 12:15).

Their balance of the two, grief and rejoicing, never losing sight of one for the other, but carrying both together in sensitivity to our broken hearts continues to bless us immensely. What a privilege and blessing it is to be part of the body of Christ: knit together through the love born of the indwelling of the Holy Spirit, filled with longing to bear one another's burdens, overwhelmed with compassion to weep with those who weep, and subject to the selflessness that rejoices with those who rejoice.

"Rejoice with those who rejoice, and weep with those who weep."
Romans 12:15

NEW MERCY FOR TODAY

~~~~

JULY 24, 2017

"For we do not want you to be unaware, brethren, of our affliction which came to us in Asia, that we were burdened excessively, beyond our strength, so that we despaired even of life; indeed, we had the sentence of death within ourselves so that we would not trust in ourselves, but in God who raises the dead; who delivered us from so great a peril of death, and will deliver us, He on whom we have set our hope. And He will yet deliver us, you also joining in helping us through your prayers, so that thanks may be given by many persons on our behalf for the favor bestowed on us through the prayers of many."
2 Corinthians 1:8-11

This passage has become my personal prayer over the past week or so. Any numbness that initially shielded our broken hearts has now fully resolved and been replaced with excruciating reality. We are acutely aware of how desperately we miss Sarah and how radically our lives were transformed on June 8, 2017.

We are *"burdened excessively"* far *"beyond our strength,"* indeed we have *"despaired even of life."* We feel the sting of death in our souls, and we cry out in the depth of our grief like Jeremiah in Lamentations, *"my soul is bereft of peace; I have forgotten what happiness is; so I say, 'My *endurance has perished; so has my hope from the LORD'"* (vv. 3:17-18 ESV).

Thankfully Jeremiah's testimony goes on to give us hope in the midst of our deep distress, His mercies are new every morning. We cling to this hope.

> But this I call to mind, and therefore I have hope: The steadfast love of the LORD never ceases; his mercies never come to an end; they are new every morning; great is your faithfulness. "The LORD is my portion," says my soul, "therefore I will hope in him." The LORD is good to those who wait for him, to the soul who seeks him. It is good that one should wait quietly for the salvation of the LORD. (Lam. 3:21-26 ESV)

As we journey this dark valley, we have learned the necessity of heeding His warning in Matthew 6:34 regarding *"tomorrow."* We must fight the constant temptation to agonize over tomorrow, we must not allow ourselves to fall into Satan's crippling snare of trying to figure out how we will survive the next painful *first*, *second*, or *third* without Sarah.

We do not currently possess the strength, grace, or mercy to meet the unthinkable challenges of tomorrow. We praise Him that His Word promises to provide each and every morning the new mercy and abundant grace uniquely necessary for that day specifically. We relate to the Word inspired through Paul in 2 Corinthians 1, *"we had the sentence of death within ourselves so that we would not trust in ourselves, but in God who raises the dead"* (v. 9).

So we fix our eyes on Him and strive to daily rest in the grace and mercy provided for that day. Encouraged by the knowledge He has faithfully provided our every need each new morning for the past forty-five days, and trusting like Paul that *"He will yet deliver us."*

> So do not worry about tomorrow; for tomorrow will care for itself. Each day has enough trouble of its own. (Matt. 6:34)

Also like Paul in 2 Corinthians, we continue to ask for prayer, that you may join *"in helping us through your prayers, so that thanks may be given by many persons on our behalf for the favor bestowed on us through the prayers of many"* (v. 1:11).

People naturally watch those who suffer, so our prayer is that we may suffer in a way that points to God's abundant provision. May we keep our hope fixed on Him, and may He continue to faithfully deliver us daily. May His mercy and grace be evident in us, and His surpassing power overrun in our lives as a testimony to His faithfulness for His glory and the expansion of His kingdom.

> But we have this treasure in earthen vessels, so that the surpassing greatness of the power will be of God and not from ourselves; we are afflicted in every way, but not crushed; perplexed, but not despairing; persecuted, but not forsaken; struck down, but not destroyed; always carrying about in the body the dying of Jesus, so that the life of Jesus also may be manifested in our body. (2 Cor. 4:7-10)

Like Sarah, we long to finish well but the path before us is so painfully long, dark, and daunting without her. We covet prayers that our focus will stay fixed on Him and His provision for today, that we may receive the outpouring of grace, mercy, and strength necessary to continue in Him. May we also hold unswervingly to the hope we profess so that in the end we, too, may be confident and unashamed before Him.

LIVE redeemed

WAITING IN THE PIT

JULY 26, 2017

"I waited patiently for the LORD; And He inclined to me and heard my cry. He brought me up out of the pit of destruction, out of the miry clay, And He set my feet upon a rock making my footsteps firm. He put a new song in my mouth, a song of praise to our God; Many will see and fear And will trust in the LORD." Psalm 40:1-3

Last night I finally washed Sarah's sheets and blankets and made her bed, neatly placing her favorite blankets and stuffed animals back in their places. It shattered my already broken heart a little further.

So this morning I find myself still in this pit I've been stuck in for several days now. I see the light of His new mercy in the morning as I spend time in His Word, but in the depth of the pit, I don't feel it fully washing over me as I do when I am on solid ground. For now, the shadow of death seems to block its warmth. I have no energy to claw or climb my way out, and even if I did have the energy to somehow get out it would never be sufficient to keep me from eventually sliding back in. So as I sit here in the mire of this pit this morning I once again look to His Word longing for encouragement.

David *"waited patiently for the LORD"* in the pit. That alone is an encouragement to me this morning. Not only did he, the man after God's own heart, fall into the pit just like me, but he also realized he was incapable of getting out by his own strength. So he waited—he sat in the pit and waited. He waited, but he did not wait silently.

He says God *"inclined to me and heard my cry."* He was crying out to God from the depths of the miry pit, and God heard and inclined Himself to David. Not only was David crying out, but as he was waiting, it says specifically that he was waiting *"patiently."* Some think the word for patiently here is better understood as intently. Either way, the implication is the same, as David was waiting in the mire he was expecting his God to answer. The man after God's own heart knew the character and nature of God just as we can through His Word, and he knew that his God prides Himself on His faithfulness and lovingkindness to His children.

> Know therefore that the LORD your God, He is God, the faithful God, who keeps His covenant and His lovingkindness to a thousandth generation with those who love Him and keep His commandments (Deut. 7:9)

My prayer through tears this morning before opening His Word was that He would remind me of His faithfulness and that He would give me the confidence to wait on Him. I'm so thankful His Word is living and active, that through the power of the Holy Spirit, He faithfully speaks exactly what our aching hearts need to hear.

So once again in the midst of this suffering, I will entrust my soul to my faithful Creator and I will choose to wait patiently and intently for Him in this pit (1 Pet. 4:19). Like David, I will cry out knowing He will hear and eventually answer me. *"My voice rises to God, and I will cry aloud; My voice rises to God, and He will hear me"* (Ps. 77:1).

I find courage in knowing He will lift me out, providing my way of escape, in His time. In the meantime, I know He is faithful and will supply my every need to endure however long He chooses to leave me here.

HEALING OR ADAPTING?

JULY 31, 2017

*"'For behold, the day is coming, burning like a furnace;
and all the arrogant and every evildoer will be chaff; and the day
that is coming will set them ablaze,' says the LORD of hosts, 'so that
it will leave them neither root nor branch. But for you who fear My name,
the sun of righteousness will rise with healing in its wings; and you will go
forth and skip about like calves from the stall.'"*
Malachi 4:1-2

Lately, Scott and I have talked a lot about what it means for us to be "healed." From almost the very moment Sarah left we have heard talk of our eventual healing. It's been almost eight weeks and the wound to my heart is still just as raw as it was the very first day.

Pretty much every day at some point, if not multiple points, I end up weeping, as does Scott. How can we not? Our child we have poured our hearts and lives into for seventeen and a half years has been ripped from our arms. There is a gaping hole in our family, a searing open wound simultaneously inflicted on each of our hearts and the hearts of Katelyn, Kristen, and Sophie as well.

Friends and family have offered up countless prayers for healing for us from the moment she left us, counseling and encouraging us that healing will certainly come in time. I believe what they say in a sense, but in a larger sense—I don't.

I have sure and certain hope that the Sun of Righteousness truly will rise with healing in His wings, and we will be completely healed at our reunion in heaven. On this side of heaven, however, a precious, treasured, irreplaceable part of the body of our family has been severed from us. We have suffered a traumatic amputation. We know where that precious part of us is, but she is gone for this lifetime.

As I think of healing, I think of restoration of former health, a return to completion. Healing in that regard is an impossibility for us, restoration of former health and completion as a family will not occur this side of heaven. Because a precious part of us is missing, we as individuals and a family will never again be who we were prior to June 8, 2017.

In addition, when I think of healing I think of the absence of pain. When you've had an injury you generally don't consider it healed until the pain has subsided. In the initial days after Sarah's departure the pain was suffocating and constant. Now we find ourselves able to breathe most of the time, but the pain remains constant. We know from others who have walked this path before us that the pain will always be a part of our lives. For the remainder of this earthly life, we will bear in our souls a mark of suffering.

I find myself recoiling every time I hear mention of our "healing." It seems to me to be a lofty, unattainable goal, something I would have to constantly strive for all the while not really believing it possible for the aforementioned reasons. For that reason, my personal goal has become adapting. It is liberating for me to say that because it gives me an attainable goal to set my sights on. I don't believe we will be healed here, but I know God can and will enable us to adapt to this new and different life.

Recognizing all the while, this is just part of a journey. Sarah skipped ahead of us and we will meet her there, but for the remainder of our journey, we must adapt to her absence and our pain. We are learning to do both. We are learning how to push through the pain to live this new and different life. As we do, we are offering our pain up as another fragrant offering to Him. We are trusting Him to redeem it and use it for our good and His glory, just as He has been redeeming the taking of Sarah's earthly life.

We are already seeing some of His redemption of our pain. The pain causes us to be constantly aware of our need for His grace and mercy. Though we have never been capable of making it a day in the absence of His grace and mercy, through our pain our eyes have been opened and we are acutely aware of our desperate need for His sustaining provision. At the end of each day, we offer up prayers of thanksgiving for His having sustained us through another day in Sarah's absence.

We thank Him for the comfort He provides through His Word, the love of family and friends, notes of encouragement, and a myriad of other sources. We are reminded through His Word that we are not promised to be spared from our affliction, but we are promised that the Father of mercies and God of all comfort will comfort us. He chooses to allow us to bear this pain, but He faithfully undergirds, strengthens, and comforts us in it. Though our suffering is abundant, *"so also our comfort is abundant through Christ."*

> Blessed be the God and Father of our Lord Jesus Christ, the Father of mercies and God of all comfort, who comforts us in all our affliction so that we will be able to comfort those who are in any affliction with the comfort with which we ourselves are comforted by God. For just as the sufferings of Christ are ours in abundance, so also our comfort is abundant through Christ. (2 Cor. 1:3-5)

Through our suffering, He has equipped us and called us to serve differently, and so we are adapting to this new role as well. Through our pain, He has given us a greater tenderness of heart toward those who suffer. By allowing us to walk through the valley of the shadow of death, He has made us His ambassadors there. He is calling us to speak life amid death. He has so graciously comforted us in our pain *"so that we will be able to comfort those who are in any affliction with the*

HEALING OR ADAPTING?

comfort with which we ourselves are comforted by God." We as individuals and a family are all recognizing and adapting to our calling to be vessels of His comfort in a hurting world.

We as a family will not be healed, restored to former health, complete and free from pain—but we will adapt. That is not a statement of hopelessness, to the contrary it is an expectant testimony of His ongoing grace. The hole in our family and the pain will remain, but His comfort, grace, and mercy are abundant and exceedingly sufficient.

He will continue to sustain us, just as He will continue restoring our joy, His Word promises us so. We are learning as individuals, as a married couple, as parents, and as a family to adapt to life here without our precious Sarah. Sarah's absence constantly reminds us that we are only sojourners here. At the end of each day, we rejoice that we are one day closer to our glorious reunion with our precious sustaining Savior and Lord, and sweet Sarah at His side.

> Therefore humble yourselves under the mighty hand of God, that He may exalt you at the proper time, casting all your anxiety on Him, because He cares for you. Be of sober spirit, be on the alert. Your adversary, the devil, prowls around like a roaring lion, seeking someone to devour. But resist him, firm in your faith, knowing that the same experiences of suffering are being accomplished by your brethren who are in the world. After you have suffered for a little while, the God of all grace, who called you to His eternal glory in Christ, will Himself perfect, confirm, strengthen and establish you. (1 Pet. 5:6-10)

INTERMINGLED JOY AND SUFFERING

AUGUST 8, 2017

"Beloved, do not be surprised at the fiery ordeal among you, which comes upon you for your testing, as though some strange thing were happening to you; but to the degree that you share the sufferings of Christ, keep on rejoicing, so that also at the revelation of His glory you may rejoice with exultation."
1 Peter 4:12-13

I have been very reluctant to write what the Lord has been teaching me this week because He is still teaching me about pain and suffering. I am fearful of wearying those not currently afflicted by continuing to discuss suffering, but the hope of potentially encouraging someone walking through a similar valley compels me to share now.

Prompted by ongoing staggering waves of pain, over the past several weeks I have spent much time meditating on Scripture regarding suffering. It has been such a blessing to go back to well-worn Scripture and understand many passages much more deeply through the lens of affliction.

Through His Word we know that suffering is to be expected (2 Tim. 3:12). Satan is roaming this earth desiring to steal, kill, and

INTERMINGLED JOY AND SUFFERING

destroy, and a faithful follower of Christ will not go unnoticed by him (John 10:10; 1 Thess. 2:18). We are not guaranteed deliverance from what afflicts us this side of heaven, but we are guaranteed abundant comfort in our affliction through Christ Jesus (2 Cor. 1:5). He also promises to use whatever afflicts us and our resulting pain for good, to redeem both (Rom. 8:28).

I have touched on these points in other writings since the crash, but what has come into much clearer focus this week is the fruit of suffering. While a variety of fruit is produced, the fruit most prominent in my mind this morning is that suffering stimulates an eternal focus in believers.

Our affliction creates a deep and passionate hunger and longing for the return of Christ or our homegoing. Scripture tells us if we persevere through our suffering, rejoicing in Him and His provision, when He comes we will rejoice exceedingly *"with exultation."* We will rejoice in this way because the bitterness of suffering makes the sweetness of Christ and His promises sweeter.

Though we suffer now, we will be filled with joy, exceeding joy, rejoicing with exultation in *"a little while"* (1 Pet. 1:6-7). As our eyes are fixed expectantly on Him, longing for His return, that which is temporal fades away and a greater urgency for that which is eternal emerges. The priority of knowing Christ and making Him known is heightened through suffering. In this manner, God is glorified through our suffering.

It is okay to mourn. Mourning, grieving, pain, agony, and sorrow are acceptable and appropriate responses to death. They, in and of themselves, are in no way indicative of hopelessness or a lack of faith or joy.

Scott and I regularly weep together. For almost twenty-four years I was blessed to not know the feeling of my hair wet with my husband's tears, but now I know it well. We have been deeply afflicted by the enemy, we mourn and grieve accordingly, and yet we have hope.

We cling to the sure and certain hope promised in God's Word. We have certain hope we will see Sarah again. Hope that God will redeem the taking of her physical life. Hope that God will redeem our suffering. Hope that God will comfort and sustain us. Hope that because of our suffering, we will "rejoice with exultation" at the return of Christ. Because we have this hope we have joy intermingled with our suffering.

We went on our annual beach trip last week, the first time for the rest of our lives without Sarah. The very night Sarah left us we promised Katelyn, Kristen, and Sophie that we would strive to find joy as a family again and we would make every effort to continue to live life fully with them.

As a result, we have already tearfully walked through many painful firsts. Just a few being our first family walk, our first meal at the kitchen table, our first Sunday at church, our first time getting a table for five at a restaurant, our first 4th of July, and now our first beach trip, all without sweet Sarah.

Sarah, Sophie, and Kristen sang together all the time, but especially when we traveled. For years it delighted my soul to hear their voices melded together singing everything under the sun, anything from The Jackson Five to Veggie Tales, to hymns of old, to classic eighties, to modern pop, and the Alabama fight song, of course. We all knew the first long drive would be hard in the absence of her sweet voice. Indeed it was extremely hard, but Kristen and Sophie sang. We shared precious memories of Sarah. We cried, but we sang, too—Joy and suffering intermingled.

For our family, every beach trip requires family beach pictures. Our first family picture without Sarah was at our local Chick-fil-A at the #servelikesarah event they so generously and graciously hosted. The sting of that one slipped by me because of all of the activity, but I was painfully aware that the beach pictures were coming. However, not taking the pictures was not an option for us. We as a family have never been more aware of our not knowing what tomorrow will bring, so we strive to celebrate life and create meaningful memories with one another daily, while at the same time deeply aching for Sarah (Prov. 26:1).

As I took the pictures of the girls, for the first time three instead of four, my mom snapped a picture of me taking their picture. My heart aches every time I see it, but I also rejoice because through Christ's sustaining power Scott and I are keeping our promise to Katelyn, Kristen, and Sophie.

We are confronting and pressing through painful moments, hours, days, and weeks compelled by our desire to model for them and the world the hope we possess. Certain hope that we will see Sarah again; hope that God will redeem the taking of her physical life; hope that God will redeem our suffering; hope that God will comfort and sustain us; hope that because of our suffering, we will *"rejoice with exultation"* at the return of Christ; and hope that provides joy intermingled with our suffering.

For I consider that the sufferings of this present time are not worthy to be compared with the glory that is to be revealed to us. (Rom. 8:18)

And not only this, but we also exult in our tribulations, knowing that tribulation brings about perseverance; and perseverance, proven character; and proven character, hope; and hope does not disappoint, because the love of God has been poured out within our hearts through the Holy Spirit who was given to us. (Rom. 5:3-5)

In this you greatly rejoice, even though now for a little while, if necessary, you have been distressed by various trials, so that the proof of your faith, being more precious than gold which is perishable, even though tested by fire, may be found to result in praise and glory and honor at the revelation of Jesus Christ (1 Pet. 1:6-7)

"HOW AWESOME IS THAT?"

AUGUST 14, 2017

I was reminded of Sarah's last journal entry this morning as I was having my quiet time. I once again found myself in 2 Peter seeking much-needed encouragement to persevere. As I read I could hear her voice shouting the exclamation she wrote in her final journal entry, "We get to participate in His divine nature! I mean how awesome is that?"

> Grace and peace be multiplied to you in the knowledge of God and of Jesus our Lord; seeing that His divine power has granted to us everything pertaining to life and godliness, through the true knowledge of Him who called us by His own glory and excellence. For by these He has granted to us His precious and magnificent promises, so that by them you may become partakers of the divine nature, having escaped the corruption that is in the world by lust. (2 Pet. 1:2-4)

I had memorized 2 Peter 1:2-3 a few months before the crash, they are such rich verses. They are why I was back in 2 Peter 1 this morning, reminding myself of the truth I know I must meditate on to survive. *"Grace and peace be multiplied to you in the knowledge of God and Jesus our Lord"* (v. 2). As never before, we as a family stay in constant need of grace and peace, knowing they are the only balm to our wounded souls.

What beautiful truth in this verse that they are present, not only present but multiplied through our knowledge of God and Jesus our Lord. Grace and Peace are multiplied to me through my knowledge that my precious Savior is interceding on my behalf today, that He and my Father know my pain, that my Father sees my every tear, that my Father will uphold me with His righteous right hand, and that He will not leave our pain unredeemed.

Grace and peace come in knowing that my Father knows every situation that faces us, that He recognizes every scheme of the enemy swirling about us. Though the enemy taunts us with words and thoughts of hopelessness and despair, our loving Father has already provided a way of escape from those temptations through His Word and His promises. Our escape from the hopelessness and despair that the enemy desires to ensnare us with is through the grace and peace that are readily available and multiplied through the knowledge of Him.

I don't believe it is by chance that the Lord prompted Sarah to write in her final journal entry about the need to "be alert and of sober mind" because of "the devil prowling about seeking whom he may devour, which he will especially be doing on this mission trip." The mission trip she was called to became our "mission trip" at her departure, and she was so very right. Satan struck our family with a devastating blow that day, and he continues to wage war through relentless attacks.

As his fiery darts continue to strike about us, as we walk through multiple strategic attacks at once, the temptation comes to say: "I can not do it all." "I simply can not." "It requires too much energy, too much pain, too much sacrifice, I can't."

I'm so thankful that through knowledge of His Word, He provides a way of escape from this temptation as well. I am immediately reminded of Elisha's words when he and his servant were under what seemed like an inescapable attack. Encircled by their enemies, his servant overcome by fear, Elisha implored, *"Do not fear, for those who are with us are more than those who are with them"* (2 Kings 6:16). Elisha then prayed to the Lord that He would open the servant's eyes so he could see. His eyes were opened and he beheld angel armies, the mountain full of horses and chariots of fire all around them.

Grace and peace are multiplied as I meditate on this account, this is the God I serve, the God of angel armies. The God who delivers and sustains, though the enemy pursues with death and destruction in his eyes. Grace and peace are multiplied through the knowledge that my tender Father, my Defender, my Refuge, the God of the universe holds us in the the palm of His hand where no one and nothing can pluck us out.

Grace and peace are multiplied even further, though. In addition to His omnipotent external provision in the form of His righteous right hand and His angel armies gathering about us, we also have His mighty internal provision through the gracious imparting of His divine nature.

> His divine power has granted to us everything pertaining to life and godliness, through the true knowledge of Him who called us by His own glory and excellence. For by these He has granted to us His precious and magnificent promises, so that by them you may become partakers of the divine nature, having escaped the corruption that is in the world by lust. (vv. 3-4)

Not only is He in front of me, behind me, and beside me but through the indwelling of the Holy Spirit, He and His divine power are in me. He has granted to me everything pertaining to life and godliness. That means He has given me, through His divine nature, everything I need to walk this path before me, not only to walk it but to walk it in godliness.

In my own strength, I can not do what He is calling me to do, it is impossible. He can, though. And it is only through His divine power in me that I can. It is not easy, but He warned us it would not be easy. He warned us there would be fiery trials even unto death. Amid the fiery trials, we must continue to daily take up our cross and crucify our flesh, thereby escaping *"the corruption that is in the world by lust."*

So moment by moment, hour by hour, and day by day we have a choice to make. Will we indulge the selfish desires, the lusts of our flesh, succumbing to the fiery darts of the enemy and in so doing deny the divine power that is within us? Or, will we crucify our flesh and cling with all our might to *"His precious and magnificent promises"*? May we always choose Him and His promises, knowing that through them His divine power is unleashed in us to victoriously withstand every assault launched against us.

I pray that I will never fail to appreciate the incomprehensible magnitude of the gift of power available to me through the divine nature. May my heart cry always resonate with that of my precious daughter in exclaiming with heartfelt excitement, "We get to participate in His divine nature! I mean how awesome is that?"

FOR YOU WERE ONCE
DARKNESS
BUT NOW YOU ARE
light in the Lord
LIVE children
AS of light

EPHESIANS 5:8

THE "LITTLE CRICKET" MARTYR

AUGUST 22, 2017

Sarah loved the book *Little Women*, her face lit up every time she talked about it. She identified with Beth, one of the main characters, who not only happened to be a third daughter in a family of four daughters but sadly also died at a young age.

> There are many Beths in the world, shy and quiet, sitting in corners till needed, and living for others so cheerfully that no one sees the sacrifices till the little cricket on the hearth stops chirping and the sweet, sunshiny presence vanishes, leaving silence and shadow behind.[1]

Beth was very reserved, quiet, and shy, much like Sarah. Sarah copied the quote above in her journal. She loved this quote, and I'm certain she loved it because her gentle and quiet spirit identified with it. Like Beth, Sarah was very much a "little cricket" easily missed or overlooked against the backdrop of this loud and busy world.

In addition to *Little Women*, Sarah also loved stories of faith. She was constantly devouring testimonies and books by and about those who were persecuted and martyred. She had been captivated by the faith of persecuted Christians and martyrs for several years. She

THE "LITTLE CRICKET" MARTYR

longed to possess the faith of the martyrs, she longed to be willing to lay down her life for Christ.

The day before the bus crash, as she and I discussed the most recent horrific martyring of Christians in Egypt, she shared that she used to worry if she would have the faith to persevere if she were in that situation. She shared she had found peace, though, as God had confirmed in her spirit that He would sustain and strengthen her faith if He called her to that. She had realized her confidence was not to be in self or perceived spiritual maturity, but rather in knowing that as she walked in humble surrender to God, He would fully indwell her thereby enabling her to obediently fulfill her calling, even unto death.

I can still see and hear a conversation I had with Sarah shortly before she left for Botswana. She stood in the living room next to the sofa telling me no matter what happened on the mission trip she had peace it was within God's will because she knew God had called her to go.

There was an unmistakable gleam of courageous confidence in her eyes as she spoke those words. At that moment I had a compelling realization—within my precious "little cricket" beat the heart of a lion. The faith of the martyrs was now powerfully coursing through her veins. In the traditional sense of the word Sarah was not a martyr, but this mother's heart knows that in the truest sense of the word she absolutely was.

The fear-resolving, life-sacrificing faith of the martyrs she had pondered for years had been realized through the full and humble surrender of her heart and will to the God of the universe. All of this clearly reflected and confirmed in the final words that poured from her heart into her journal in the days and weeks leading up to her departure.

> Now as they observed the confidence of Peter and John and understood that they were uneducated and untrained men, they were amazed, and began to recognize them as having been with Jesus. (Acts 4:13)

Though she did not die at the hands of men seeking to destroy the name of Jesus Christ, she did die at the hands of the enemy. God spoke to my heart immediately after the crash that Satan had requested to sift our family and that He, God, had allowed him to do so.

As the enemy unleashed his wrath on us that day, he sought to both silence Sarah through physical death and to turn our family from our faith in God. Our enemy failed to realize a powerful truth though: Our God is the mighty Redeemer. He is the mighty Redeemer who miraculously turns even seemingly absolute devastation inflicted by the enemy to be used instead for His own glory and honor.

The enemy sought to silence Sarah, but instead, our Redeemer launched the powerful testimony of our "little cricket" around the globe within forty-eight hours. I continue to be awe-struck by how God has used and is using Sarah's life and testimony. It has been such a beautiful reminder that He takes ordinary people fully surrendered to Him and uses them in extraordinary ways.

The enemy also sought and continues to seek to turn us as a family away from our Lord and Savior. But instead, by His strength, we immediately and continually run straight to the shadow of His wing: our Rock, our Fortress, and our Deliverer.

The enemy strategically hurled us into the furnace seeking to destroy our faith with his scorching flames. As we stand in the fire, our mighty Redeemer lavishly pours out His sustaining grace and mercy upon us moment by moment, hour by hour, and day by day. He tenderly ministers to us in the midst of the flames kindled to destroy us. As He faithfully sustains us through His abiding presence and precious and magnificent promises our faith is not destroyed but instead forged: strengthened and purified.

> Beloved, do not be surprised at the fiery ordeal among you, which comes upon you for your testing, as though some strange thing were happening to you; but to the degree that you share the sufferings of Christ, keep on rejoicing, so that also at the revelation of His glory you may rejoice with exultation. (1 Pet. 4:12-13)

Our family's passionate prayer for the past year and a half has been to see a mighty transforming revival sweep through our church and community. In an essay on her biblical worldview, Sarah rightly wrote, "God uses the worst times of trial and persecution to spread the gospel." Like many before her, I pray that the Lord will use Sarah's life and testimony as a seed for revival at Mount Zion Baptist Church and abroad.

I pray that the excruciating pain of her absence will be redeemed through continued testimonies of lives changed through salvation and total surrender to Him. How I long to be able to repeat the words of Joseph to the enemy, *"As for you, you meant evil against me, but God meant it for good in order to bring about this present result, to preserve many people alive"* (Gen. 50:20).

At this very moment, our precious seventeen-year-old little girl is worshipping our Lord and Savior among the martyrs whose faith she aspired to emulate. She has joined that great cloud of witnesses as they cheer us on. She and they are crying out challenging us to persevere with the same faith God provided them and longs to provide us.

> Therefore, since we have so great a cloud of witnesses surrounding us, let us also lay aside every encumbrance and the sin which so easily entangles us, and let us run with endurance the race that is set before us, fixing our eyes on Jesus, the author and perfecter of faith, who for the joy set before Him endured the cross, despising the shame, and has sat down at the right hand of the throne of God. For consider Him who has endured such hostility by sinners against Himself, so that you will not grow weary and lose heart. (Heb. 12:1-3)

FROM SARAH'S JOURNAL:
  Botswana Devotion (Day 4) 5/18/17

- Acts 11:19-26 (and Psalms 125-128 and 2 Corinthians 13)

- Isn't it incredible that we get to carry on the work of the apostles and the early church? And we have no disadvantage. The same Spirit that lived in them lives in us!
- Psalm 126:5-6
- Psalm 128:1-2 ♥ – There is a reason to keep pressing on and doing good when people even hate you for it. It may not be any time soon, but eventually you will receive your reward, it will be completely and entirely worth it.
- 2 Corinthians 13:11

> "There are many Beths in the world, shy and quiet, sitting in corners till needed, and living for others so cheerfully that no one sees the sacrifices till the little cricket on the hearth stops chirping and the sweet, sunshiny presence vanishes, leaving silence and shadow behind."
>
> —Louisa May Alcott

---

1. Alcott, Louisa May. *Little Women*. Baltimore, Penguin Books, 1953.

SOWING IN TEARS

AUGUST 24, 2017

I will risk sounding like a broken record by saying we as a family are in a season of suffering. Because of Sarah's absence pretty much everything we do brings a staggering sting of pain with it. In addition, there are some other unresolved issues surrounding her death that have proven to be extremely painful as well.

Only days after Sarah's departure I found myself regularly saying both to myself and our girls, "Just do the next right thing." It became a mantra of sorts that persists to this day, a basic plan of survival amid the crippling trauma: Seek the Lord, determine the next right thing, and do it.

Not too far into this journey, I began quoting 1 Peter 4:19 along with the mantra, recognizing that each choice to do the next right thing, particularly the painful right things, was an act of worship and obedience to my faithful Creator.

> Therefore, those also who suffer according to the will of God shall entrust their souls to a faithful Creator in doing what is right. (1 Pet. 4:19)

Last Monday night brought with it the realization of a painful challenge we knew was a looming possibility. Our wounded hearts ache all the more now, as what was a very disappointing possibility the day before has become a painful reality we must now deal with.[1] That night my weary flesh wanted to give up and run away, wave a white flag, and cry defeat. I was too tired and the next right thing was too much, but then I sat down and began reading Sarah's journals.

She reminded me "There is a reason to keep pressing on and doing good when people even hate you for it" and that in the end "it will be completely and totally worth it." Tuesday morning I included that entry from her journal in "The Little Cricket Martyr."[2] I included it because what she wrote reflected her faith and heart for perseverance in spite of potential opposition, which went well with the topic.

There were a few of her other entries I read the night before that I thought about using, but at the last minute felt led to go with this one instead. It wasn't until afterward, though, that I went back and meditated on the passages of Scripture she had referenced. I started by reading Psalms 125-128, what a blessing each verse was for me. But when I came to Psalm 126:5-6, I was moved to tears. I immediately knew the Lord had prompted me to include this specific journal entry because I desperately needed the blessing of this particular passage:

> Those who sow in tears shall reap with joyful shouting. He who goes to and fro weeping, carrying his bag of seed, Shall indeed come again with a shout of joy, bringing his sheaves with him.

As we continue to plod through this long dark valley I realize now I was wrongly beginning to view my persistent flow of tears as failure in some way, starting to entertain the lie that perhaps it meant I was no longer trudging on in pursuit of my Lord. As I read this passage, though, I was flooded with the reassurance and comfort of His truth.

I weep. I weep because my heart is shattered. I weep because my husband's heart is shattered. I weep over my children's pain. I weep over our parents' pain. I weep over sinful circumstances beyond my control. I go *"to and fro weeping."*

If I stop there, if I only weep and no longer sow, If I no longer "carry my bag of seed," if I no longer do the next right thing—that would be the failure, that would be sin. Oh, how I praise God for His Word of encouragement that He sees our tears as we continue to sow; He sees us obediently carrying and scattering our "bag of seed" through the pain, and He assures us a joyful harvest is coming. As we persevere in doing the next right thing, in sowing through our tears, we are promised we will *"reap with joyful shouting."*

I was blessed beyond measure as I studied Psalm 126, looking at context, original language, and reading commentaries. After I finished studying it, I went on to read the other passages she shared, 2 Corinthians 13 and Acts 11:19-26, each a blessing and encouragement. But it wasn't until I finally read further down in her journal entry that I realized that my sweet Sarah had been so struck by the same two verses, Psalm 126:5-6, that she listed them out separately, what a treasure.

If you are also journeying a dark valley, take heart and cling to this hope with us. We will see a mighty harvest and rejoice all the more over the fruit of the precious seed we have sown through tears and weeping. May we never put down our bags of seed. Though tears readily flow and weeping persists may we continually persevere in spreading seed. May we continually trudge forward in obedience as we entrust our suffering souls to our faithful Creator in doing the next right thing and making Him known.

---

1. Because many grieving parents endure secondary challenges of the judicial process, sharing context seems appropriate and beneficial: We met with the bus driver, a fellow church member, hopeful he would rightly accept responsibility and plead guilty to the state's misdemeanor vehicular homicide charge. Instead, he denied responsibility and told us he intended to fight the charge. Scott was the primary witness to the crash, going to trial would require him to testify in court about all he had seen that day. He was struggling with traumatic flashbacks so this was a gut-wrenching blow that brought many additional painful challenges and loomed oppressively heavy for the next sixteen months.
2. see "The Little Cricket Martyr," pp. 60-64.

LEARNING TO WALK

SEPTEMBER 7, 2017

"God is our refuge and strength, A very present help in trouble. Therefore we will not fear, though the earth should change and though the mountains slip into the heart of the sea; Though its waters roar and foam, Though the mountains quake at its swelling pride. Selah." Psalm 46:1-3

I am learning on this journey through the valley that the terrain is continually changing, constantly bringing with it new and unexpected challenges. Some days I think as a family we might be learning how to walk, but then suddenly it feels like the earth is shifting and quaking beneath our feet and we once again find ourselves struggling just to stand. The goals we set for ourselves daily are continually changing along with the shifting terrain.

In the immediate days following the crash, we were inundated and overwhelmed by all the terrible details that accompany an unexpected death. Our goal at that time was set for us, we had to move through all that was required of us, focusing on one task after another.

After the funeral the majority of those details were complete and we moved into a period where the goal was very much basic survival. We were learning how to breathe again, how to simply exist moment by moment as a family with a precious and cherished part of us now painfully missing.

The goal shifted again slightly as we faced having to learn how to do all the things we routinely did together, but with sweet Sarah now gone: going to church, going out to eat, going to the store, running errands, on and on the list goes. All simple activities of daily life, but all so excruciatingly hard while bearing the crippling weight of the heartbreak of her absence.

About three weeks after the crash it became clear that the enemy was not done with his attempt to sift us. Spiritual warfare was raging about us. A new urgent goal emerged as a situation beyond our control wreaked of the stench of his handiwork. We realized Sarah's admonition in her final journal entry was providential as it was imperative that we now be alert and sober-minded to recognize the enemy prowling about us just as she had warned.

I immediately began to question, "How do I walk in righteousness?" "How do we as a family walk in righteousness?" "What does righteousness look like in our situation?"

I long to be righteous. I long to be obedient. But I am so weary and my flesh wages war with the Spirit. I hurt. I ache beyond words. I get angry. I get discouraged. I want to quit. I want to give up. I don't want to walk this detestable course that has been set for my family and me.

In the end, I only have two options, though. It's an either-or situation: either I will live for Christ, or I won't. I know the price with which I have been bought, so there is no choice at all. I must live for Christ. I must "Live Redeemed."

For weeks I have wrestled with how to do that practically, though. Right now, in this painful moment, in this war, plagued by this weary flesh, how do I walk in righteousness? I needed Him to break it down into simple steps for me through His Word, to give me a clear guide, one breath after the other, and one foot in front of the other. I need Him to take me by the hand and teach me how to walk each part of this constantly shifting and quaking path in righteousness, one step at a time.

Last week in His faithfulness He led me back to Psalm 37. I have been clinging to it as a lifeline ever since. When I find myself struggling to breathe, struggling to hope, struggling to take another step, I recite the simple yet challenging commands contained in that passage.

I made a very simplified list of just the commands and have them up all the time on my laptop and posted on the refrigerator. The full text of Psalm 37 is beautiful and powerful, I meditate on it every morning and evening. But my simplified list is like a compass in my hand, I can quickly and repeatedly glance at it throughout the day to be certain I am walking in the right direction.

Do not fret.
Be not envious.
Trust in the Lord.
Do good.
Dwell in the land.
Cultivate faithfulness.
Delight yourself in the Lord.
Commit your ways to the Lord.
Trust the Lord.
Rest in the Lord.
Wait patiently for the Lord.
Do not fret.
Cease from anger.
Forsake wrath.
Do not fret.
Wait for the Lord.

As the earth repeatedly shifts and quakes beneath our feet and I am left struggling to stand and walk in this valley, I am strengthened through the power of the indwelling Holy Spirit and His Word. I am learning to consistently cry out to God immediately, the very moment the earth tremors.

As I cry out for help I also affirm His truth that He sees our plight and has not abandoned us. I frequently look to the heavens and tell Him at that moment that I trust Him and I am waiting on Him. He is good and faithful, He is righteous and just, He will neither abandon nor forsake my family or me. His Spirit and His Word testify within me that He holds each member of my family by the right hand and He will not allow us to be overtaken. He alone is our refuge.

Lord, help me to not fret, and to not be envious when evil seems to prevail. Help me to fix my eyes on You alone and to trust You fully. Open my eyes to see the good I need to do, and strengthen me to do it. Help me to live with a focus to bring glory and honor to You as I dwell in this land, and to daily long to dwell in Your land yet to come.

Cultivate faithfulness in me as I regularly feed on Your Truth. Cause my heart to continually delight in You. Open my eyes to every outpouring of Your grace, thereby restoring to me the joy of Your salvation. Enable me to commit my way to You, and to trust You. Give me grace to cease striving, to rest in You, and to wait patiently for You.

No matter the challenges before me, may my eyes be so fixed on You that I am not even tempted to fret. Empower me to surrender to You that which angers me, and to forsake the wrath that is so easily justified. May Your Word so richly indwell me that that which is designed to cause me to fret will instead strengthen my faith to wait all the more eagerly for You.

Lord, lead me, teach me, equip me, strengthen me, and sustain me to walk in righteousness as "a child of Light" that Your name may be praised (Eph. 5:8).

> Mark the blameless man, and behold the upright; For the man of peace will have a posterity. But transgressors will be altogether destroyed; The posterity of the wicked will be cut off. But the salvation of the righteous is from the LORD; He is their strength in time of trouble. The LORD helps them and delivers them; He delivers them from the wicked and saves them, Because they take refuge in Him. (Ps. 37:37-40)

SHELTER IN THE STORM

SEPTEMBER 15, 2017

"The LORD is my rock and my fortress and my deliverer, My God, my rock, in whom I take refuge; My shield and the horn of my salvation, my stronghold." Psalm 18:2

As I watched footage of Hurricane Irma as it swept across islands and parts of the U.S. it reminded me of our plight. Our experience has been much like that of the impact of a hurricane, the primary exception being there was no forecast for our disaster.

I was particularly struck as I watched landscapes and buildings gradually being swept away. People clamored to a structure thinking they had found shelter from the storm only to realize it was incapable of protecting them, and they were sent frantically searching for another. In some cases, no doubt, people went to several places seeking shelter before they found refuge.

In much the same way, God has been solidifying in my mind and heart the reality that He alone is my Refuge, all others will fail.

> But let all who take refuge in You be glad, Let them ever sing for joy; And may You shelter them, That those who love Your name may exult in You. (Ps. 5:11)

I initially hoped or maybe even assumed our local church would be my place of shelter in this storm, my refuge. However, our first week back at church took me to my knees in brokenness. It was so devastatingly hard. It caught me completely off guard but, in retrospect, I realize I should have seen it coming. We always go to church as a family, we always walk through the same doors, greet the same people, sit in the same places, and always worship and serve together.

Church membership and service is a reflection of our faith, which is the heart of who we are as a family and individuals. We are one: Scott, Karen, Katelyn, Kristen, Sarah, and Sophie. Outside of our home, no place reveals more clearly the devastation that has befallen our family than our local church. It is the most difficult place for us to be right now.

The pain of church attendance for us is compounded by various factors related to how Sarah left us, but we have learned that it is quite common for bereaved parents to find church attendance and corporate worship extremely painful. While I've read multiple theories as to why, I personally believe it is not one reason, but many.

Regardless of the reasons, though, that very real pain prevents our local church from being our refuge. When I first realized this I was heartbroken at the thought and cried out to God in distress, "Church is supposed to be our refuge, how can it not be?"

Almost immediately in my crying out, His Word began echoing in my heart reminding me that He never said church is our refuge, local or universal. He said He alone is our shelter and refuge.

> Be gracious to me, O God, be gracious to me, For my soul takes refuge in You; And in the shadow of Your wings I will take refuge until destruction passes by. (Ps. 57:1)

Surrounded by friends, acquaintances, and even deeply compassionate strangers in the initial days and weeks, I sometimes found myself unintentionally taking refuge in them. All of those shelters eventually gave way with time and the sustained winds of this massive storm, though.

It's not at all that anyone has failed us, they have not. It was never God's design for them to be our refuge. They are neither equipped nor called to shelter and sustain us through the destructive winds of this storm. We must not expect them to protect us and meet our needs, that is not their role.

They are called to bring cups of cold water as He leads, and we are so very blessed that they are faithful to do so. But, He alone is able, worthy, willing, and waiting to be our Refuge.

> But as for me, I shall sing of Your strength; Yes, I shall joyfully sing of Your lovingkindness in the morning, For You have been my stronghold And a refuge in the day of my distress. (Ps. 59:16)

I frequently refer to Scott as the rock of our family. I could not ask for, or even imagine a better husband for me and father for our girls. He is a godly, gentle, humble, sacrificial servant leader. He longs to be a shelter for us, to carry our pain, grief, and burdens for us, but he can not. He is incapable and he would collapse under the weight if he somehow actually managed to lift it from our shoulders.

He is the little "r" rock of our family, but the Rock and Refuge for each of us individually must be Christ alone, all others will fail. I can not, *I must not* expect Scott to be my shelter and sustainer in this storm. We are both grieving and painfully wounded and we both must run to the Rock that is higher than us. He alone is our Shelter in this storm.

> Trust in Him at all times, O people; Pour out your heart before Him; God is a refuge for us. Selah. (Ps. 62:8)

A couple of days ago I went to the visitation for a dear friend since childhood, I love him and his family deeply. I intended to stay for the funeral as well, but after hugging and crying with his family I realized I simply was not able to stay. I went home and sat alone in silence. My heart ached for them and us. I thought about Sarah and how desperately I miss her, I even felt a little jealous that my friend is with her now.

I spent a lengthy amount of time studying Scripture and searching for encouragement, but the oppressive weight of my sadness lingered. I went downstairs to distract myself with a project and ended up looking for a piece of plywood in our storm shelter. When we built our house I let the girls write Scripture on the storm shelter walls, and periodically they would add more. Providentially, the board I was looking for was strategically beneath two verses recently added by Sarah that I had not previously seen:

Because He bends down to listen, I will pray as long as I have breath. (Ps. 116:2)

The Lord will fight for you, you need only to be still. (Ex. 14:14)

God is so faithful. I went around the storm shelter reading all the verses the girls have written through the years. Sarah had traced her little hand five years ago and written her name. I laid my hand across the outline of hers and wept, longing to feel her hand beneath mine.

Even so, I was encouraged alone in our storm shelter surrounded by His Word. I was encouraged because I was reminded who my Shelter is in this storm, my Rock, and my Refuge. I have a gentle loving God who inspired my sweet Sarah to write on a wall in our storm shelter two verses I could cling to in this moment. My tender Shepherd then led me to them to remind me that as the winds continue to howl about us, He bends down to listen to my cry, and I need only to be still.

ALL TO JESUS, I SURRENDER

&

SEPTEMBER 21, 2017

"If anyone comes to Me, and does not hate his own father and mother and wife and children and brothers and sisters, yes, and even his own life, he cannot be My disciple. "Whoever does not carry his own cross and come after Me cannot be My disciple. "For which one of you, when he wants to build a tower, does not first sit down and calculate the cost to see if he has enough to complete it? "Otherwise, when he has laid a foundation and is not able to finish, all who observe it begin to ridicule him, saying, 'This man began to build and was not able to finish.' "Or what king, when he sets out to meet another king in battle, will not first sit down and consider whether he is strong enough with ten thousand men to encounter the one coming against him with twenty thousand? "Or else, while the other is still far away, he sends a delegation and asks for terms of peace. "So then, none of you can be My disciple who does not give up all his own possessions. "Therefore, salt is good; but if even salt has become tasteless, with what will it be seasoned? "It is useless either for the soil or for the manure pile; it is thrown out. He who has ears to hear, let him hear." Luke 14:26-35

One morning the week before Sarah left, I vividly remember sitting on the porch having my quiet time and being prompted to turn my palms up to the Lord as I prayed a familiar prayer, "all that I am and all that I have, my life and my family, I surrender to You, use it all for Your glory." I had a slight sense of foreboding prior to praying, which is actually what prompted the prayer.

At the time I assumed it was my health, well-being, or physical life that might be impacted. I think that is a natural assumption as a parent, rather than the very unnatural idea of something terrible happening to our child or children. However, as I prayed I surrendered everything I held dear to Him, including that which is most precious to me, my children.

It wasn't the first time I felt led to surrender all in prayer. I had done it many times in the past, each time recognizing the priceless value and weight of the offering. But each time I surrendered all in the past, like Abraham, my Isaac(s) left the altar with me, physically alive and well. That is, each time until this time.

I've pondered the significance of that specific prayer of total surrender on that specific morning many times since Sarah left. For three and half months I have not prayed that prayer again. I came close to praying it when we sent Sophie on another mission trip and I in obedience entrusted her, as well as Katelyn and Kristen, to God. In my heart and mind, though, there was a difference between entrusting and sacrificially offering or surrendering.

I recognize my inability to protect, preserve, and sustain the lives of my children, so I entrust them to His care and plead with Him to protect and preserve them as only He can. In the process of entrusting I recognize His sovereignty and I surrender my futile sense of control and my fears to Him.

However, when I with open palms before the Lord offer up to Him my life and all that I treasure, namely my family, I am symbolically surrendering all on the altar before Him, saying, "Take it and do with it whatever You please, for Your glory."

Katelyn, Kristen, and Sophie are all traveling out of town without us this weekend. Kristen and Sophie will be going with our student ministry for their Fall Retreat. The students are traveling in charter buses.

They were both uncomfortable with the thought of riding in the bus, not for fear of the bus, but because they were both too raw to sit in a bus for a prolonged period, knowing it would trigger the agony of thinking nonstop about the details of what happened to our sweet Sarah. Kristen's boyfriend will be driving them to their location, and Katelyn will be riding with her boyfriend's parents to an out-of-town wedding.

Fear so easily creeps in as I think about them traveling, especially apart from us. As I was praying for them today, entrusting them to the Lord once again, I felt that tug, that calling I knew would eventually come my way again. He was prompting me to place all on the altar once again, to lift my heart, my life, my family, my all to Him in surrender with open hands, palms up.

Today, after three and half months, by His grace alone, I did it. I moved beyond entrusting my family to Him while pleading for their protection, to praying with palms open before Him, saying, "Whatever You choose to do with my family and my life, I surrender all to You, for Your glory."

My family and I have once again counted the cost, this time through the lens of fiery trials and excruciating pain, and He is still worthy. He is worthy of our full trust and our total surrender to His will and working, whatever it may be. So, with a shattered heart and weary arms and hands, I stand before Him, palms up, saying, "All to Jesus, I surrender."

> Therefore I urge you, brethren, by the mercies of God, to present your bodies a living and holy sacrifice, acceptable to God, which is your spiritual service of worship. And do not be conformed to this world, but be transformed by the renewing of your mind, so that you may prove what the will of God is, that which is good and acceptable and perfect. (Rom. 12:1-2)

HEART, SOUL, AND MIND

OCTOBER 2, 2017

"Teacher, which is the great commandment in the Law?" And He said to him, " 'YOU SHALL LOVE THE LORD YOUR GOD WITH ALL YOUR HEART, AND WITH ALL YOUR SOUL, AND WITH ALL YOUR MIND.'"
Matthew 22:36-37

Walking through this valley I have repeatedly been struck afresh by Scripture. Each time, the subtle yet profoundly deepened understanding leaves me wanting to shout it from the rooftop. It has happened again, this time with the passage above. I've read and heard it thousands of times, no doubt, but only now is it unfolding before me.

We regularly talk of loving God with all our hearts and surrendering our hearts to the Lordship of Christ, but it seems there is very little mention of the role of our minds in our faith. Likewise, I periodically pray offering my whole life to Christ, all that I am and have, but sadly I realize I've not spent much time meditating on what it means to love God with all of my mind.

I frequently feel there is a chasm between my mind and my heart these days, particularly as I serve in various ministry roles at church. My mind tells me to look past the pain in my heart to focus on those I am called to minister to. As a result, I regularly smile, laugh, and interact casually while at the same time, my heart and soul feel crushed within me. At first, I was concerned this was hypocrisy, but prayer and study revealed that was not the case.

Scripture is replete with references regarding the vulnerability of the heart and soul to the afflictions of grief, sorrow, pain, and troubles. While my heart and soul are set on following the Lord, they bear the excruciating sting of indescribable earthly loss. They long to follow Him but for now, they limp in pain and are sometimes so faint within me that I feel I can not go on.

My mind now takes the lead in my pursuit of Him. It testifies to my heart and soul of the truths it has spent countless hours meditating on through the years. It reminds them of the urgency of kingdom work (2 Cor. 6:1-10), it reminds them that we each only have *"a little while"* to be used (James 4:14). My mind reminds my heart and soul that God has prepared good works in advance for me to do, and that I don't want to miss a single one (Eph. 2:10). As I am reminded of these things, I am compelled to look beyond my own pain to ache for a lost and dying world.

Like Paul in 1 Corinthians 9, my surrendered mind reminds me I must make myself a slave to the gospel. In circumstances where my tears and pain can be used for the sake of the gospel I will share them, but when they may impede it, I must discipline them into submission.

I praise God that He captivated my mind years ago with the wonder of His Word. I praise Him that prior to entering this dark valley many a night watch had been spent meditating on the riches of His truths. I praise Him for causing me to love Him with my mind through the power of His Word.

Now, through the whispering of the Holy Spirit, those pondered truths once again swirl mightily through my mind enabling me to persevere through the pain in the valley, even when my heart and soul are faint within me.

> My soul cleaves to the dust; Revive me according to Your word. I have told of my ways, and You have answered me; Teach me Your statutes.

HEART, SOUL, AND MIND

> Make me understand the way of Your precepts, So I will meditate on Your wonders. My soul weeps because of grief; Strengthen me according to Your word. Remove the false way from me, And graciously grant me Your law. I have chosen the faithful way; I have placed Your ordinances before me. I cling to Your testimonies; O LORD, do not put me to shame! I shall run the way of Your commandments, For You will enlarge my heart. (Ps. 119:25-32)

I long to be obedient to love Him with all of my heart, soul, and mind. I am challenged afresh to hunger and thirst relentlessly for His Word. I recognize how vitally important it is that I love Him with all of my mind. It is the portal to the heart, it is through the meditations of my mind that my heart gleans truth.

To strengthen my weary heart and soul I must focus my mind all the more on the rich truths of His Word. In His faithfulness, He continues to teach and unfold it before me in such a way that captivates my heart and reminds me of His sure and steadfast hope that is the anchor for my wounded soul (Heb. 6:19).

DO justly
LOVE mercy
WALK humbly

BROKEN HALLELUJAH

❦

OCTOBER 17, 2017

"As the deer pants for streams of water, so my soul pants for you, my God. My soul thirsts for God, for the living God. When can I go and meet with God? My tears have been my food day and night, while people say to me all day long, "Where is your God?" These things I remember as I pour out my soul: how I used to go to the house of God under the protection of the Mighty One with shouts of joy and praise among the festive throng. Why, my soul, are you downcast? Why so disturbed within me? Put your hope in God, for I will yet praise him, my Savior and my God. My soul is downcast within me; therefore I will remember you from the land of the Jordan, the heights of Hermon--from Mount Mizar. Deep calls to deep in the roar of your waterfalls; all your waves and breakers have swept over me. By day the LORD directs his love, at night his song is with me--a prayer to the God of my life. I say to God my Rock, "Why have you forgotten me? Why must I go about mourning, oppressed by the enemy?" My bones suffer mortal agony as my foes taunt me, saying to me all day long, "Where is your God?"
Psalm 42:1-10 NIV

I'm sitting here with my Bible open before me, its pages wet and wrinkled from a seemingly endless flow of tears. I hear the ticking of the clock on the wall next to me and it reminds me of the steady passage of time, yet time seems to stand still for us in so many ways.

Sarah left us 131 days ago, that's almost nineteen weeks without my child. My heart aches with the same intensity it did that very first day. I miss her desperately. While we as a family do find joy in each day, my pillow is still wet with tears of longing and pain most nights, if not every night.

I've said it many times, but I will say again how much I miss the sound of her singing filling our home. Sarah had a song in her heart that constantly overflowed and brought such joy to our home. Missing Sarah's constant singing has prompted me to think a lot about the importance of our songs.

The four-month anniversary of her death was two Sundays ago. It was an exceptionally raw day for Scott, the girls, and me. In our church service that morning as we worshipped we sang a song that had "holy, holy, holy" in it. Instantly I vividly imagined Sarah before the throne of God singing and worshipping with all of her heart. It took my breath away and prompted a flood of tears.

After that, we sang of falling down and laying our crowns at the feet of Jesus. I envisioned Sarah doing just that, her face glowing and eyes sparkling with joy as she set her crowns before Him. I celebrate for her as I envision her in His presence. God graciously set a passionate longing for His presence and heaven in her heart and then He fulfilled it. Her faith has become sight and I am confident she is rejoicing and praising Him with the song of her heart at this very moment.

Both Scott and I long for the day when we, like Sarah, stand before Him singing "holy, holy, holy," but for now we instead stand here, so very far away, with shattered hearts in our hands. We cry out with the voice of the Psalmist in Psalm 42, *"Our tears have been our food day and night, our souls are in despair and are poured out within us as breakers and waves have swept over us."* In the midst of the pain, He is so faithful, though.

Like the Psalmist we acknowledge that He commands His lovingkindness toward us in so many ways. He pours out grace and mercy upon grace and mercy in His dealings with us. Each day He has been faithful to put a song in and on our hearts to sustain us and minister to us, as well as to offer praise back to Him. Sometimes the same song resonates over and over again for a week or even weeks, and sometimes just for one day, but every day our hearts lift a song to Him.

As I was meditating on Psalm 42, I was struck by verse 8, *"And His song will be with me in the night."* As I read that I was immediately reminded of Zephaniah 3:17, *"The LORD your God is in your midst, a mighty one who will save; he will rejoice over you with gladness; he will quiet you by his love; he will exult over you with loud singing"* (ESV).

I wonder if this is what the Psalmist had in mind as He was inspired to write of God's song being with us in the night. Nighttime is the worst for this shattered heart. In the still of the night, I feel the pain with each pulse. Perhaps in the darkest moments of the night, He is singing over me, singing for me as I lie there too shattered to lift my voice. Perhaps the reason I am able to rise in the morning is because He has quieted me with His love in those moments, as He alone can.

Perhaps in the shattering of our hearts, He has given us a more beautiful song to sing. Perhaps the brokenness that our hallelujah flows from makes it a more fragrant offering to Him.

In the hours I frantically drove to Atlanta on June 8th, I sang "Even If" by MercyMe, over and over again. In those hours I pleaded with Him to move the mountain and not let Sarah be taken from us, but He did not.

Even so, like the lyrics of that song, and like Sarah wrote in her journal, I proclaim again—though He did not move the mountain I longed for Him to move, I will praise Him still. I will trust Him to give me a new song, like the Psalmist, knowing that my hope is in Him alone, and I will yet praise Him.

After Sarah left we found a recording on her iPod of her singing "Hallelujah" by Leonard Cohen. She knew it was a secular song, but she loved the fact that even as a secular song it reflected the beauty of people in brokenness singing "Hallelujah" (Praise the Lord). So today I am singing with her, lifting high my broken heart and broken hallelujah as a fragrant offering to the King of Kings and Lord of Lords.

From Sarah's Journal:

October 27, 2016

Psalm 42:1-5 – this is a great example of how God won't always move mountains when we ask him to and through that, we should still praise God

The Heavens declare the glory of God, The skies proclaim the work of His hands.

—PSALM 19:1

THE SANITIZING OF GRIEF

NOVEMBER 3, 2017

"He will swallow up death for all time, And the Lord GOD will wipe tears away from all faces, And He will remove the reproach of His people from all the earth; For the LORD has spoken. And it will be said in that day, "Behold, this is our God for whom we have waited that He might save us. This is the LORD for whom we have waited; Let us rejoice and be glad in His salvation."
Isaiah 25:8-9

I'm not working through the stages of grief. To be frank, I have grown to rather deeply resent the phrase, "the stages of grief." Let me say it again, I am not working through the stages of grief. I am missing my child. I am learning to live life moment by moment, hour by hour, day by day, week by week, and now month by month in the wake of the death of my daughter. I am learning to live life without my child. I am learning to press on while no longer hearing her singing, her laughter, or her quirky sense of humor.

I am learning to leave the house in silence instead of hearing her cries of "Wait! Wait!" as she bounds up the steps because she needs to hug me just one more time. I am learning what it means to cling to the hope of the resurrection unlike ever before. I am learning what it truly means to let the joy of the Lord be my strength. I am learning and doing a myriad of other things, but I am not "working through the stages of grief."

I first learned about the stages of grief in a health occupations class in high school. As a senior in high school, I worked in the cardiac care unit at our local hospital. I saw many people die there. I remember watching dying people and their families and trying to identify where they were in the stages of grief. True to what I had been taught, I observed some who were in denial right up to the very last seconds, some who were filled with rage, others bargaining, many depressed, and now and then even someone who seemed to have reached acceptance. My black-and-white, meticulous personality that loves to categorize things found it very intriguing. In my immaturity, it was a neat, tidy little outline, another medical process to be observed and analyzed.

Later in college, I took a class titled "Death and Dying." We looked at how different cultures respond to death; it was there that I was first confronted with the concept of "the sanitizing of death." I don't remember if that was the exact phrase used in our discussions, but it was very much the thrust of what we discussed. As you look across cultures in comparison, it becomes clear that Western culture strives to hide death as much as possible. We clean it up, or "sanitize it" to make it more palatable or to hide it all together. It's uncomfortable and awkward to discuss, and its aftermath, grief, is equally uncomfortable and awkward, so we make every effort to neutralize the sting of both.

Sadly, along with death, I fear we are sanitizing grief through standardizing and medicalizing "the stages of grief." While outlines of the stages of grief may be beneficial in recognizing the gamut of emotions and feelings many walk through as they grieve, the manner in which many now apply "the stages of grief" has become a detriment to the bereaved. The prevalence of referring to bereaved family members as "working through the stages of grief" may well be another way we are sanitizing death.

We shift the focus from the tragic death of their loved one and the details of the legitimate and horrific pain they are experiencing to instead focusing on a standardized process that even in its title lacks the impact of the word death. It is an impotent encapsulation of the heart-shattering reality of the bereaved. It distances the observer from the full impact of death because now the bereaved are working through a defined process that has a conclusion. It's neat, it's tidy, and it's much more comfortable to discuss.

Those who are better educated on the stages of grief are quick to tell the bereaved that they may go through the stages in any order, skip some of the stages, and go back and forth between stages as well. The educated will also tell the bereaved there is no set timeline for working through the stages, and that everyone does it in their own time and way. But the implication remains that there is to be a conclusion, and the bereaved are charged with working toward it.

If we switched our terminology back to what I shared in the first paragraph though, would there be a conclusion? What if instead of talking about "working through the stages of grief" we talked about me no longer "missing my child," or for better clarity yet, you not missing your child?

If your child is gone when do you stop missing them? Think about the last time your child was gone, if it was more than a few days, say a week or even a month, did you miss them more the first day or after many days? Because my child is physically dead and I can not see her again this side of heaven, does that mean that changes for me?

It does not. I miss her more today than I did the first day. That deep sorrow I feel as I miss her, that throbbing pain in my heart is "grief." There are no stages, processes, or procedures that will strip away my longing to see and hold my child, or the grief that results from my inability to see and hold her. There will be no conclusion or resolution to my grief on this side of heaven.

But saying that undoubtedly made someone reading this very uncomfortable. It sounds hopeless, perhaps someone even had a desire to clean it up a bit, to sanitize it.

Don't do it. Don't sanitize grief. Grief hurts and it is raw, but grieving is not bad or wrong. It is not a disorder to be cured, and it is not a list of stages or steps to be completed. It is simply deep sorrow in response to deep loss.

The presence of grief does not eliminate the possibility of joy and happiness. Grief and joy exist simultaneously. I grieve the absence of Sarah, but I have great joy that she is in the presence of our Lord and Savior, and even greater joy that I will one day join her there. I am able to celebrate the victories and blessings of others while at the same time bearing the pain of her absence in my heart.

The permanence of my grief does not define or enslave me, but it does change me and mold me. God, who uses all things for the good of those who love Him, is using my grief as a sanctifying flame to refine and transform me more and more into His image.

In my pondering, I have frequently wondered if Satan plays a role in the sanitizing of death. It makes sense that the very one who comes to steal, kill, and destroy would want us to avoid meditating on the weight and ramifications of death. Death and grief should not be hidden away or sanitized. Instead, they should be harnessed as powerful reminders of the consequence of sin—the fallenness of this world and the origin of death itself. Death and grief are reminders of the brevity of this life. We should use them as catalysts to teach ourselves and others *"to number our days that we may get a heart of wisdom"* (Ps. 90:12). They also provide profound opportunities *"to make a defense to anyone who asks you for a reason for the hope that is in you"* (1 Pet. 3:15).

I am not working through the stages of grief. But God is working through my grief to transform me, to equip me, and to use me in ways that He has foreordained (Eph. 2:10). My grief is part of my offering to Him. Just as I offer up my life to Him, I offer up my grief, knowing that He who is faithful will use it, too, for His glory and my good.

> Why are you in despair, O my soul? And why have you become disturbed within me? Hope in God, for I shall again praise Him For the help of His presence. (Ps. 42:5)

WAITING IN SOLITUDE

NOVEMBER 14, 2017

"My soul is bereft of peace; I have forgotten what happiness is; so I say, 'My endurance has perished; so has my hope from the LORD.' Remember my affliction and my wanderings, the wormwood and the gall! My soul continually remembers it and is bowed down within me. But this I call to mind, and therefore I have hope: The steadfast love of the LORD never ceases; his mercies never come to an end; they are new every morning; great is your faithfulness. 'The LORD is my portion,' says my soul, 'therefore I will hope in him.' The LORD is good to those who wait for him, to the soul who seeks him. It is good that one should wait quietly for the salvation of the LORD." Lamentations 3:17-26 ESV

Sometimes we choose solitude. But other times solitude is unexpectedly thrust upon us, carrying with it the potential sting of isolation and loneliness.

I had a season of undesired solitude years ago when I was a young stay-at-home mother to my preschool-aged children. At that time I longed for an intimate circle of friends like everyone else seemed to have. But God used that extended season of solitude to redirect my focus to Him. During that time I learned to lean hard into Him to meet my every need, and more importantly to be the source of my peace, joy, hope, and love. Though I went into that season of solitude kicking and screaming against it, I look back on it as one of the sweetest seasons of my life. Through solitude and the power of His Word, He drew me into His presence and taught me the richness of intimately abiding in Him.

I have been feeling increasingly isolated and lonely over the past few months. I am physically alone far more than I used to be prior to Sarah leaving, but it is a much deeper loneliness than just being physically alone. In fact, sometimes I feel most alone when I am in a crowd of people actively engaging in superficial conversation. I'm confident I appear just fine in those moments. I certainly do not look alone, but my heart and soul feel desperately alone.

I often think of Proverbs 13:14, *"Even in laughter the heart may ache, and the end of joy may be grief."* I know many commentators relate this passage to the folly of fools, but I so relate to a literal reading of it. I frequently find myself surrounded by people yet alone, laughing yet aching, and experiencing joy yet grieving.

There have been some extenuating circumstances related to Sarah's death that have played a significant role in my sense of isolation. However, after reading and speaking with others who are grieving the absence of their children as well, I am realizing I probably would have struggled with some sense of isolation even in the absence of those other painful circumstances.

My loneliness in no way reflects any type of failure of Scott, my family, or my friends. I'm suspicious a degree of loneliness following the physical death of one's child may be inevitable. There is a staggering void in our family where she once was, and I desperately miss her presence and companionship. She is the last thought on my mind as I go to sleep, and the first thought the moment I wake, both instances spurring a deep ache within me.

Everywhere I go and everything I do, my mind is flooded with memories of Sarah with each location and activity. I long to step back in time to be with her there, and can easily get lost in those thoughts. I am lonely because I uniquely grieve as Sarah's mother; I painfully miss my child.

Additionally, in my uncertainty of how to answer people's inquiries I have probably contributed to my isolation. Increasingly I sense in those who love us an urgency for us to be okay or better. When asked expectantly how I am, I am confronted with a choice to be transparent or to make the person questioning feel better by speaking only the positives. The majority of the time I opt for speaking only the positives.

While the positives are true, they are only half of the story. The reality is that Scott's heart and mine ache deeply. With each pulse, we bear a throbbing, indescribable sadness. In the midst of the indescribable sadness, though, we experience God's grace, mercy, strength, and provision. While mourning our unfathomable loss through Sarah's absence we also simultaneously celebrate God's many rich blessings.

We are painfully broken yet we have great hope and joy. I am so thankful to be able to boldly proclaim the truth of all the positives. But at the same time, I recognize that my failure to acknowledge the magnitude of the lingering pain contributes to my isolation.

Regardless of the causes, though, it is clear I have entered another season of solitude. As an extrovert, my flesh resists and even dreads being alone, my natural reflex is to frantically fight against it. But remembering well the sanctifying power of that season of solitude so many years ago compels me to lean into Him in this new season as well.

Instead of focusing on my solitude as an additional source of pain, I am striving to set my heart to seize this time as an intimate retreat with Him. As I seek His face through His Word and prayer, I am continually hearing the same thing over and over again, "Wait." As I've meditated on what it means to wait, I believe there are three specific modes of waiting He is calling me to amid my pain and solitude.

I am called to wait on Him in His Word.

God's Word is living and active and speaks to my every need (Heb. 4:12). He speaks to us through the unfolding of His Word by the power of the Holy Spirit who indwells each of us as believers (1 John 2:27).

Aside from spending regular time in His Word, for me in the mornings and frequently again before going to bed, I also harness each sting of loneliness throughout the day as an impetus to meditate on His Word. Whenever the solitude overwhelms me giving way to feelings of isolation and loneliness, I open His Word and meditate on it waiting expectantly for Him to speak. As I wait on Him in His Word, He is so faithful to speak exactly what I need.

> My soul clings to the dust; give me life according to your word! When I told of my ways, you answered me; teach me your statutes! Make me understand the way of your precepts, and I will meditate on your wondrous works. My soul melts away for sorrow; strengthen me according to your word! (Ps. 119:25-28 ESV)

I am called to wait on Him in prayer.

In addition to waiting on God in His Word, I wait on Him in prayer, the two go hand in hand. As I wait on Him in prayer He uses the power of His Word to answer and sanctify me. I regularly pray Scripture back to God, often using the prayers lifted by David and the other Psalmist as my own. Prayer is powerful because the God of the universe hears and answers our prayers. This simple yet revolutionary truth should continually drive us to our knees.

I say that as the one who prayed fervently for my precious child, Sarah, to be safeguarded and to remain with me. He did not answer how I desired that day, but as I listened in prayer He did answer, and His answer was powerful. He spoke to my heart that Satan had asked Him for permission to sift us and He had granted it, but if we would cling to Him He would carry us through. He has been and continues to be faithful to that answer.

Through time in prayer, He also reveals those areas of my life that are not fully surrendered to Him, the areas where I have allowed sinful thoughts or attitudes to creep back in. As I repent and surrender those areas back to Him I am drawn closer to Him. As I cry out to Him daily entrusting my pain to Him and asking Him to strengthen me yet again, He is faithful to do so. Through His continued faithfulness to speak and answer as I wait on Him in prayer, I am learning to abide more and more deeply in Him.

> He who dwells in the shelter of the Most High will abide in the shadow of the Almighty. I will say to the LORD, 'My refuge and my fortress, my God, in whom I trust.' For he will deliver you from the snare of the fowler and from the deadly pestilence. He will cover you with his pinions, and under his wings you will find refuge; his faithfulness is a shield and buckler. (Ps. 91:1-4 ESV)

I am called to wait on Him in service.

Most recently He has been teaching me that I am also to wait on Him in service. Previously I had viewed waiting on Him in a more passive sense, but I am now convinced I am to actively wait on Him as well. I am called to wait on Him much as a waiter waits on a table of dinner guests.

In His gentleness He has shown me my act of waiting on and serving Him doesn't have to be an in-depth, far-reaching, complicated commitment, but instead continues to be simply perceiving and doing the next right thing. As I daily wait at His feet, He tenderly leads me in the next right thing—moment by moment, hour by hour, and day by day.

When I fail to wait with my gaze fixed upon His face, focusing instead on my circumstances and future, my heart invariably grows faint within me. But then my gentle Shepherd patiently reminds me once again, *"Do not be anxious about tomorrow, for tomorrow will be anxious for itself. Sufficient for the day is its own trouble"* (Matt. 6:34 ESV).

As I shift my focus back to Him, my fears are alleviated as He faithfully comforts, encourages, leads, and directs me; simultaneously equipping and sustaining me to actively wait on Him day by day.

Come to me, all who labor and are heavy laden, and I will give you rest. Take my yoke upon you, and learn from me, for I am gentle and lowly in heart, and you will find rest for your souls. For my yoke is easy, and my burden is light. (Matt. 11:28-30 ESV)

So I thank Him today for using my solitude for good. Through it, He continues to teach me to abide in Him and no other. In the silence, He is teaching me to wait on Him through His Word, prayer, and service. Causing my heart to cry out with the heart of Jeremiah this morning, *"'The LORD is my portion,' says my soul, 'therefore I will hope in him.' The LORD is good to those who wait for him, to the soul who seeks him. It is good that one should wait quietly for the salvation of the LORD. It is good for a man that he bear the yoke in his youth. Let him sit alone in silence when it is laid on him; let him put his mouth in the dust–there may yet be hope"* (Lam. 3:24-29 ESV).

Above all else, guard your heart for everything you do flows from it.

— Proverbs 4:23

SORROWFUL YET ALWAYS REJOICING

NOVEMBER 21, 2017

Thanksgiving and Christmas are here, such exciting and precious times to celebrate family and the rich blessings of God. Greetings of "Happy" and "Merry" are at every turn. The words "Joy" and "Rejoice" are in the air now more than at any other time of year. As a result, I've been meditating at length on what it means to rejoice, particularly what it means to rejoice while walking through the valley of the shadow of death.

I think sometimes when we talk about rejoicing we mistakenly interpret it as gleeful exuberance, perhaps accompanied by visions of singing in the rain or dancing in the park. We may even mistakenly believe that if sorrow or grief are present then rejoicing can not or must not be present. To believe so would rob us of one of the most poignant expressions of rejoicing, though.

Saved and lost alike rejoice in the good times of life. Times of health, wealth, and blessing are welcomed with giddy excitement and celebration appropriately called rejoicing. But there is a deeper rejoicing than this.

There is a deeply resonating joy derived from hope in the midst of tribulation and tragedy (Rom. 12:12). This rejoicing is not evidenced by the expression of festive celebratory feelings but is instead characterized by the peace of confident hope that rests squarely on God and His promises. This is the rejoicing of the redeemed that defies worldly logic as it exists even amid piercing pain and streams of tears.

I am convinced there is a uniquely sweet and profound expression of rejoicing forged only in the hearts of those who walk in intimacy with Christ through fiery ordeals. Paul wrote, *"Rejoice always,"* yet he also wrote, *"I am telling the truth in Christ, I am not lying, my conscience testifies with me in the Holy Spirit, that I have great sorrow and unceasing grief in my heart"* (1 Thess. 5:16; Rom. 9:1-2). In 2 Corinthians he describes the tremendous hardships and abuses he has endured and describes himself as *"sorrowful yet always rejoicing"* (v. 6:10).

There is an incomparable rejoicing that is birthed through the marriage of steadfast faith and great sorrow. It is a rejoicing that is reverent, sober, and soul-stirring. It is the rejoicing evidenced by praise flowing out of immeasurable heartbreak, as tear-streaked faces proclaim, *"Though He slay me, yet will I trust in Him"* (Job 13:15).

Our risen Savior was described as *"a man of sorrows and acquainted with grief"* (Isa. 53:3). He Himself wept at the sting of death (John 11:35). He is our Great High Priest who sympathizes with our weaknesses. He was tempted in all things as we are and He lives to intercede continually for us. He's beckoning all, but particularly the broken-hearted, weary, and heavy-laden among us to confidently draw near to His throne of grace. He lovingly waits to lavishly dispense His grace and mercy to powerfully enable us to persevere, *"sorrowful yet always rejoicing"* (Heb. 4:15-16; 2 Cor. 6:1-10).

> I BELIEVE IN CHRIST
> like I believe in the sun
> NOT BECAUSE I CAN SEE IT,
> BUT BY IT
> I can see everything else
> —C. S. LEWIS

THE STEWARDSHIP OF PAIN

NOVEMBER 30, 2017

"As each one has received a special gift, employ it in serving one another as good stewards of the manifold grace of God. Whoever speaks, is to do so as one who is speaking the utterances of God; whoever serves is to do so as one who is serving by the strength which God supplies; so that in all things God may be glorified through Jesus Christ, to whom belongs the glory and dominion forever and ever. Amen." 1 Peter 4:10-11

I periodically wrestle with feelings of insecurity about continuing to share our family's painful journey. I realize that there are varying views regarding the appropriateness of speaking so openly about the intimate details of the deep heartache of grief. I also recognize that some say there are limits to how long it is appropriate to discuss the pain of the death of a loved one and that continuing to do so may reflect a lack of desire to "move on."

I am confident those who say the latter have not had the experience of walking this path or they would recognize the grotesque fallacy of that line of thinking. Nonetheless, these realizations trigger insecurity by causing me to think that perhaps continuing to acknowledge our pain will only serve to weary those around us, and in so doing will alienate us as well. As I've recently taken a short break from social media and writing this has been one of my primary focuses of prayer.

We all know as believers we are called to steward our finances, material resources, gifts, abilities, and skills for the glory of God. But as I have been praying over how God desires me to walk through this painful valley, I have a growing conviction He is calling me to wisely steward my pain and suffering as well. The most costly experience we can ever have or offer is that of our suffering.

I would give every dollar and possession I have ever had, or ever will have, along with my very life to have Sarah back in my arms, even for just one moment. The pain I bear because of her absence is the most expensive possession I have to offer my Lord. I am confident I am called to be a wise steward of it. I am to prayerfully seek His face and counsel to understand how He is calling me to offer it up to Him, or invest it, so that He may multiply it for His glory.

In 1 Peter 4:10, we are called to be *"good stewards of the manifold grace of God."* According to Strong's Concordance, the word translated "manifold" here can also be understood to mean divers or various in character.[1] It is through His manifold grace that we as His children are beckoned, comforted, convicted, chastened, rebuked, exhorted, forgiven, restored, and healed, just to name a few.

The same grace that carries us through the refining flames of fiery tribulation also binds our wounds on the other side. The same grace that provides new mercies each morning to soothe our aching hearts also opens our eyes to sin and convicts and chastens our wandering hearts. Recognizing this, I hold my open hands before Him and plead with Him to continue to use my pain as an investment to be multiplied through teaching and refining me personally, to continue the process of purifying my heart so that I may be increasingly used for His glory.

In addition to stewarding the pain and suffering by requesting and allowing God to refine me personally through it, I am also to steward His grace that has been given to me through sharing our pain and suffering. As I transparently expose my shattered heart to others, it affords me the opportunity to boldly testify to His manifold grace. It is His abundant, amazing grace alone that sustains us and enables us to persevere through the heartache. Our pain and suffering is a stage upon which His grace can be boldly displayed as we testify to His faithfulness to meet our every need. We share our pain and suffering as a means to testify to His provision *"so that in all things God may be glorified through Jesus Christ to whom belongs the glory and dominion forever and ever. Amen"* (1 Pet. 4:16).

I am also realizing that the ability to find the words to communicate both the pain and the provision is a special gift from Him to be stewarded as well. In the middle of the time I had set apart to pray over how God would have me steward this painful journey, our pastor preached a sermon on the account of Paul and Silas in Acts (16:16-40). After they had been beaten with many blows and shackled in a dingy prison cell they were praying and singing hymns at midnight.

Every time I've read that account I've been amazed by their faith and God's sustaining grace in their lives, but it wasn't until this week that I was struck by the last part of verse 25, *"and the prisoners were listening to them."* From the very first entry I wrote after Sarah's death, my intent has consistently been to glorify God through sharing His provision and all that He is teaching us through this valley.

I will continue to acknowledge the cold metal bars of earthly death that now separate my family, the open wounds of the attacks of the enemy, and the weight of the shackles of grief because through acknowledging them the power of God's grace in our lives is magnified. I will tell of the pain and then sing of His grace because the prisoners are listening.

Sarah's death was not a gift of God, but Sarah's life and the outpouring of His marvelous grace that sustains us are His gifts. The tremendous hope of the knowledge of Sarah's present ongoing eternal life and our promise of joining Him and her in His presence is the pinnacle promise of His grace about which we are called to testify.

I will continue to vulnerably and transparently expose my shattered heart because in so doing I am able to expose the grace of God that is greater than all my pain. I will join with Paul and Silas as I sing in this prison cell because as He said to Paul, He also says to me, *"'My grace is sufficient for you, for power is perfected in weakness.' Most gladly, therefore, I will rather boast about my weaknesses, so that the power of Christ may dwell in me. Therefore I am well content with weaknesses, with insults, with distresses, with persecutions, with difficulties, for Christ's sake; for when I am weak, then I am strong"* (2 Cor. 12:9-10).

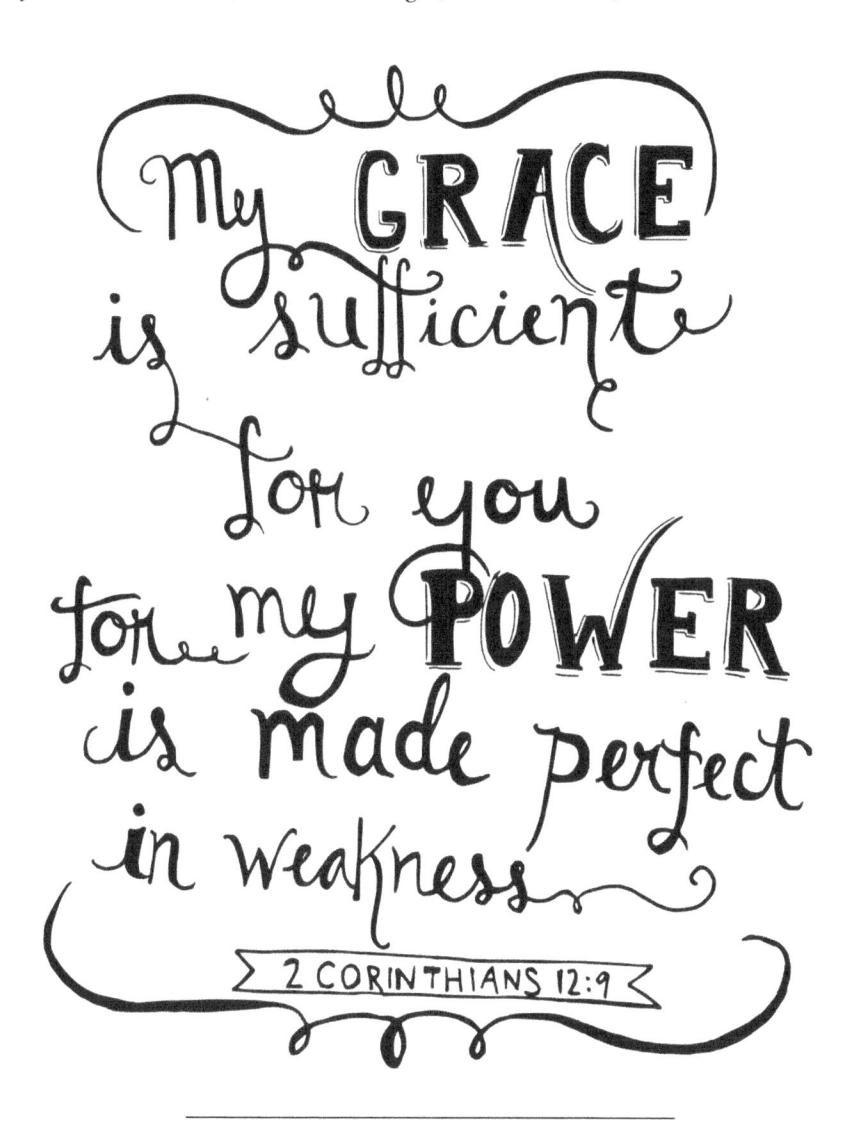

> My GRACE is sufficient for you, for my POWER is made perfect in weakness
> 2 CORINTHIANS 12:9

---

1. "G4164 - poikilos - Strong's Greek Lexicon (kjv)." *Blue Letter Bible*, blueletterbible.org/lexicon/g4164/nasb95/mgnt/0-1/.

MY CHILD DIED. GOD IS GOOD?

DECEMBER 5, 2017

Sunday at church a song was sung that has been stuck in my head ever since. I say "it was sung" instead of "we sang," because both Scott and I found ourselves unable to sing it. We were not familiar with the song so we were particularly attentive to the words. It repeatedly said about God, "You are good, good," followed by repeatedly saying, "You're never gonna let me down."

After several choruses of "You're never gonna let me down," I leaned over to Scott to ask him what exactly he thought it meant. Perhaps the song is written by someone much younger than us and the meaning of that phrase has changed. For us, "never gonna let me down" means I will never be disappointed. Afterward, I looked up the definition in a few resources, similar to our understanding the consensus was it means a failure to do what someone expected or hoped. But in the songwriter's defense, maybe he or she meant God will never forsake us, which is most certainly true.

As I've thought about those lyrics from that song I've been reminded of how we as believers frequently report good news and follow it with a euphoric exclamation of "God is good!" For years, long before Sarah's departure, I've been bothered by stating the truth that "God is good" in the context of good things happening to us.

Linking good circumstances with a statement of God's goodness seems to beg the question, what if it had not been good news? Would God still be good then? Certainly, those good circumstances are blessings of God, but if they are the evidence of God's goodness, what are the terrible circumstances evidence of? I've often wished we instead reserved the statement "God is good" as a battle cry for the wounded rather than an "amen" to everything that goes our way.

The reality is God didn't just let our family down. "Disappointing us" or "letting us down" sounds far too mild. Instead, in the blink of an eye He allowed our family to plummet into a deep, dark, unimaginably painful pit. We had bathed our precious child in prayer, pleading for her safety. I had wrestled with putting her on that bus that morning and had prayerfully gone through the process of entrusting her to Him and His providential care as I allowed her to walk up its steps. I was completely and hopefully expecting him to honor those prayers to keep her safe, and I was wretchedly, horribly, excruciatingly disappointed.

Our family identifies with Paul. Our good God has allowed us to be afflicted, perplexed, persecuted, and—not just let down—*struck down*. We, too, bear *"great sorrow and unceasing grief"* in our hearts. (2 Cor. 4:8-9; Rom. 9:2). Our good God allows His children to be let down, disappointed, wounded, broken, grieved, persecuted, and even killed. He told us in His Word that He would. He repeatedly warns us we live in a fallen world, and that we have an enemy who has come to steal, kill, and destroy (John 10:10). He warns us that we will endure fiery trials (1 Pet. 4:12). And if that's not clear enough, He tells us, *"Indeed, all who desire to live godly in Christ Jesus will be persecuted"* (2 Tim. 3:12).

His goodness is completely independent of our circumstances. His goodness is not contingent on health, wealth, or prosperity. His goodness is not compromised by tribulation or suffering. On the contrary, His goodness is most powerfully experienced and displayed when He, our mighty Deliverer, plunges into the pit with us (Ps. 40).

He is faithful to be there with us as the mire of heartbreak and agony press in tight and we struggle to breathe; He upholds us by His righteous right hand (Isa. 41:10). Though the waters rise, He will not allow us to be completely overtaken (Ps. 69). In the midst of our pain and suffering His sustaining grace is poured out enabling us to persevere and testify, *"we are afflicted in every way,* BUT NOT CRUSHED; *perplexed,* BUT NOT DESPAIRING; *persecuted,* BUT NOT FORSAKEN; *struck down,* BUT NOT DESTROYED*"* (2 Cor. 4:8-9).

Some have mocked our faith since the crash, presuming out of finite imagination that a good god would only allow good circumstances, and would certainly never allow us to be let down or disappointed in such a way as we have suffered. Such a view fails to take into account the totality of Scripture and the fact that this life is not the focus, it is but a flicker. When we look with earthly eyes at the painful circumstances of this temporal life there seems no option but hopelessness and despair.

However, when we view the struggles of this life through the lens of Scripture and eternity, God's goodness is clearly revealed. *"After you have suffered for a little while, the God of all grace, who called you to His eternal glory in Christ, will Himself perfect, confirm, strengthen and establish you"* (1 Pet. 5:10). *"Therefore we do not lose heart, but though our outer man is decaying, yet our inner man is being renewed day by day. For momentary, light affliction is producing for us an eternal weight of glory far beyond all comparison, while we look not at the things which are seen, but at the things which are not seen; for the things which are seen are temporal, but the things which are not seen are eternal."* (2 Cor. 4:16-18).

For most of us, there will come a day when the mountain before us is not moved, the flood is not diverted, or the flames are not quenched. When that day comes we can persevere knowing that, though the path before us is unspeakably hard, we do not go alone.

Our good God was not absent or unaware the day Sarah died. He did not abandon us or forsake us. The mountain was not moved, the flood was not diverted, and the flames were not quenched for our family on June 8, 2017. Even so, He was with us, and we still testify, shouting the battle cry of the wounded—"God is good!"

LONGING TO DIE

DECEMBER 11, 2017

A couple of months after Sarah's departure I had the opportunity to visit with a friend I had not spent time with for several months. I was sharing with her some of our experiences surrounding the crash and in the process had a very candid moment in which I said that I would welcome death. As soon as the words parted from my lips I realized she might not understand. It was as if I could see the words tumbling through the air in slow motion from my mouth to her ears. The moment they hit her ears, her eyes widened and I saw fear in them, possibly even horror. I immediately tried to explain that I was not suicidal, that I was just torn between heaven and earth now more than ever before. I'm not certain I was successful in alleviating her fears that day, and I felt terrible for having traumatized her.

As a result, I've been exceptionally guarded in saying anything of the sort since. What I failed to explain to her that day was that I was not just longing for an escape from the pain. My heart indeed continues to ache and throb. I do long for the day that He will wipe the tears from my eyes, and all the anguish will be as waters gone by (Rev. 21:4; Job 11:16).

More than that, though, I am simply longing for home. As Christians we know that we are aliens here, this world is not our home (1 Pet. 2:11). But to my shame, I have to admit I felt pretty cozy here until June 8th. I clearly saw the waywardness of the world around us, but our family had a little bubble that felt a bit like heaven on earth. I loved it, I was content. I had a desire to be with Christ eventually, but as a mother, my longing to be here to parent and disciple my girls was clearly more compelling. I deeply dreaded the thought of leaving.

Sarah is now home and my heart is torn. I long to be with her there, but I also long to be with her sisters here. My comfortable bubble, my little bit of heaven here has been shattered. Everywhere I go I am constantly reminded this is not home. Particularly in our house, our earthly home—every room, every picture, every memory that floods my mind as I look around reminds me this is not my home. I am so very homesick.

I also long for home because I am warworn. In addition to the weight of the pain of grief, there continues to be spiritual warfare (Eph. 6:12). We don't get a reprieve from the war with our flesh as we grieve, we continue to be responsible for walking in righteousness. When I am tired and weary, my fleshly desires, selfishness, and pride rise threatening to consume me.

I must be alert and sober-minded to crucify them, as well as to avoid the schemes of the enemy (Gal. 5:2; 1 Pet. 5:8-9). I am convinced our enemy, the predator of our souls, joins forces with our flesh and intensifies the attack when he sees us struggling, wounded, and limping. So in the midst of our pain, we must press on in fighting the war against our sinful flesh, while simultaneously buffeting the fiery arrows of the enemy (Eph. 6:16).

I long for the day when this great war is over, for the day I am stripped of this sinful flesh with all its worldly passions and desires. I long for the day when the schemes and arrows of the enemy can no longer reach me. To die will be great gain.

I save for last the greatest reason I am longing for home. I long to be with the Father and the Son, the very One who makes heaven home. I long to be with my loving Father who sacrificed His Son for me. My Father who gives us His song in the night when we are too weak or broken to sing (Job 35:10). My Father who catches my every tear, takes account of each one, and holds them in His bottle (Psa. 56:8). My precious Lord and Savior, the one who gave His life for me. My compassionate risen Lord who I believe stood at the death of Sarah on June 8th, just as He stood at Stephen's (Acts 7:55). Our Good Shepherd who softly and gently leads us, and carries us when we are wounded (John 10:11). Our Great High Priest who lives to intercede for us (Heb. 7:25). Our merciful Savior who beckons us to come to His throne of grace, *"that we may receive mercy and find grace to help in time of need"* (Heb. 4:16). Indeed, to die and be with Him will be great gain.

> For to me, to live is Christ and to die is gain. But if I am to live on in the flesh, this will mean fruitful labor for me; and I do not know which to choose. But I am hard-pressed from both directions, having the desire to depart and be with Christ, for that is very much better; yet to remain on in the flesh is more necessary for your sake. Convinced of this, I know that I will remain and continue with you all for your progress and joy in the faith, so that your proud confidence in me may abound in Christ Jesus through my coming to you again. (Phil. 1:21-26)

Paul's words written from prison to the Philippians resonate so deeply in my soul. *"I am hard-pressed from both directions, having the desire to depart and be with Christ, for that is very much better"* (v. 23). The word "desire" in verse 23 is translated elsewhere as "lust" and "coveting." Paul was deeply longing for home, acknowledging it as *"very much better."* However, he immediately goes on to say, *"Yet to remain on in the flesh is more necessary for your sake."* Paul was emulating Christ in surrendering his personal desire, to desire instead that which is best for his brothers and sisters in Christ.

Jesus Christ left His throne in glory, His and our home, to come to earth to redeem and reconcile us. His act of coming, enduring, and dying on earth was sacrificial from start to finish, not just at the climax of the cross. Jesus told the disciples at the Last Supper, *"A new commandment I give to you, that you love one another, even as I have loved you, that you also love one another"* (John 13:34). The second greatest commandment, to *"love your neighbor as yourself"* (Matt. 22:39), was being intensified through this new commandment. As He was preparing to be crucified, He was telling His disciples, watch me closely because you are to love one another in the way I demonstrate for you.

Paul was responding in obedience to this command to love others as he had been loved by Christ. Compelled by fervent love he chose to persevere in sacrificially pouring his earthly life out for those who had and would come to know Christ. He embraced his call to live, recognizing that to live is Christ.

Though we may be imprisoned by pain, suffering or discouragement, and longing for home, we must choose like Paul to say, *"If I am to live on in the flesh, this will mean fruitful labor for me."* However many days the Lord leaves us here we should long for them to be full of fruitful labor for Him. As we look at those around us, family, friends, acquaintances, and strangers, the words of Paul should ring in our ears, *"to remain is more necessary for their sake, for their progress and joy in the faith."*

God has called us and longs to equip us to impact the lives of others through His love in us if only we will humbly submit to Him and seek His face. Like Paul, fervent love for others should compel us to live and to live fruitfully. We are not our own, we have been bought with a divine price (1 Cor. 6:20). As Christ-followers we are His bondservants to do His bidding. We must embrace our call to live, recognizing that to live is Christ.

> not one of us lives for himself, and not one dies for himself; for if we live, we live for the Lord, or if we die, we die for the Lord; therefore whether we live or die, we are the Lord's (Rom. 14:7-8)

The anguish of my child's death is a sanctifying flame being used by the Refiner to melt away my temporal desires and interests, leaving a piercing focus for that which is eternal. More than ever before I am acutely aware of the race I am running, the purpose for living.

The charge from the book of Hebrews echoes in my mind, *"Therefore, since we have so great a cloud of witnesses surrounding us, let us also lay aside every encumbrance and the sin which so easily entangles us, and let us run with endurance the race that is set before us, fixing our eyes on Jesus, the author and perfecter of faith, who for the joy set before Him endured the cross, despising the shame, and has sat down at the right hand of the throne of God. For consider Him who has endured such hostility by sinners against Himself, so that you will not grow weary and lose heart"* (vv. 12:1-3). So then, let us run this race with endurance, recognizing that to live is Christ.

There is much life to be lived and I want to urgently and obediently live every second of every day ordained for me (Ps. 139:16). His Word tells us we are *"His workmanship, created in Christ Jesus for good works, which God prepared beforehand so that we would walk in them"* (Eph. 2:10). I long to live the remainder of my days with my eyes so fixed on Jesus that I don't miss a single appointment or opportunity that God prepared beforehand for me.

The promises contained in His Living Word will guide and strengthen me to persevere. I will find hope in the midst of pain by meditating on the magnitude of the eternal weight of glory being produced through affliction (2 Cor. 4:17). Through the outpouring of His sustaining grace I will not lose heart until, finally, I will have completed the race on the day appointed for me. On that glorious day, through the power of Christ in me, I will join that great cloud of witnesses joyously proclaiming, *"I have fought the good fight, I have finished the course, I have kept the faith"* (2 Tim. 4:7). For to me, to live is Christ and to die is gain.

NOT SO MERRY CHRISTMAS

DECEMBER 14, 2017

Merry:
1: full of gaiety or high spirits : mirthful
2: marked by festivity or gaiety
archaic: giving pleasure : delightful [1]

It wasn't long at all after the crash that Katelyn, Kristen, and Sophie voiced they wanted to go away over Christmas. They couldn't bear the thought of being at home for Christmas without Sarah. I was so relieved when they said it. I had wanted to run away as well, but above that wanted to do what was best for them.

We are a traditions family, we love traditions and are faithful to them every year, predictable like clockwork. To make matters worse, Sarah embodies a high percentage of our Christmas spirit as a family. She loves Christmas, appropriate since she is our Christmas baby born on December 20th. She and Katelyn are the only two who will push through in decorating the tree each year. Sophie and Kristen will bail out about halfway through, curling up on a sofa or chair under a blanket instead.

But Sarah loves the ornaments. She loves reminiscing over each picture, popsicle stick craft, handprint angel and melt bead ornament.

The thought of hanging each ornament and going on with each tradition without our sweet Sarah is unbearable.

A few weeks after the crash we chose a home on Tybee Island to rent from December 22nd through the 29th. Our parents planned to go with us, and some of our siblings and their families would be joining us part of the time as well. Quiet time away from home, on the beach in particular, would surely be healing to our wounded souls.

As time passed, though, the girls started expressing concern about being away from home so long over Christmas. They were nervous about the possibility of having so much quiet and stillness there that the sadness would somehow be intensified.

So a couple of months ago we decided to cancel the Tybee Island reservation and book a shorter trip to Pigeon Forge, Tennessee, instead. With all the shows and activities there, surely there would be no time for the boredom that allows the mind to dip into the depths of despair. We had our plan, we would busy ourselves with activities to distract ourselves from the pain in our hearts.

We planned to put our Christmas tree up and decorate it on December 3rd. I spent the preceding days trying to brace my heart for the pain that would accompany pulling out each precious memento of years gone by. More than that I was already having to suppress the dread of taking each of those ornaments off the tree to box them up in January. The night finally came. Scott brought the pre-lit tree in and we carefully connected the lights only to discover they would not turn on. We were so disappointed, especially me.

The days leading up to decorating the tree had been like the slow climb up the largest peak of a roller coaster—visions of treasured ornaments popping into my mind like that repeated clicking leading up to the plunge. I had braced for the plunge, I was as ready as I could be, and now I was trapped on the peak. I responded in agitation, "The tree is broken. Of course, the tree is broken. If it can go wrong, it will. This is where we are."

This reveals something about me. I am trusting God with the incomprehensible, with the death of my daughter, but I'm frustrated that He won't "give me a break" on the small stuff. It's the small stuff that I slip into sin over. Through tears, I gave voice to my frustration, "It feels like if you're enduring your worst nightmare, then all the small stuff should work!" But that's not reality, a broken heart earns you no breaks. We have a long list of ongoing fiascos to prove it.

Scott took the tree wiring apart and found the transformer had gone bad. He ordered one online and we waited. In the meantime a precious family friend mailed us a rustic wood cross ornament with "He Comforts" scrolled across it. We hung it alone in the center of our lightless tree.

That week we talked several times about our plans to go to Pigeon Forge, but no one was looking forward to it. One of the girls expressed uncertainty saying "We may just be sad there instead of here, I'd rather be sad at home." After several family discussions, we concluded there is no escape, we can't run away. It's going to be painful wherever we are, so we will stay home and confront it. We will strive for joy but brace for the ongoing inevitable waves of grief and sadness.

On December 8th, the six-month anniversary of the crash and Sarah's departure, the transformer finally arrived. That same day Scott's company had their Christmas party. After applying my makeup and crying it off three separate times, I finally gained enough composure to be able to get out the door. Tears brimmed and drained several times on the way to the party.

Scott wanted to go and I wanted to go for him, but I was dreading it. His company is wonderful and we have been so well loved by them, but my heart was not merry, it was and is shattered. With the ticking of the clock throughout that day and into the night I was repeatedly and unwillingly drifting into thoughts of all the things I had done and experienced "six months ago today at this time."

My goal for the party was simply to not cry through it. I did my best to muster a "not crushed in spirit" face and pressed through. I made it, only allowing the tears to overflow once at the very beginning, and again when we prayed before the meal.

I was confronted with a dilemma at that party, though. Up until then, I had managed to avoid Christmas for the most part. But now, for almost four hours we were surrounded by festive celebration with repeated cheerful exclamations of "Merry Christmas!" When it was spoken to me directly, my eyes still brimming with tears from the quiet drive there, my heart recoiled in my chest. What do I say in response? This is not a merry Christmas at all, my heart is broken, how can I possibly say those words?

I had not thought about how to answer, all I knew was my lips would not form those words, not then, and not now. "Thank you." That's all I could come up with in response. My mind was suddenly reeling with questions, is my lack of merriness reflective of a lack of faith? Is it a sin to not think Christmas is merry? Am I not appreciating Christ by not enjoying Christmas this year? So many thoughts, and in the midst of the torrential flood of emotions, so few answers.

The next day was Katelyn's college graduation. My goal for the day was to celebrate Katelyn. I wanted to remind her how very much she is loved and how proud we are of her, not because of a college degree but because of who she is. I believe we celebrated her well. At the end of the day, the five of us were in the living room, the lights of the tree twinkling with our single ornament in the center. I believe it was Sophie who said it first, "I like the tree like that." My heart leapt in my chest, "Yes, I do, too!" Everyone agreed it was the perfect way to keep the tree this year. The lights are glistening like the hope that remains in our hearts, but only a singular message to be spoken for us this Christmas, "He Comforts."

It wasn't until two days later that I realized the blown transformer had been more of God's tender care for me, His comfort. By delaying the decorating of the tree, He had graciously delivered my shattered heart from a task that was certain to crush the remaining shards. Conviction immediately fell over me. I have no explanation for why I trust Him when my world completely falls apart, but I so frequently fail to trust Him with the small stuff. Perhaps I am too quick to assume He's not in the small stuff. It never entered my mind He could be working through those broken lights, but oh how my loving Father was working on my behalf. Lord, I believe, help my unbelief.

For our family, this is not a merry Christmas, and that's okay. It is not a sin for us to not feel merry. It's not a sin to not feel like celebrating the holiday. The absence of merriness does not reflect an absence of faith. The reality is we have never celebrated more the arrival and provision of our precious Savior. We boldly proclaim He is our only hope. He is our only Redeemer. He is our only Sustainer. He is our only Deliverer. He is our only Comforter. He is the one who sometimes blows transformers to spare our wounded hearts suffering upon suffering.

I am celebrating Him in the depths of my heart, just not with "gaiety, high spirits, and festivity." Not right now, and maybe not even next year, either. If not, that's okay, too.

If there's one thing I'm learning in all of this, it's to trust Him and walk in obedience to Matthew 6:34, *"So do not worry about tomorrow; for tomorrow will care for itself. Each day has enough trouble of its own."*

> Be Comforted dear soul! There is always light behind the clouds.
> —LOUISA MAY ALCOTT

---

1. "Merry, *Adj.* (1-3)." *Merriam-Webster Dictionary,* merriam-webster.com/dictionary/merry. Accessed 14 Dec. 2017.

A MOTHER'S PAIN

DECEMBER 20, 2017

"Whenever a woman is in labor she has pain, because her hour has come; but when she gives birth to the child, she no longer remembers the anguish because of the joy that a child has been born into the world."
John 16:21

December 20, 1999, was a day marked by intense pain followed by consuming joy. John 16:21 is perfectly true regarding the birth of Sarah Lauren Harmening. As I sit here this morning, eighteen years later, I can not recall the pain of that day, but I very much recall the thrill of holding that beautiful baby girl in my arms.

Unlike the pain of December 20, 1999, I'm certain the pain of December 20, 2017, will not be forgotten. As I sit here in the dark of early morning I recall the excitement as we traveled to the hospital eighteen years ago today. I would soon be holding the precious baby who felt so long awaited. Today I again find myself longing to hold that same precious baby, but recognizing my wait has the potential to be so very much longer.

As I was lying awake through the night watches I was thinking about the oppressive weight of the pain in my heart. In my mind's eye,

I once again traced the pain to its source, the fall of man. The pain I felt eighteen years ago and the pain I feel today both originated in the exact same moment. Both the pain of childbirth and the pain of death entered in Genesis 3. The pain of childbirth is only a fleeting memory, particularly in comparison to the debilitating sting of death.

With the prevalence of the prosperity gospel some have mistakenly come to believe that we as believers should be free from pain and hardship, and to experience otherwise is evidence of a lack of faith. It is wrongly implied living victoriously in Christ means we live free of the impact of the fallenness of this world. It is presumed we are to be free from pain, suffering, grief, trials, and tribulations.

Joy in Christ is wrongly understood to mean the absence of pain and the presence of perpetual happiness. These beliefs and teachings can result in unintentionally pious Christians who meticulously hide away their pain, fearing that acknowledging its brutal grip will indicate a failure to abide in Christ. I'm convinced this is another brilliant scheme of our adversary.

Experiencing and acknowledging pain and grief is not evidence of a lack of faith or joy in the life of a believer. They are simply evidence we live in a fallen world and suffer some of the consequences of that fallenness. Every twinge of pain should be a reminder of the consequences of sin: Adam and Eve's sin, and our sin. Pain should be a powerful reminder harnessed to propel us toward righteousness.

Pain, suffering, mourning, grief, trials, and tribulations are acknowledged as ongoing realities throughout Scripture. As followers of Christ we are never promised to be spared from these things, but we are promised His grace and mercy to sustain and uphold us. As Brother Jimmy shared having heard someone else say, "God's grace is sufficient, but it's not novocaine."

Though we as believers have been gloriously redeemed, we are not spared the painful, temporal consequences of sin. In this life, we will all taste the hardships of the fall: brokenness, pain, and death. Just as pain should propel us toward righteousness, it should also compel our sharing of the gospel. We are called to be Christ's ambassadors to a broken, hurting, and dying world.

Our tasting of the pain of brokenness and death powerfully equips us to be effective ambassadors. If I am unwilling to experience and transparently share about the deep sting of pain and death, how can I testify to His faithfulness and provision as the great comforter (2 Cor. 1:3-4)? If I am unwilling to acknowledge the hurdles of this life, how can I testify to the joy that perseverance brings amid the hurdles and pain (Job 6:10)? If I refuse to acknowledge the depths of the sting of death, how can I adequately testify to the weight of the glorious truth that the day is coming when there shall be no more death (Rev. 21:3-4)?

> Blessed be the God and Father of our Lord Jesus Christ, the Father of mercies and God of all comfort, who comforts us in all our affliction so that we will be able to comfort those who are in any affliction with the comfort with which we ourselves are comforted by God. (2 Cor. 1:3-4)

> But it is still my consolation, And I rejoice in unsparing pain, That I have not denied the words of the Holy One. (Job 6:10)

Therefore, I am compelled to transparently share this morning that my heart is still shattered. I desperately long to hold my child, to feel her hair brush across my face as she hugs me, to hear her laugh, and to see her eyes light up as she tells a story. I ache beyond words that there will be no birthday celebration with my child today.

In the midst of all that pain, though, He is faithful. Though He allows the pain to persist, He faithfully comforts me in it. He is faithful to graciously uphold me by His righteous right hand, and I confidently know He will remain faithful. More glorious than that, though, is the hope of knowing there is coming a day when He will wipe away every tear from our eyes, and there will be no more death, no more mourning, no more crying, and no more pain. *"He who testifies to these things says, 'Yes, I am coming quickly.' Amen. Come, Lord Jesus"* (Rev. 22:20).

EXTRACTING THE PRECIOUS

DECEMBER 27, 2017

Why has my pain been perpetual And my wound incurable, refusing to be healed? Will You indeed be to me like a deceptive stream With water that is unreliable? Therefore, thus says the LORD, "If you return, then I will restore you– Before Me you will stand; And if you extract the precious from the worthless, You will become My spokesman. They for their part may turn to you, But as for you, you must not turn to them." Jeremiah 15:18-19

I have wrestled for a couple of weeks with the thought of sharing this part of my journey. I've been inhibited by a pervasive concern that it is too intimate to effectively share. Not too intimate in the sense that it will require too much vulnerability. But too intimate in the sense that it might be such an intimate encounter with the Lord that I can not adequately convey the magnitude of what happened.

However, it has impacted me so profoundly that I have repeatedly felt prompted to share for two weeks now, so I will do my best to put to words at least a portion of what He impressed upon my heart.

Before I share what happened, I need to share my life verse and how I came to choose it as my life verse. I believe it was shortly before Valentine's Day of 2005. My mom asked me what my favorite verse was. I am generally stumped by that question, I'm not certain how to choose one "favorite." I might have a favorite for battling discouragement, another for inspiring me to persevere, another for reminding me of the attributes of God, and so forth. To narrow it down to one overall favorite verse seems impossible to me.

She explained she was wanting to have matching bracelets made for my dear friend and me, each with our favorite verses. Touched by her idea, I told her I would pray and think about it, which I did. I can't remember now how I ended up in Jeremiah. I'm unsure if that's where I happened to be in my quiet time reading when she asked, or if the Lord led me there on a quest. But somehow I ended up reading Jeremiah 15:16, and in that moment I knew that was the verse for me. I claimed it not as my favorite verse, but as my life verse; I long for it to be the verse that characterizes my life. From that day forward that verse has been very precious to me.

> When your words came, I ate them; they were my joy and my heart's delight, for I bear your name, LORD God Almighty. (Jer. 15:16 NIV)

Fast forward to the week of December 10th, 2017. Several things had recently happened that amplified my awareness of my solitude. My heart was aching with the pain of longing for Sarah, but it was compounded by deep loneliness and the stings of circumstances beyond my influence or control. As I sought the Lord through tears of discouragement the morning of December 13th, I laid my hands on my Bible and pled with Him to encourage my weary heart, and to strengthen my weak and trembling legs to enable me to continue to stand.

In the desperation of my aloneness, I searched His Word for encouragement by doing a word search on BlueLetterBible.org for "alone." Skimming the verses that showed in the results, Jeremiah 15:17 instantly caught my eye and resonated with my heart. I immediately flipped to it in my Bible.

I did not sit in the circle of merrymakers, Nor did I exult. Because of Your hand upon me I sat alone, For You filled me with indignation. (Jer. 15:17)

It wasn't until I opened my Bible to Jeremiah 15 that it connected in my mind that this verse that now resonated with my broken heart was the very next verse following my life verse, claimed and clung to for more than a decade. I read the remainder of the chapter, and I wept both bitterly and joyfully.

It was simultaneously convicting and encouraging. It was as if the Lord audibly spoke and told me He had given me that life verse so long ago for a reason. I thought I had claimed that verse as a goal, but He had claimed it for me as a promise. It was given to me as my identification and my reminder for such a time as this.

I clearly discerned Him impressing on my heart that now the remainder of that chapter is His direction for me as well. I have a choice to make: I can wallow in and waste time dwelling on the worthless, or I can extract the precious and allow Him to wash the worthless away.

The enemy of our souls throws so much worthless our way. He devises scheme after scheme seeking to distract, cripple and destroy us. Worthless thoughts he whispers in our ears to breed fear, doubt, and insecurity. Worthless words of gossip he circulates through flaming tongues speaking in ignorance, then delivers to our ears to scorch our wounded hearts. Worthless tasks and pursuits he dangles before us to distract us from the only truly worthy goal. On and on the adversary's list of schemes and "worthless" lures goes.

He seeks to bury all the precious that the Lord has for us beneath mounds of worthless. But we are called to extract the precious from the worthless. I am called right now, in the midst of my brokenness, to continue to extract the precious from the worthless. In fact, what more opportune time to clearly discern the precious and distinguish it from the worthless than in the flames of adversity?

> In this you greatly rejoice, even though now for a little while, if necessary, you have been distressed by various trials, so that the proof of your faith, being more precious than gold which is perishable, even though tested by fire, may be found to result in praise and glory and honor at the revelation of Jesus Christ (1 Pet. 1:6-7)

Amid the flames of pain, longing, and loneliness my desire to be used by Him compels me to beg Him to use those very flames to refine me, clearly revealing that which is precious. Each time I feel the burn of one of the enemy's schemes I will ask Him to use it, too, to reveal the precious to me so that I may "extract it" as a costly gem. I will also ask Him to simultaneously reveal to me that which is worthless so I can forsake it and allow Him to purge it.

I long to become the spokesman He has called me to be (Col. 3:16). May I never allow that which is worthless to blind me to or distract me from that which is precious. Nothing worthless is worthy of sacrificing His plan for me. So through His divine power in me, I commit to set my heart to discern and throw off the worthless, so I may increasingly possess and share the precious for my good and His glory.

> Grace and peace be multiplied to you in the knowledge of God and of Jesus our Lord; seeing that His divine power has granted to us everything pertaining to life and godliness, through the true knowledge of Him who called us by His own glory and excellence. For by these He has granted to us His precious and magnificent promises, so that by them you may become partakers of the divine nature, having escaped the corruption that is in the world by lust. (2 Pet. 1:2-4)

MOMENT BY MOMENT

JANUARY 1, 2018

Within days of Sarah leaving, we as a family began dreading the upcoming Christmas season. We were certain it, combined with Sarah's December 20th birthday, would be filled with devastatingly hard days. In the months leading up to December, we tried to come up with a strategy to somehow reduce the pain of those days, all to no avail. In early December we finally accepted that we could not avoid the coming hard days and the pain they would bring with them. We resolved as a family to make our way through the season one day at a time.

 I didn't sleep the night before Sarah's birthday, I was instead reliving the hours leading up to her arrival. I arose early and wrote what had been on my heart through the night watches. I then spent some time reading her baby book and reminiscing, moments accompanied by both smiles and tears. Later that afternoon we were so blessed as some of our dear church family came to our home to pray with and for us. After they left, a florist delivered a beautiful arrangement from a precious family who also knows the pain of losing a child. After the florist left, a sweet friend showed up at the door with a stack of cards from other friends, acquaintances, and strangers sharing their thoughts and prayers with us.

Our birthday tradition for each of the girls is a family dinner at home and a dessert of their choosing. We decided to break away from the sting of that tradition for Sarah's birthday; Katelyn, Kristen, and Sophie requested we go eat dinner at a restaurant instead, which we did. When we got home, Scott and I sat on the sofa reading each of the cards that had been delivered by the friend, as well as others that arrived in the mail. What a blessing each card and note was to our aching hearts.

The day as a whole was very reminiscent of the days immediately after Sarah's departure. It was a day marked by a clear ebb and flow of pain and tangible grace. Multiple moments of stark heart-wrenching reality followed by clear outpourings of God's grace through the touch of His people; we were so richly blessed by our brothers and sisters in Christ this day.

Christmas Eve and Christmas Day we decided to push through our family traditions with the exception of Christmas stockings. The girls did not have strong feelings about what to do with stockings this year, so I elected to not get them out of storage. Whenever they come out again, they will all be out, Sarah's included. But this year I didn't think my shattered heart could withstand seeing hers alone and empty Christmas morning, so we had Christmas bags instead, and it was just fine.

We played lots of games on Christmas Eve and Christmas Day, both days being full of moments of special family time and laughter as well as moments of heart-crushing anguish; two more days marked by the ebb and flow of pain and grace. Grace is evidenced in special moments of love and joy with family, times which now more than ever, we do not take for granted. But more importantly, we were also aware of the grace we were celebrating, the very reason we have confident hope we will soon see Sarah again—the coming of our Lord and Savior.

Now that we have survived those dreaded "hard days," more of the big "firsts" without Sarah, I've learned it's better for me to think in terms of moments rather than days. There were many exceedingly hard and painful moments within those dreaded days, but there were also moments where God's grace and provision were palpable. There were moments of laughter and joy interspersed with moments of the overwhelming, indescribable pain of longing for our child.

The reality is those daunting days we had dreaded for so long were not all that different from all the other days since June 8, 2017. Each day has held moments of joy and pain; sometimes the balance tips to one side or the other, but both are always present. While it would have been very easy for the balance of these particular days to tip fully to pain, and there certainly was much pain, through fervent prayer and God's grace there were also many moments of joy, laughter, love, and peace.

The daunting days and dates may hold more ripe cumulative opportunities for piercing pain, but they lack the element of surprise. I expected them to be dreadful, and while they were in many ways dreadful, the depth of pain was not new or surprising. It was the same deep indescribable pain I have felt in waves regularly for months.

In fact, in some ways, I may actually struggle more when I am caught off guard on an otherwise nonsignificant day or date by an unexpected wave of the same pain. I was hit by such a wave when we took Katelyn, Kristen, and Sophie ice skating a few days after Christmas. After we had been there for a little while and were enjoying our time together, a man came out to the center of the rink with his little girl. He was bald like Scott and she had brunette hair much like Sarah's. They remained in the center of the rink for the majority of our time there. Seeing them together was like a living flashback of Scott playing with Sarah. Each time I passed them hugging and laughing together it was like the twisting of a dagger in my heart. I found myself skating faster and faster, partially to avoid focusing on them and partially to ensure the streams of tears now running down my face would dry before they were noticed.

I was hit by another such wave the next day when the girls and I were sitting in a waiting area near another mother and daughter. The mother looked in our direction, but not at anyone specifically, and asked if the girls were three sisters. I attempted to change the subject but she asked again, this time looking directly at me, "So you have three girls?" I recognized the potential string of questions probably getting ready to ensue so I attempted to subvert them by answering candidly, "I have four daughters but we lost one in an accident." She carried on with the conversation as if nothing out of the ordinary had been spoken, but my heart was rent, every ounce of energy I had was refocused into trying to hold back the impending cascade of tears rising in my eyes.

Those are just the two most recent among many unexpected waves of pain. Perhaps one or both are unrelatable in the absence of having lost your child, but for me, both bore a similar sting to many of the stings of the dreaded days. As I write this I am reminded there is another moment that my heart is pierced daily, and that is bedtime. Bedtime brings a nightly aching of my arms as I long to hug my child and tell her how much I love her. Each night finds me seeking the balm of His Word as I go to bed missing that treasured nightly ritual of seventeen and a half years.

I share all of that to say—thinking in terms of moments rather than days has proven helpful in encouraging me and casting out fear, particularly as I approach painful days and dates. There are still many "firsts" to be trudged through without Sarah, and after all of those are completed, there will be the entire collection of "seconds" and then "thirds." Thinking of my time in moments rather than days guards my heart from despair. It reminds me that though each day continues to bring indescribably hard and painful moments, those moments will continue to be flanked by moments where joy and peace dominate.

Each day will continue to have the ebb and flow of pain and grace. In the moments that breathtaking pain dominates I can remind myself it is momentary, and He will soon provide moments dominated again by joy and peace. No day, no matter how excruciatingly painful, is ever void of His grace and mercy. As I think of my days in terms of moments, I can acknowledge the often consuming pain in the midst of the painful moments but cling to the hope that with the certainty of the ocean tides, a fresh wave of grace is coming any moment now.

LAUGHTER IN THE VALLEY

JANUARY 8, 2018

"A joyful heart is good medicine, but a crushed spirit dries up the bones."
Proverbs 17:22 ESV

Our home has always been one characterized by joy and laughter. We find humor in almost everything, and we delight greatly in evoking laughter in one another. The day of the crash I promised Katelyn, Kristen, and Sophie that we would find our way back to joy. I promised them we would smile and laugh again, but I had no idea how we would get there. In those moments, it was unfathomable that this oppressive pain we were only just beginning to feel the full weight of could possibly lift enough to allow any joy, let alone actual laughter.

My first laugh...

The day after the crash we found ourselves over twenty-four hours without sleep and needing to get back to Huntsville. It would have been unsafe for either Scott or me to drive at that point, and the thought of being trapped in the van for hours on the same course we had so traumatically driven the day before was unbearable. A family friend graciously agreed to come get us in his eight-passenger jet to take us back to Huntsville. It would be a twenty-six-minute flight, rather than a three and half hour drive, we were so thankful.

Neither Kristen nor Sophie had ever flown, so when we told them we would be flying, Sophie expressed some apprehension. In what was probably not one of my better parenting moments, I told her it was a win-win situation: "We'll be there in twenty-six minutes or we'll be with Sarah, either way—we'll be fine." She hesitantly agreed to go. It was such a blessing to not have to go through a commercial airport, we walked straight out to the jet and boarded.

Scott and I sat in the back seats in the tail, Sophie sat knee to knee with me, Kristen was knee to knee with Scott, Katelyn was in the front row back to back with Sophie, and Katelyn's boyfriend was in the front seat right next to the door, back to back with Kristen. After what seemed like a prolonged period of taxiing, we finally took off.

While we were still climbing in a somewhat steep ascent, we began to turn to the right. As we turned, suddenly the door of the jet flew open revealing mostly sky, and earth far below. Katelyn's boyfriend, who was sitting right next to the door, quickly grabbed it and pulled it to. He was unable to completely close it or latch it, though, so he held it in place as best he could and looked back to Scott and me for help.

Katelyn, assuming her boyfriend was about to be sucked out of the jet, was frantically clinging to his arm and telling me to do something. Scott sat leaning back in his seat with his arms crossed, no reaction at all. Sophie and Kristen were silent, just looking around to see what was going to happen. To everyone's surprise, mine included, my reaction was to laugh.

The pilot and co-pilot had headphones on and couldn't hear us talking, or me laughing. As Katelyn's boyfriend's panic grew, we all, with the exception of Scott, joined together in repeatedly shouting toward the cockpit, "The door is open!" Finally, after what seemed like several minutes but was probably only seconds, the co-pilot heard us and told the pilot.

We turned back to the airport and landed safely. When we landed, Katelyn looked at me with a smirk and proclaimed with a stern accusatory tone, "I thought you had prayed us down! [to our demise]" Which evoked more laughter from me. Our friend re-latched the door, and we took off again for an uneventful flight, safely landing in Huntsville twenty-six minutes later.

I still look back on that event with such great gratitude. When laughing seemed so very unthinkable, this story was one of the few that possessed the power to make all of us laugh, not a little superficial laugh, but a genuine hearty laugh. If you were around us at all in the early weeks after Sarah's departure, you no doubt heard this story as it was a lifeline of laughter for us.

From the very first moments after the crash, it was vitally important to me that our remaining daughters knew we as a family would have joy and laughter again. Their lives and joy had not "ended" because Sarah's physical life had "ended." I was and am convinced that the restoration of Scott's and my joy and our ability to laugh is part of our testimony to our girls and others that the hope that we profess is real and certain. We can experience joy and laughter because we know Sarah is safely home rejoicing in the presence of our Lord and Savior. Laughter has returned to our home, we laugh often and heartily. We have the joy of Christ that enables us to laugh despite the persisting, indescribably deep pain of Sarah's absence.

I have heard many who have lost loved ones, particularly those who have lost a child, express deep guilt over experiencing joy and laughter. I am convinced this is yet another cunning strategy of our adversary. With his choice weapon of lies, the enemy clamors to convince us to stifle even the faintest glimmers of joy that begin to glisten in the darkness of grief.

He whispers, "Your joy and laughter would surely mean you are not appropriately or adequately grieving your loved one." If that lie is not effective, he may whisper, "Others will think you are fine, that your heart is no longer shattered," "If they see you laughing they will question your love for the one who is gone." Or, "How can you laugh now or enjoy this when your loved one doesn't get to experience it?" Any thought that implies we must not laugh or experience joy while in the valley of the shadow of death is a flaming arrow from the father of lies (Eph. 6:16).

Each moment of joy, whether in the valley or not, is a precious gift of God's grace, peace, and mercy. But in the valley, moments of joy bathed in His grace are the *"good medicine"* that strengthens and refreshes us to withstand the ongoing waves of pain that continue to take our breath away (Prov. 17:22). The enemy targets those moments and our joy because he knows they are vital to our faith and witness.

As believers, we are called to rejoice in Him and His salvation. Through the power of His Holy Spirit indwelling us, His eternal joy can prevail over our temporal anguish. Perhaps first appearing and experienced only as glimmers, and then fleeting moments that gradually run longer and deeper. Our greatest and most elaborate joy here on earth pales in comparison to the joy our believing loved ones are experiencing in the presence of our Lord and Savior. Their joy did not end with their physical deaths but was instead transformed into uninterrupted, never-ending, eternally perfected *"joy inexpressible and full of glory"* (1 Pet. 1:8).

As Scott has said many times, if Sarah could come back, she wouldn't want to. She has fully tasted and knows the richness of His presence. Her faith has become sight, and I'm confident she is exuberantly worshipping Him at this very moment. There is no place she would rather be. She is experiencing eternal joy, and I greatly rejoice in His gracious promised provision of that for her and us.

Because of this certainty, the hope of His salvation, I can and should rejoice in this very moment. As I choose to rejoice, His joy penetrates the shroud of my grief, shining forth its light even in the deepest pit of affliction and pain. The restoration of His joy in us is both blessing and obedience, and contrary to the accusations of the enemy it is absolutely not a cause for guilt or shame.

The restoration of joy and laughter does not indicate "healing" of the gaping wound of Sarah's absence. The pain of my child's absence is ever-present and often excruciating. I desperately long for my child. My arms and my heart ache for her. But we *"do not grieve like the rest of mankind, who have no hope"* (1 Thess. 4:13). Praise God, through His hope I can rejoice, because I know with certainty I will see her again.

In the meantime, pain and joy will continue to collide, weeping and laughter will co-exist, and suffering and hope will endure in unison. And eventually, on that coming glorious day, *"He will wipe away every tear from [our] eyes, and death shall be no more, neither shall there be mourning, nor crying, nor pain anymore, for the former things [will] have passed away"* (Rev. 21:4).

> Rejoice in hope, be patient in tribulation, be constant in prayer. (Rom. 12:12 ESV)

Let me hear joy and gladness; let the bones that you have broken rejoice. Hide your face from my sins, and blot out all my iniquities. Create in me a clean heart, O God, and renew a right spirit within me. Cast me not away from your presence, and take not your Holy Spirit from me. Restore to me the joy of your salvation, and uphold me with a willing spirit. (Ps. 51:8-12 ESV)

> I WOULD Always RATHER be HAPPY THAN Dignified
> — CHARLOTTE BRONTË

RAINS OF REFRESHING

❦

JANUARY 11, 2018

"Come, let us return to the LORD.
For He has torn us, but He will heal us;
He has wounded us, but He will bandage us.
He will revive us after two days;
He will raise us up on the third day,
That we may live before Him.
So let us know, let us press on to know the LORD.
His going forth is as certain as the dawn;
And He will come to us like the rain,
Like the spring rain watering the earth."
Hosea 6:1-3

Two days a week I take Sophie to classes at a church across town. Because she only has three classes, one class one day and two the other, there's not enough time to return home while she's in them. As a result, both days I typically sit in the parking lot in the car and wait. More often than not these forced times of stillness result in the spilling of my tears.

I have repeatedly tried to productively use these hours of parking lot time, but only with marginal success. My raw heart has very much grown to dread my time there. From the start, I have never doubted that the preciousness of the drive time with Sophie is worth any pain the parking lot time holds. Nonetheless, I was greatly relieved to have a break from those trying hours of entrapment once Christmas break arrived.

School resumed on January 8th, as did my parking lot time. Seven months to the day from when Sarah left us, and there I sat trapped alone again with my shattered heart. I sat in the parking lot facing the church, battle-ready, Bible in hand, and worship music playing. I closed my eyes and communed in prayer with Him. I opened my eyes and watched the raindrops steadily landing on and rolling down the windshield.

As I shifted my focus, I noticed in the distance the cross on the church before me. In that moment I was reminded how just as I shifted my focus from the raindrops to the cross, I am called to look through this raging storm that currently engulfs me to fix my focus on Him (Isa. 26:3-4).

I was reminded that He promises to sustain through the storms of this life those who are founded upon Him (Matt. 7:25). I was reminded that He promises to satisfy, strengthen and comfort us like the rains that replenish scorched lands (Isa. 58:11). Though our souls may be dry and parched from suffering and pain, as we continue to hunger and thirst for righteousness, He promises we will be filled (Matt. 5:6). As we fix our eyes on Him, we will be fully satisfied in Him (Psalm 22:26).

I'm so thankful for His gentleness and faithfulness to meet us in our brokenness. The dispenser of the rain and the collector of my tears sees me, knows me, and loves me. He has not forgotten me, forsaken me, nor abandoned me. Though He has torn and wounded me in allowing Sarah's death, He promises to bind up and eventually heal me. And through the blood of Jesus Christ, raised on the third day, He has graciously enabled me to live before Him.

So in the midst of the storm, I will focus on Him. I will press on to know Him, confident in the certainty of His coming, and with Him the rains of refreshing.

So let us know, let us press on to know the LORD. His going forth is as certain as the dawn; And He will come to us like the rain, Like the spring rain watering the earth. (Hos. 6:3)

Sarah's journal entry from one year ago today included a one-line note from our church's student worship service, so divinely timed and appropriate.

January 11, 2017

> "When things get dark, you can focus on Jesus."
>
> — SARAH HARMENING

Above all else guard your heart for everything you do flows from it.
— PROVERBS 4:23 —

MORNING IS COMING

JANUARY 17, 2018

*"My soul waits for the Lord More than the watchmen for the morning;
Indeed, more than the watchmen for the morning."*
Psalm 130:6

It happened again in the depths of the darkness last night. Exactly the same as it has happened almost nightly for over six months now. Six months, not seven, because I was unable to sleep at night the first month after Sarah left. It happens most frequently between 2:30 and 2:40 a.m.

It's as if grief is an enormous bird of prey that recognizes the vulnerability of my desperately needed slumber, and opportunistically and violently strikes. I am jolted awake by its talons abruptly clutching my chest, piercing my heart, and squeezing the breath from my lungs. Two thoughts join as one and instantaneously shock me with the impact: "The bus crashed" and "Sarah is gone."

Both ever-present thoughts and undeniable realities, but in the depth of night especially—completely incomprehensible. My mind races. I know it is true. I have borne the months of pain that testify it is true. Yet, somehow in the dark of night, my shattered heart pulses with hope as it tries to convince me, "Surely we have been deceived, it can not possibly be true!" My mind and my heart cry out against each other.

In the darkness of the night, seconds are as minutes, and minutes as hours. My mind replays memory after memory. I can feel her snuggled in the bed beside me. I can hear her sweet voice laughing and chatting away, recounting all the day's events. I can smell her freshly washed hair. I can feel the bed shift slightly as she drapes herself across the edge next to me, begging me to rub her back, and delighting when I do.

With each memory, the talons tighten. The gripping pain becomes unbearable. My soul cries out with that of King David: *"I am weary with my sighing; Every night I make my bed swim, I dissolve my couch with my tears. My eye has wasted away with grief"* (Ps. 6:6-7a). The darkness of night prevails as the light of hope is shrouded by the blackness of despair.

I focus my mind on praying, hoping my heart and soul will soon follow. I cry out to God for mercy, compassion, comfort, and grace. I intercede for my family and others. I meditate on and cling to the truths of His Word. Gradually, as minutes have ticked away to hours, the talons loosen. I can breathe again, though the pain of their gaping wounds remains. I drift off to sleep.

A couple of hours later my eyes open once again, this time absent the violence of the sudden strike. No need, the pressure of the grip and the wounds of the talons from a few hours before linger as painful reminders. Light filters through the blinds on the windows as the sun rises and I am confronted with the reality of yet another day without my precious child. Another day of mustering resolve to go through the day in a way that brings honor and glory to the Lord and strengthens and supports my family.

The sun has risen but morning has not yet come. Night remains as we trudge through the dark valley of the shadow of death. But morning is coming. That glorious long-awaited morning is coming; as certain as the rising of the sun. We are told of that morning: *"But for you who fear My name, the sun of righteousness will rise with healing in its wings; and you will go forth and skip about like calves from the stall"* (Mal. 4:2).

Oh, brokenhearted brothers and sisters, we must remind ourselves, *"Weeping may last for the night, But a shout of joy comes in the morning"* (Ps. 30:5b). There is a coming dawn when we will joyously proclaim with all the saints, *"You have turned for me my mourning into dancing; You have loosed my sackcloth and girded me with gladness, That my soul may sing praise to You and not be silent. O LORD my God, I will give thanks to You forever"* (Ps. 30:11-12).

On that glorious morning, we will joyfully proclaim His lovingkindness. In the meantime, through the remaining darkness of this night, we will experience and boldly proclaim His faithfulness (Ps. 92:2). He is perfectly faithful, even in the darkest of nights. He is near to the brokenhearted, giving us His song to sustain us in the night (Ps. 34:18; 42:8). Our mighty yet gentle Shepherd beckons, *"Come to Me, all who are weary and heavy-laden, and I will give you rest. Take My yoke upon you and learn from Me, for I am gentle and humble in heart, and YOU WILL FIND REST FOR YOUR SOULS. For My yoke is easy and My burden is light"* (Matt. 11:28-30).

Surrendered to Him and empowered by His grace, I will persevere. I will expectantly fix my eyes on the Good Shepherd, the Sun of Righteousness, and follow wherever He leads, for it is He, One with the Father, alone, *"who changes deep darkness into morning."* (Amos 5:8).

He who testifies to these things says,
"Yes, I am coming quickly." Amen. Come, Lord Jesus.
The grace of the Lord Jesus be with all. Amen.
Revelation 22:20-21

REDEEM MY PAIN, O GOD.

FEBRUARY 4, 2018

"Look upon my affliction and rescue me,
For I do not forget Your law.
Plead my cause and redeem me;
Revive me according to Your word."
Psalm 119:153-154

Since the moments immediately following Sarah's earthly death, I have clung to the hope that God would use both her death and our indescribable pain to further His kingdom. The pain of Sarah's absence drives an urgency within my spirit: a longing to "do" something and a desperation to be used by God in a way I can see. I hoped and believed that this deep pain would surely be met with "big redemption." Big redemption being something of broad, tangible, visible, powerful, and ongoing impact.

I've prayed over and over again with hands open before Him and tears flowing, pleading with Him to show me what He would have me do. If led by Him, I would be willing to move around the globe to share His name, to go to school for broader ministry opportunities, or to pour myself into ministry locally. I am willing to follow Him wherever and however He leads. I've offered it all up to Him, the pain, and my life as a whole, but all He has spoken in response is *"Wait."* Over and over again, both through prayer and His Word He repeatedly says only—*"Wait."*

> I would have despaired unless I had believed that I would see the goodness of the LORD In the land of the living. Wait for the LORD; Be strong and let your heart take courage; Yes, wait for the LORD. (Ps. 27:13-14)

For months, *"wait"* was the only response He gave my petitions, until a couple of weeks ago. A couple of weeks ago through His Word and prayer He gently spoke another word to my heart, and what He whispered was not what I wanted to hear.

In the stillness of my quiet time, I felt Him asking if I would be content if the only redemption I ever saw was the refining of my own heart. He prodded my heart asking if I would be satisfied if the only lasting change to come from all the pain associated with Sarah's death, as well as the excruciating circumstances surrounding it, is my personal sanctification.

My transparent response was one of great disappointment. The Holy Spirit within me boldly testifies that personal sanctification is more than enough redemption for the agony I bear. But my aching heart resists that notion as it longs instead for what it perceives as big redemption.

My flesh cries out for redemption that it deems more worthy of the excruciating pain being redeemed. Others who bear the same or similar pain get to see redemption in the form of foundations and ministries that have a tremendous ongoing impact for His kingdom. Yet, the Lord is speaking to my shattered heart that it must be willing to be content with the possibility of its own refining being the only redemption.

The truth is, I deeply longed for the big redemption to be the spark of heart-transforming revival in our church and community. We as a family, Sarah included, had prayed for revival in our church and community throughout the year preceding her death. How can I possibly be content if instead, my heart is the only one meaningfully impacted?

> Sow with a view to righteousness, Reap in accordance with kindness; Break up your fallow ground, For it is time to seek the LORD until He comes to rain righteousness on you. (Hos. 10:12)

As I wrestled with the Spirit through Scripture and prayer, I was confronted with the reality of my misplaced focus. I recognized the sanctifying work the Lord was doing in my heart through the pain, but I failed to appreciate the immeasurable worth of it. I was so focused on a desire for external redemption, being called to "go" or "do," or seeing others impacted, that I failed to rightly appreciate the big redemption He had already provided: His ongoing sanctifying work in my heart in the midst of the flames.

Progressive personal sanctification is "big redemption." Sanctification turns the soil of our hearts, rips out the weeds of fleshly tendencies and desires, and enables the fruit of the Spirit to flourish in abundance. That priceless fruit is both visible and tangible redemption. Through the sanctifying flames of adversity *"the proof of our faith"* is found (1 Pet. 1:6-7). This sanctified faith that emerges, forged and fortified through the flames, is *"more precious than gold."* Precious redemption—priceless, powerful, imperishable redemption.

> In this you greatly rejoice, even though now for a little while, if necessary, you have been distressed by various trials, so that the proof of your faith, being more precious than gold which is perishable, even though tested by fire, may be found to result in praise and glory and honor at the revelation of Jesus Christ (1 Pet. 1:6-7)

I am still in the flames. He is still refining and sanctifying me through the relentless pain. He is still saying *"wait,"* but He is also saying *"be content"* in the wait. He is specifically challenging me to be content to *"lead a quiet life"* as I wait on Him (1 Thess. 4:7-12). He is gently calling me to choose to joyfully embrace and celebrate His ongoing transforming work in my heart as "big redemption."

Perhaps one day soon He will no longer say *"wait,"* but will instead say *"go"* or *"do."* If He does, I will rejoice in that day knowing that He has prepared my heart for *"such a time"* through His sanctifying work in the flames. Whatever my calling may be, whether *"wait," "go,"* or *"do,"* may my obedience to it, and my sanctification through it *"result in praise and glory and honor at the revelation of Jesus Christ."*

> For God has not called us for the purpose of impurity, but in sanctification. So, he who rejects this is not rejecting man but the God who gives His Holy Spirit to you. Now as to the love of the brethren, you have no need for anyone to write to you, for you yourselves are taught by God to love one another; for indeed you do practice it toward all the brethren who are in all Macedonia. But we urge you, brethren, to excel still more, and to make it your ambition to lead a quiet life and attend to your own business and work with your hands, just as we commanded you, so that you will behave properly toward outsiders and not be in any need. But we do not want you to be uninformed, brethren, about those who are asleep, so that you will not grieve as do the rest who have no hope. For if we believe that Jesus died and rose again, even so God will bring with Him those who have fallen asleep in Jesus. (1 Thess. 4:7-14)

LIVE redeemed

"FAKING FINE" IN THE MIDST OF GRIEF?

FEBRUARY 13, 2018

"I pray that the eyes of your heart may be enlightened, so that you will know what is the hope of His calling, what are the riches of the glory of His inheritance in the saints, and what is the surpassing greatness of His power toward us who believe. These are in accordance with the working of the strength of His might which He brought about in Christ, when He raised Him from the dead and seated Him at His right hand in the heavenly places, far above all rule and authority and power and dominion, and every name that is named, not only in this age but also in the one to come. And He put all things in subjection under His feet, and gave Him as head over all things to the church, which is His body, the fullness of Him who fills all in all."
Ephesians 1:18-23

Over the past eight months, I've read countless articles imploring grieving people to not "fake being fine." Many of the articles express deep concern over the importance of being open with everyone about your pain and never suppressing or stifling your emotions which is to the detriment of your own well-being.

Others express concern from the viewpoint that grieving people who "fake" well-being unintentionally reinforce or perpetuate false beliefs and unrealistic expectations regarding the depth and longevity of grief, particularly the grief of parents who have lost a child.

I understand both concerns and the validity of each, but have struggled to understand what exactly constitutes "faking fine." I'm suspicious some would deem me "a faker" as I have struggled to navigate feeling lost between two seemingly opposing realities.

One reality is my family's and my ongoing inner brokenness from Sarah's sudden departure. This reality finds my husband's heart and mine equally shattered, and our remaining children deeply wounded. It is a reality characterized by deep, inexpressible pain that regularly reverberates through our souls. None of us are who we were prior to Sarah's departure. We have each been transformed by the cavernous wound of her absence.

This reality requires inordinate amounts of energy and effort to be invested in understanding who we are now, both as individuals and as a family. Nurturing our remaining nuclear family relationships and seeking to ensure the well-being of each individual as we learn how to move forward together is a staggering responsibility. On a nightly basis, it takes Scott and me to our knees together in brokenness and desperation seeking God's sustaining grace, wisdom, and strength to persevere. This is the heart-rending and exhausting reality of "child loss." We are aware of this reality every moment of every day.

The other reality is equally unavoidable, it is the mundane reality of "everyday life." We must persevere in living daily life in a world that has more or less moved on without our daughter. In this reality, there is Scott going to work each day, both of us meeting the daily needs of our remaining children, household management tasks, various errands, and church commitments, just to name a few.

In this reality, I interact superficially with most of the people I encounter. My focus in this reality is the task at hand, as well as the people each task brings me into contact with. I smile and answer "Fine" when casually asked as a greeting, "How are you?" I reciprocate small talk and I strive to be politely attentive and engaged in whatever topics, interests, or concerns others choose to discuss. Sarah and our desperately missing her are rarely mentioned by anyone in this reality. In this reality, my pain is not visible and I appear fine.

I've recognized from very early on the apparent dichotomy between these two realities. I have repeatedly pondered the possibility that I am "faking fine." My concern that I might be perceived that way was recently reinforced by a friend. After I shared my perception of the two realities with her she interjected, "But that's faking it."

I was not surprised by her assessment but I was disappointed because that was definitely not my intention. In my mind, instead of opposing realities where one is "real" and one is "fake," they are actually both "real" or "true" realities. The more I've pondered it, I have come to believe they are both joined together within a third overarching reality, the reality of our hope.

> Therefore we do not lose heart, but though our outer man is decaying, yet our inner man is being renewed day by day. For momentary, light affliction is producing for us an eternal weight of glory far beyond all comparison, while we look not at the things which are seen, but at the things which are not seen; for the things which are seen are temporal, but the things which are not seen are eternal. (2 Cor. 4:16-18)

Sarah is alive. Though she died, she lives (John 11:25). She is absent from the body and present with the Lord, alive with Him in paradise today (2 Cor. 5:8; Luke 23:43). Though death has not been destroyed yet, it has been defeated through the shed blood and resurrection of Jesus Christ. As I fix my eyes on the hope I have in Christ, my heart becomes keenly aware of the distinction between the temporal and the eternal.

My separation from Sarah is temporal, for a season. My deep heartache and that of my family is temporal and temporary. My opportunity to be used by Christ in this life to make an eternal impact is also temporary, a fleeting opportunity.

I can't say it any better than Sarah did in one of her last text messages:

> "For you have been born again, not of perishable seed, but of imperishable, through the living and enduring word of God. For, 'All people are like grass, and all their glory is like the flowers of the field; the grass withers and the flowers fall, but the word of the Lord endures forever.'" 1 Peter 1:23-25 [NIV]
>
> "This is such a great reminder! We are like a wisp of smoke. We are only here a moment. And this is not about us. Life is not about us. It's about God who is eternal. So I want to dedicate the one moment I'm here completely and entirely to him."
>
> — SARAH HARMENING

The clashing of the pain and hope within me sparks an overwhelming awareness of the brevity of life and an urgent longing for my remaining days to be full of fruitful labor (Phil. 1:22). I am consumed with a desire to finish well (1 Tim. 4:7-8). Hope compels me to fix my eyes on the goal before me (Phil. 3:14).

Obedience to my Lord in running the race marked out before me takes precedence over my pain (Heb. 12:1-3). Every day I acknowledge the presence of the pain to Him, the only One who can help. I entrust it to Him daily and then I fix my eyes on the goal and seek His leading for the day ahead. If He prompts the sharing of my testimony or pain to comfort or encourage another I will gladly share, but I am content to be silent about it otherwise.

I'm not faking fine, I am just learning to be content in Him. In accordance with His great faithfulness, He pours His sustaining grace and strength into my shattered heart alongside the pain and hope to enable me to cry out with the Apostle Paul, *"...I have learned in whatever situation I am to be content. I know how to be brought low, and I know how to abound. In any and every circumstance, I have learned the secret of facing plenty and hunger, abundance and need. I can do all things through him who strengthens me"* (Phil. 4:11b-13 ESV).

ALONE, YET NOT ALONE

FEBRUARY 22, 2018

"Behold, an hour is coming, and has already come, for you to be scattered, each to his own home, and to leave Me alone; and yet I am not alone, because the Father is with Me. These things I have spoken to you, so that in Me you may have peace. In the world you have tribulation, but take courage; I have overcome the world." John 16:32-33

Loneliness is a formidable foe for me these days. Much of my time is spent alone, but surprisingly, I sometimes feel most alone when I am in a group of people. It's a deep loneliness not satisfied by just being in the presence of others. Instead, it's a loneliness characterized by a longing to be authentically understood and intimately related to. It's a hunger to be understood without explanation, a yearning for someone to simply but fully "get it." In its depths, this loneliness can only be comforted by one who comforts from the well of grace that only experience supplies.

Praise God, my blessed Savior has gone before me having experienced deepest pain, greatest grief, and stinging loneliness. My aching heart resonates with His words as He wept in the Garden that night as overwhelming grief threatened to consume Him.

And He said to them, "My soul is deeply grieved to the point of death; remain here and keep watch." And He went a little beyond them, and fell to the ground and began to pray that if it were possible, the hour might pass Him by. And He was saying, "Abba! Father! All things are possible for You; remove this cup from Me; yet not what I will, but what You will." And He came and found them sleeping, and said to Peter, "Simon, are you asleep? Could you not keep watch for one hour? Keep watching and praying that you may not come into temptation; the spirit is willing, but the flesh is weak." Again He went away and prayed, saying the same words. And again He came and found them sleeping, for their eyes were very heavy; and they did not know what to answer Him. And He came the third time, and said to them, "Are you still sleeping and resting? It is enough; the hour has come; behold, the Son of Man is being betrayed into the hands of sinners." (Mark 14:34-41)

"My soul is deeply grieved to the point of death." These words reverberate through my heart with the crash of each tidal wave of grief that washes over me. What tremendous comfort that my Comforter knows the agony of greatest grief. He knows the throbbing in my heart, the aching of my arms, and my desperate longing for home.

As He entered the garden He shared the magnitude of His grief with His disciples and implored them to remain and keep watch. He fell to the ground just a little beyond them, and as He was crying out from the depths of His grief to the Father through tears and sweat dripping as blood—they fell asleep. They abandoned Him to slumber in the midst of His incomprehensible grief, not once, not twice, but three times. Surely His heart was pierced by that solitude, the bitter sting of loneliness in greatest grief.

When in the depths of my grief it feels as if those around me are unaware, and loneliness overtakes me, He meets me there. He who knows the sting of unimaginable aloneness reminds me He neither sleeps nor slumbers, and He will never leave me nor forsake me. He sees my every tear, feels my every pain, sympathizes with my every weakness, and understands my every temptation.

My steadfast and loving Savior beckons me, *"Therefore, since we have a great high priest who has passed through the heavens, Jesus the Son of God, let us hold fast our confession. For we do not have a high priest who cannot sympathize with our weaknesses, but One who has been tempted in all things as we are, yet without sin. Therefore let us draw near with confidence to the throne of grace, so that we may receive mercy and find grace to help in time of need"* (Heb. 4:14-16).

My God, my Father, my Savior, my Lord, my Comforter, my Counselor, my Healer, my Great High Priest, my Refiner, my Shepherd, my Redeemer, my Defender, my Rock, my Refuge, my Deliverer sees me. He hears me. He knows me. He deeply understands and intimately relates to me. He is with me. He will never leave me. I am not alone.

O LORD, You have searched me and known me. You know when I sit down and when I rise up; You understand my thought from afar. You scrutinize my path and my lying down, And are intimately acquainted with all my ways. Even before there is a word on my tongue, Behold, O LORD, You know it all. You have enclosed me behind and before, And laid Your hand upon me. Such knowledge is too wonderful for me; It is too high, I cannot attain to it. Where can I go from Your Spirit? Or where can I flee from Your presence? If I ascend to heaven, You are there; If I make my bed in Sheol, behold, You are there. If I take the wings of the dawn, If I dwell in the remotest part of the sea, Even there Your hand will lead me, And Your right hand will lay hold of me. If I say, "Surely the darkness will overwhelm me, And the light around me will be night," Even the darkness is not dark to You, And the night is as bright as the day. Darkness and light are alike to You. (Ps. 139:1-12)

THIS THORN OF MINE

MARCH 4, 2018

"... there was given me a thorn in the flesh, a messenger of Satan to torment me..." 2 Corinthians 12:7

As we approach the nine-month mark of Sarah's homegoing, we seem to be hearing more people routinely mentioning our "healing" as something they believe has already taken place to one degree or another. As I've continued to ponder and pray about the concept of our healing I believe the Lord has continued to instead confirm an alternate concept I first shared in July.[1]

While I do not believe we will be healed this side of heaven, I am confident God will continue to faithfully sustain us. He will continue upholding us by His righteous right hand and strengthening us to endure and adapt (Isa. 41:10). I was recently reminded of Paul's "thorn in the flesh" and it resonated in a new way with the pain of Sarah's absence.

With bone-crushing pain, Satan struck and pierced us on June 8, 2017. Like the fang of his bite, he thrust his thorn deeply and painfully into our flesh. He left it there as his messenger of torment, a reminder that we have a strong and cunning adversary intent on stealing, killing, and destroying.

Like Paul, I pleaded repeatedly with the Lord, begging Him to remove the painful thorn, but instead, He gently spoke to my heart, *"My grace is sufficient for you, for power is perfected in weakness."* The thorn torments, distresses, and weakens me; I am broken by the thorn.

> Concerning this I implored the Lord three times that it might leave me. And He has said to me, 'My grace is sufficient for you, for power is perfected in weakness.' Most gladly, therefore, I will rather boast about my weaknesses, so that the power of Christ may dwell in me. Therefore I am well content with weaknesses, with insults, with distresses, with persecutions, with difficulties, for Christ's sake; for when I am weak, then I am strong. (2 Cor. 12:8-10)

The piercing wound of the thorn of Sarah's absence hurts no less today than it did the day it was inflicted. What appears to some to be our healing is instead the grace of God's upholding strength shining through our weakness and brokenness. When the peace and contentment of His sustaining grace are presumed to be the result of "healing" it diminishes the power of what God is doing in sustaining us.

He is miraculously strengthening us to bear up under the weight of the thorn and the pain that remains constant. The miracle of His sustaining grace is that we actually are sustained to experience peace, contentment, and even joy amid the pain.

To presume the thorn and the pain must be removed or diminished through healing in order to allow peace and joy to enter in is to deny the miraculous nature and power of the provision of our Sustainer. To the contrary, through His sufficient grace, His power in me makes me *"well content with weaknesses, with insults, with distresses, with persecutions, with difficulties, for Christ's sake; for when I am weak, then I am strong."*

> But we have this treasure in earthen vessels, so that the surpassing greatness of the power will be of God and not from ourselves; (2 Cor. 4:7)

The thorn requires me to adapt just as if it were a visible tangible thorn protruding from my flesh. It, like a physical thorn, brings unique vulnerabilities. Part of my adapting involves realizing that there is a very delicate balance between my pain and His sustaining grace. My experiencing the sufficiency of His sustaining grace is directly related to my obedience to fix my focus on the eternal rather than the temporal, and to *"approve the things which are excellent"* and dwell on them (2 Cor. 4:18; Phil. 1:10; 4:8).

I am adapting to my thorn by learning it is acceptable and wise for me to move away from or avoid, whenever possible, situations and interactions that unfruitfully amplify the pain of the thorn of Sarah's absence. Unfruitful situations and interactions are those that magnify the temporal rather than the eternal by unduly drawing my focus to Sarah's physical death and absence rather than her life, her testimony, and His gracious provision for us.

> And this I pray, that your love may abound still more and more in real knowledge and all discernment, so that you may approve the things that are excellent, in order to be sincere and blameless until the day of Christ; having been filled with the fruit of righteousness which comes through Jesus Christ, to the glory and praise of God... Finally, brethren, whatever is true, whatever is honorable, whatever is right, whatever is pure, whatever is lovely, whatever is of good repute, if there is any excellence and if anything worthy of praise, dwell on these things. (Phil. 1:9-11; 4:8)

Similarly, I must also adapt to the reality that bearing the thorn depletes my emotional and physical strength. I must be very thoughtful and, more importantly, prayerful about what I commit to each day. I long to walk righteously, and the thorn is a constant reminder that the only way to do so is to walk in the center of His will where His grace abounds.

The thorn brings an urgent awareness that I must continually seek His will to wisely steward the strength He alone provides. I am adapting to the thorn by learning I must inquire of the Lord first before committing to anything, even seemingly inconsequential things. Recognizing and adapting to my weaknesses allows me to function within His grace and strength in a manner that some may view as healing.

The Lord has confirmed this thorn in my flesh will not be removed. The pain of my separation from Sarah will not end here, I will not be healed on this side of heaven. But, praise God, there is coming a day when this corrupt flesh will be stripped away, and this thorn along with it. On that marvelous day, in the twinkling of an eye, I will be gloriously set free when my flesh and my thorn fall away as temporal chaff. I will be instantaneously transformed in the presence of my precious Savior and Lord, and with joy inexpressible I will be reunited with my sweet Sarah.

In the meantime, I will not deny or hide the ongoing reality of the pain, distress, weakness, and brokenness the thorn of Sarah's absence brings. Instead, I will humbly acknowledge its painful impact as the bleak backdrop upon which His grace and strength are gloriously displayed through His powerfully and miraculously sustaining us.

Our otherwise inexplicable contentment, peace, and joy are the power of Christ in us, for His glory. My thorn remains. I am not healed, but I am lovingly, graciously, and miraculously sustained by God, my Helper and the Sustainer of my soul. (Ps. 54:4).

> But when this perishable will have put on the imperishable, and this mortal will have put on immortality, then will come about the saying that is written, "DEATH IS SWALLOWED UP in victory. "O DEATH, WHERE IS YOUR VICTORY? O DEATH, WHERE IS YOUR STING?" The sting of death is sin, and the power of sin is the law; but thanks be to God, who gives us the victory through our Lord Jesus Christ. Therefore, my beloved brethren, be steadfast, immovable, always abounding in the work of the Lord, knowing that your toil is not in vain in the Lord. (1 Cor. 15:54-58)

---

1. see "Healing or Adapting?" pp. 48-51.

THE GOD OF THE VALLEYS

MARCH 8, 2018

Then a man of God came near and spoke to the king of Israel and said, "Thus says the LORD, 'Because the Arameans have said, "The LORD is a god of the mountains, but He is not a god of the valleys," therefore I will give all this great multitude into your hand, and you shall know that I am the LORD.'" 1 Kings 20:28

Nine months ago today I hugged my precious daughter for the last time on this earth. Nine months. I can't say or hear that phrase without thinking of the period of time I carried her within my womb as the Lord knit her beautifully together beneath my heart. The time from realizing you are pregnant to giving birth seems so very long amid such great anticipation. The nine months of missing Sarah has seemed equally long in many ways, but dauntingly short in others.

As I approached my time with the Lord this morning, hungering for His encouragement, I purposefully did not seek out Scripture specifically to soothe my soul as I frequently do. Instead, I chose to read and meditate on the Old and New Testament books I have been systematically working through. Not surprisingly at all, my ever-faithful Lord met me there, turning His living Word as a multifaceted gem to minister to my yet wounded heart and spirit.

The account of an Aramean war was my source of encouragement today. I never would have discovered this one had I gone digging specifically for encouragement, but what an encouraging gem it is. Israel had just defeated the Arameans. The response of the servants of the King of Aram was as follows:

> Now the servants of the king of Aram said to him, "Their gods are gods of the mountains, therefore they were stronger than we; but rather let us fight against them in the plain, and surely we will be stronger than they. Do this thing: remove the kings, each from his place, and put captains in their place, and muster an army like the army that you have lost, horse for horse, and chariot for chariot. Then we will fight against them in the plain, and surely we will be stronger than they." And he listened to their voice and did so. (1 Kings 20:23-25)

The enemies of Israel are basically telling their king, "Bring them low, down into the valley, their God will be powerless there, we will be stronger than they, and we will defeat them in the valley." Typing that finds my eyes brimming with tears. I am confident those are the words my adversary uttered the day he flipped that bus, crushing my child beneath the weight of it. I can hear him proclaiming to his minions, "They are preserved and victorious as long as they are on that mountaintop, but watch as I force them into the valley where I will overcome and destroy them."

Never confuse valleys for places of respite conducive to healing, or "no combat zones" free from battles. There are no truces in the valleys. On the contrary, entry into a valley frequently brings with it the painful ramping up of existing battles, as well as unexpected engagement in brand-new battles.

Just like the Arameans, our adversary still regularly employs this tactic today. He loves to get us into the valley to fiercely fight against us there with every intention of defeating us. He delights in forcing

God's people into the valley and then taunting them during his attacks, "Your God is not here" and "With certainty, you will be defeated in this valley." Lies uttered from a frothy mouth prepared to devour.

Through a man of God, the unchanging God of the universe spoke to the King of Israel regarding the Arameans, *"Thus says the LORD, "Because the Arameans have said, 'The LORD is a god of the mountains, but He is not a god of the valleys,' therefore I will give all this great multitude into your hand, and you shall know that I am the LORD"* (1 Kings 20:28). God gave the Arameans over to be slaughtered because they said He was "not a god of the valleys."

Our God clearly finds it vitally important that all people know He is not only the God of the mountains, He is the God of the Valleys as well. Oh, what precious encouragement to be reminded of that truth.

If you, like me, find yourself in a valley today, take courage that whatever valley you are in, He is still God there. He is the God of the valleys, and He longs for you to know that. Whether on the highest heights of the mountain tops or in the deepest pits of the lowest valleys, we are never beyond the reach of His righteous right hand.

He longs to uphold us and carry us. His amazing grace is sufficient to sustain us in our darkest valleys, and it is free-flowing through the precious blood of Jesus Christ. I testify to this truth today, nine months in the valley, so that you, too, may know He is the LORD, the God of the valleys (1 Kings 20:28).

Come to Me, all who are weary and heavy-laden, and I will give you rest. Take My yoke upon you and learn from Me, for I am gentle and humble in heart, and YOU WILL FIND REST FOR YOUR SOULS. For My yoke is easy and My burden is light. (Matt. 11:28-30)

TAKING HOLD OF HOPE

MARCH 29, 2018

"In the same way God, desiring even more to show to the heirs of the promise the unchangeableness of His purpose, interposed with an oath, so that by two unchangeable things in which it is impossible for God to lie, we who have taken refuge would have strong encouragement to take hold of the hope set before us. This hope we have as an anchor of the soul, a hope both sure and steadfast and one which enters within the veil, where Jesus has entered as a forerunner for us, having become a high priest forever according to the order of Melchizedek." Hebrews 6:17-20

I deeply miss Sarah. Just below the surface of my smile, there is a pervasive sadness encompassing my heart. My aching heart is so very thankful that the backdrop of hopelessness is repeatedly present throughout the inspired Word of God. Over and over again we see accounts of God's extension of hope to those in hopeless situations. Joseph, Job, David, Esther, Israel, and the judges, over and over again our unchanging ever-faithful God gives hope to the hopeless.

> Let us hold fast the confession of our hope without wavering, for He who promised is faithful (Heb. 10:23)

I find myself identifying with a degree of the weight of grief that First Good Friday must have held for those who loved our Lord. High expectations and great hopes were completely dashed as they saw and heard of His crucifixion and death. The Son of Man, the Messiah, the King of Kings, and the Lord of Lords was dead. The crushing blow of hopelessness and despair must have fallen like a gauntlet.

Praise God, Sunday came. And with it the divine unfolding message of hope for the hopeless climaxed through the resurrected Lord Jesus Christ. I can only imagine the disciples' euphoric rejoicing at seeing Him again. Their hope was renewed that He would be restoring the kingdom to Israel (Acts 1:6).

They thought they understood His plan, but they did not. Our risen Lord had to shift their focus from a temporal hope to His eternal hope. Their hope and ours is not an earthly kingdom but the eternal risen Savior Himself.

> Blessed be the God and Father of our Lord Jesus Christ, who according to His great mercy has caused us to be born again to a living hope through the resurrection of Jesus Christ from the dead, to obtain an inheritance which is imperishable and undefiled and will not fade away, reserved in heaven for you, who are protected by the power of God through faith for a salvation ready to be revealed in the last time. (1 Pet. 1:3-5)

My heart deeply aches at the thought of celebrating Easter without Sarah for the first time this year, but I am so very thankful for the eternal hope of Easter: the sure and steadfast hope of the gospel of Jesus Christ freely offered as an anchor for weary souls. Because of the death and resurrection of Jesus Christ, we have confident assurance of a living hope, the certainty of our eternal future.

> For in hope we have been saved, but hope that is seen is not hope; for who hopes for what he already sees? But if we hope for what we do not see, with perseverance we wait eagerly for it. (Rom. 8:24-25)

If you, like me, are approaching this Easter with a heavy heart and deep sadness, join me in seeking encouragement through the truths of His Word. Like the disciples, we must shift our focus from our temporal pain and shattered hopes to Him and His eternal hope. The hope of His Salvation is the helmet that will guard our minds and thoughts, but we must choose to put it on (1 Thess. 5:8).

Let's diligently fix our minds on His truths and the eternal hope of living together with Him. In so doing we will be divinely strengthened to fruitfully persevere the remainder of our days with eager anticipation of His coming. We're only here a little while longer, this life is but a vapor (James 4:14). So let's take hold of the hope set before us, urgently and diligently grasping it as a lifeline, the anchor of our souls.

> But since we are of the day, let us be sober, having put on the breastplate of faith and love, and as a helmet, the hope of salvation. For God has not destined us for wrath, but for obtaining salvation through our Lord Jesus Christ, who died for us, so that whether we are awake or asleep, we will live together with Him. Therefore encourage one another and build up one another, just as you also are doing. (1 Thess. 5:8-11)

I Will Not Cause Pain Without Allowing Something new to be born, Says the Lord.

Isaiah 66:9

WHEN DELIVERANCE DOESN'T COME

APRIL 7, 2018

"It is good to give thanks to the LORD And to sing praises to Your name, O Most High; To declare Your lovingkindness in the morning And Your faithfulness by night," Psalm 92:1-2

The success of Walt Disney has safely proven most of us love knights in shining armor delivering damsels in distress, true love prevailing, good conquering evil, and fairy tale endings of happily ever after. We love stories of deliverance. In Christian circles, some of the most repeated biblical accounts are those of miraculous deliverance: Noah and the Ark, Abraham and Isaac, Daniel in the lions' den, Shadrach, Meschach and Abednego, David and Goliath, and the list goes on.

Ten months ago a bus full of people was miraculously delivered, but our precious Sarah was not. We as her family were and are not delivered from enduring the earthly sting of her death. We did not get our fairy tale ending. It is incomprehensibly illogical, but there are still multiple moments every single day that I must convince myself she is actually gone. A mother's heart is not wired to process that she will never touch or hold her child again, that she will never again hear their voice, laughter, or singing.

Each time the reality washes over me, it bears a sting similar to the first. In between those sharper stings of reality, the aching is constant. I bear an ever-present longing for someone and something, and deliverance will not be granted this side of heaven.

In Christian culture riddled with prosperity theology, there is a pervasive lie that God's faithfulness always brings deliverance. It's overtly seen in claims that God's will is always to physically heal and provide financial wealth, but more insidiously in the belief that He will not allow us to suffer or hurt indefinitely.

This is not a new belief though, we see it recorded in Scripture when the disciples question Jesus about the man blind from birth: *"Rabbi, who sinned, this man or his parents, that he was born blind?"* (John 9:2). Their wrong presumptions about God's will regarding physical well-being caused them to believe someone sinned to cause the suffering this man had endured since birth.

Praise God for the recorded Word of Christ Jesus refuting the false presumptions of the disciples, *"It was not that this man sinned, or his parents, but that the works of God might be displayed in him"* (John 9:3).

In this instance, this man was allowed to suffer from birth through adulthood so that God would be glorified through His eventual healing. Some might argue that this account still fits within the belief that God's will always includes temporal healing and deliverance. He did, after all, eventually deliver this man through healing.

Thankfully we have the account of Paul and his thorn as well. We know from Scripture that Paul pleaded for healing or deliverance from the thorn but it was not granted. Paul accepted that He was not to be delivered, and he affirmed the choice of God, saying, *"For the sake of Christ, then, I am content with weaknesses, insults, hardships, persecutions, and calamities. For when I am weak, then I am strong"* (2 Cor. 12:10).

As I was struggling with the deep discouragement of desperately missing Sarah earlier this week, I once again went to the Psalms for comfort and encouragement. It was not a Psalm of lament that captivated my heart, though. Instead, it was a Psalm of Thanksgiving, Psalm 92. Verse 1-2 instantly resonated within my broken heart, *"It is good to give thanks to the LORD And to sing praises to Your name, O Most High; To declare Your lovingkindness in the morning And Your faithfulness by night".*

In Scripture, morning is often associated with times of deliverance or blessing, and night with times of hardship and difficulty. Through the shadow of death, nighttime has fallen on our family, but like the Psalmist we can still declare His faithfulness. He did not deliver Sarah from death, and He will not deliver us from the pain of her absence on this side of heaven, but He has been, is, and will continue to be faithful.

God's faithfulness and our faith do not guarantee our temporal deliverance. Likewise, ongoing pain and lack of deliverance do not indicate a lack of faithfulness on God's part or a lack of faith in us. God does not miraculously numb grieving parents to the pain of the absence of their children. Those who have journeyed far longer than I without their children testify the pain and longing never fully subside.

However, they and I can also testify that His faithfulness is beautifully displayed as He miraculously and faithfully sustains us in the midst of the pain and longing. It is His faithfulness that strengthens us to persevere and endure (2 Thess. 3:3), and it is His faithfulness that restores the joy of our salvation even in the presence of our tears (Ps. 51:12). His faithfulness empowers our faith.

God's promised faithfulness is not a promise to spare us from that which we dread, it is a promise to faithfully walk with us and sustain us should that which we dread become our reality.

Stephen, the first martyr, was not granted deliverance but instead a brutal death by stoning. In Stephen's final earthly moments, God demonstrated His faithfulness as He revealed Himself in His glory to Stephen. As Stephen's life was being poured out through the blows of the rocks, he also saw His ever-faithful Savior, Jesus Christ, looking upon Him from the right hand of God, no longer seated but standing (Acts 7:55-56). Great is His faithfulness.

He is faithful. When He delivers, He is faithful. When He doesn't deliver, He is faithful. He is faithful in the valley of the shadow of death (Ps. 23:4). He who is faithful weeps with us (John 11:33). He collects our tears and takes account of each one (Ps. 56:8). He gives us His song in the night, and He sings over us (Ps. 42:8; Zeph. 3:17). He pours out His new mercies for us each morning (Lam. 3:22). He upholds us by His righteous right hand (Isa. 41:10). His faithfulness persists no matter how desolate or dire our circumstances may be (Ps. 46:1-3). Because of His faithfulness, my broken heart sings (Ps. 57:7).

> But this I call to mind, and therefore I have hope: The steadfast love of the LORD never ceases; his mercies never come to an end; they are new every morning; great is your faithfulness. (Lam. 3:21-23 ESV)

I can not conclude without recounting the greatest story of deliverance ever. That of Jesus Christ crucified and resurrected, offering to all mankind deliverance from the captivity of sin and death. Though we will not all receive the temporal deliverance we desire this side of heaven, all we who follow Christ will ultimately be eternally delivered. Armed with this hope, I will continue to give thanks and declare His faithfulness in the night as I eagerly anticipate the deliverance of that glorious reunion day morning when the Sun of Righteousness will rise with healing in His wings, making all things new.

> But for you who fear My name, the sun of righteousness will rise with healing in its wings; and you will go forth and skip about like calves from the stall. (Mal. 4:2)

> And I heard a loud voice from the throne, saying, "Behold, the tabernacle of God is among men, and He will dwell among them, and they shall be His people, and God Himself will be among them, and He will wipe away every tear from their eyes; and there will no longer be any death; there will no longer be any mourning, or crying, or pain; the first things have passed away." And He who sits on the throne said, "Behold, I am making all things new." And He said, "Write, for these words are faithful and true. (Rev. 21:3-5)

WHEN GOD IS SILENT

APRIL 17, 2018

To my dismay, over the past week and a half, as I've spent time in God's Word and prayer, He has been silent. Each passing day has compounded my urgency and longing for Him. After spending hours in the Word and prayer today seeking His face and not finding Him, my desperation for Him climaxed with deep anguish and weeping. Late in the afternoon, I felt a gentle nudge to go back to the Book of Job. I quickly found myself, my circumstances, and my heart in chapter 23.

> Behold, I go forward, but he is not there, and backward, but I do not perceive him; on the left hand when he is working, I do not behold him; he turns to the right hand, but I do not see him. (Job 23:8-9 ESV)

My raw eyes burned with tears once again as I read Job's words that so clearly reflected the agony of my soul. Like Job, I have been desperately searching for Him in every direction and yet not finding Him. I intimately know the comfort of His presence, His voice, and His song, which makes their perceived absence unbearable. With great anticipation, I read on.

> But he knows the way that I take; when he has tried me, I shall come out as gold. (Job 23:10 ESV)

"But He knows the way I take." Though Job could not find, see, or perceive God, he was steadfastly confident that God was present and actively watching Him. I am reminded of the song, "His Eye Is On the Sparrow." Through my own misunderstanding, I used to find false comfort in that song and the Scripture it is based on.

I wrongly thought, "His eye is on me, so no evil will befall me." Indeed, His eye is on the sparrow, and according to Matthew 10:29, not one of them will fall to the ground apart from Him. Not one will fall to the ground apart from Him, but they will all fall to the ground eventually.

In the same way, I am on the ground, broken and cleaving to the dust in search of Him. But what blessed assurance that I was not cast here apart from His watchful eye.

There is great comfort in knowing His eye is on me as I strive to persevere through the many shadows of this dark valley. He knows the way that I take. He sees this desolate, lonely path I am on. Though I can't see or find Him in this moment, He sees me urgently groping and searching for Him.

Job perceived God's silence toward him as his being tested or tried. I do as well. Job knew the silence would only be temporary, and as he walked in obedience he knew he would *"come out as gold."* His confidence that he would come out as gold was rooted in his confidence in God's faithfulness to His Word, and the fact that Job was actively choosing to walk in obedience to His Word.

> My foot has held fast to his steps; I have kept his way and have not turned aside. I have not departed from the commandment of his lips; I have treasured the words of his mouth more than my portion of food. (Job 23:11-12 ESV)

Inspired by Job's confidence I, too, will continue to cling to the truths of His Word. I will continue to search for Him as a precious jewel; my relationship with Him being my most treasured possession. I will persevere in faith and obedience, longing to be found walking in His righteousness. I will fervently seek Him through His Word and prayer, knowing His silence is only temporary, and assured by Job that—*"I shall come out."*

He will once again make His face shine upon me. He will again speak to my heart and sing His song over me in the night. In the meantime, I will cling to the promises of His Word as I urgently wait for Him. I will persevere through the silence, encouraged by the assurance of Job that *"He knows the way that I take; when he has tried me, I shall come out as gold."*

but He knows where I'm going & when He tests me I will come out as pure gold

JOB 23:10

DEATH'S STING IS RIGHT HERE, RIGHT NOW

APRIL 26, 2018

"O DEATH, WHERE IS YOUR VICTORY? O DEATH, WHERE IS YOUR STING?" 1 Corinthians 15:55

On occasion, the scriptural passage above is carelessly lobbed at grieving families as an exhortation to stop grieving. With a victorious gleam in their eyes some will subtly rebuke in ignorance, "Take hope, rejoice, death has been defeated, it has no sting!"

Indeed there is truth in what they say, but oh what unnecessary shame and pain can be inflicted by failure to present scripture in context. Proper context includes the preceding verses that reveal this bold proclamation of complete victory will be shouted at the final trumpet, when Christ returns and the last enemy, death, is completely and finally abolished.

> Behold, I tell you a mystery; we will not all sleep, but we will all be changed, in a moment, in the twinkling of an eye, at the last trumpet; for the trumpet will sound, and the dead will be raised imperishable, and we will be changed. For this perishable must put on the imperishable, and this mortal must put on immortality. But when this perishable will have put on the imperishable, and this mortal will have put

on immortality, then will come about the saying that is written, "DEATH IS SWALLOWED UP in victory." "O DEATH, WHERE IS YOUR VICTORY? O DEATH, WHERE IS YOUR STING?" (1 Cor. 15:51-55)

Death is already eternally defeated through the shed blood of Christ, but it is not yet abolished. Death has no eternal sting. Death has no sting for our believing loved ones who have gone before us. In the blink of an eye, they were liberated from the momentary grip of death to glorious life eternal. With the rest of the saints in glory, they can shout the victory cry over death. Death is powerless against them for all eternity. Likewise, we Christ-followers who remain should have no fear of death. We can each confidently face impending death as a defeated foe through the victory granted in Christ Jesus.

Death is eternally defeated, but until it is abolished at Christ's return it still possesses a temporal sting. For we who remain, death's most potent sting is that of separation from our loved ones. In addition, it can bring with it countless other stings as well, such as the sting of unfulfilled longing, the sting of shared grief, the sting of regret, the sting of isolation, and the sting of loneliness, just to name a few.

Within the walls of our home, five people have been individually impaled by the temporal sting of death: Five people trying to learn to live with the ever-present absence of a person deeply loved by each of us. Five people who know with certainty that our precious Sarah is living, yet we can not get to her, we can not see her, hear her, hug her, talk with her, or laugh with her. We are separated from her by death, and its sting is excruciatingly painful. Every time we feel that piercing sting, we are reminded that this is not what God intended. The searing pain pulses as a testimony to the grave consequence of sin—the sting of death.

It is so easy to think so little of our sin, to dismiss or excuse it as minor. It's not "big sin," after all. But as I bear the magnitude of the pain of the sting of death in my soul, I am reminded it is proportionate to the magnitude of my sin. *"The sting of death is sin."* There is

DEATH'S STING IS RIGHT HERE, RIGHT NOW

no clarification of the type of sin that gave death its sting because all sin is sin, and according to James, we are guilty of it all.

> For whoever keeps the whole law and yet stumbles in one point, he has become guilty of all. (James 2:10)

My sin deeply grieved the heart of my Heavenly Father. My sin separated me from Him. My sin required the atonement provided through the death of my precious Lord and Savior, Jesus Christ.

> For the wages of sin is death, but the free gift of God is eternal life in Christ Jesus our Lord. (Rom.6:23)

I am convinced we as believers would do well to readily acknowledge the very real and painful temporal sting of death. We are misguided if we imply or pretend it does not exist. Instead, we should readily acknowledge the wretchedness of death this side of heaven, and the heartrending pain of the separation it brings. We should allow the reality of the pain to serve as a powerful reminder to guard our hearts and minds from losing sight of the magnitude and ramifications of our sin.

Our sin birthed death. The greater our understanding of the magnitude of our sin and its consequences, the greater our celebration will be in appreciation of the victory we have been given through Christ Jesus.

> but thanks be to God, who gives us the victory through our Lord Jesus Christ. Therefore, my beloved brethren, be steadfast, immovable, always abounding in the work of the Lord, knowing that your toil is not in vain in the Lord. (1 Cor. 15:57-58)

While we acknowledge the agony of the temporal sting of death as we grieve our separation from those we love, we should simultaneously rejoice that though we grieve, we do not grieve as those who have no hope. (1 Thess. 4:13). We confidently hold to the certain hope that in *"just a little while"* the separation will be no more, *"he who is coming will come and will not delay"* (Heb. 10:37). Armed with this blessed hope we can and will persevere, *steadfast, immovable, always abounding in the work of the Lord, knowing that our toil is not in vain in the Lord* (1 Cor. 15:58). Be it through our deaths or His return we will soon see Him, and our precious loved ones along with Him, face to face, O glorious day. Come, Lord Jesus.

> For the Lord Himself will descend from heaven with a shout, with the voice of the archangel and with the trumpet of God, and the dead in Christ will rise first. Then we who are alive and remain will be caught up together with them in the clouds to meet the Lord in the air, and so we shall always be with the Lord. Therefore comfort one another with these words. (1 Thess. 4:16-18)

Where O Death is your sting? Where O Hell is your victory?

I'M SUPPOSED TO BE STOIC?

MAY 10, 2018

It finally happened. An acquaintance made it clear that my time to grieve Sarah's absence must draw to an end, it's time to move on. I had heard horror stories of gut-wrenching rebukes received by many veteran bereaved parents who have journeyed this path for years, but thankfully I had been spared from personally experiencing it until now, just eleven months after my sweet Sarah left.

If I thought it was an isolated incident unique to me, it wouldn't be worthy of discussion—but it isn't. Practically every bereaved mom I know has had a very similar experience, so it certainly seems worthy of thoughtful consideration. It's an opportunity to educate for the benefit of the wounded moms and dads who will be journeying behind us.

In some circles, stoicism has somehow become equated to Christian spiritual maturity. As a result, many wounded and suffering followers of Christ have been the recipients of unfounded disapproval, chastisement, and even outright rebuke.

For bereaved parents specifically, many of these comments are centered around the notion that the parents have an unhealthy fixation on their deceased child and his or her absence. It is often expressed as a concern that their continuing to share, speak about, or reference their child and their longing for them indicates they are "stuck in their grief" and "not moving on." Other times it's their acknowledgment of the ongoing pain that ends up being wrongly interpreted as an indication they are failing to exercise faith and choose joy.

I have purposefully listened to, processed, and prayed over these comments of concern or criticism and am impressed that each one is ultimately a demand for the wounded believer to be stoic instead of transparent. In addition, I believe they each stem from the profoundly flawed misconception that Christian spiritual maturity is evidenced by a stoic response in the face of trials and tribulation, rather than a transparent sharing of their impact.

This is particularly true of long-term or permanent trials and tribulations. In the name of spiritual maturity, a time limit has been placed on experiencing and sharing struggles, pain, longing, and heartbreak.

I am immediately reminded of Jesus in the garden. As Jesus approached the cross He was not stoic. My savior who is fully God and was simultaneously fully man, was *"deeply grieved, to the point of death"* (Matt. 26:38). Similarly, when Jesus saw the pain of those He loved at the death of Lazarus, *"He was deeply moved in spirit and was troubled"* to the point that He wept, even though He, being God, knew He could and would raise Lazarus from the dead (John 11:33-35).

I am reminded of Paul who was not stoic but transparent as he repeatedly, candidly, and descriptively shared his pain, weaknesses, trials, and tribulations in his letters. In Romans he wrote regarding the Jews' rejection of Jesus as Messiah, *"I have great sorrow and unceasing grief in my heart"* (Rom. 9:1). When he spoke of going to Macedonia, he acknowledged both his struggles and his fears, *"our flesh had no rest, but we were afflicted on every side: conflicts without, fears within"* (2 Cor. 7:5). In his letter to the church at Philippi, He spoke sharply of His aloneness except for Timothy, and referenced thankfulness to God for sparing the life of Epaphroditus because his death would have brought Paul *"sorrow upon sorrow"* (Phil. 2:27).

I am reminded of the Psalms of David, so many reflecting deep passion, pain, and emotion. David was transparent, not stoic. *"Be gracious to me, O LORD, for I am pining away; Heal me, O LORD, for my bones are dismayed. And my soul is greatly dismayed; But You, O LORD– how long? Return, O LORD, rescue my soul; Save me because of Your lovingkindness. For there is no mention of You in death; In Sheol who will give You thanks? I am weary with my sighing; Every night I make my bed swim, I dissolve my couch with my tears. My eye has wasted away with grief; It has become old because of all my adversaries"* (Ps. 6:2-7).

There is not a scriptural basis for pressuring wounded believers to be stoic. The transparent words and examples of these and many others included by God in Scripture have provided life-breathing encouragement to weary and wounded saints for centuries.

It is through the transparent telling of their pain and struggles that they allow us to connect with them in our pain and follow their examples of endurance. Christ in the garden teaches us to respond, *"Father, if You are willing, remove this cup from Me; yet not My will, but Yours be done"* (Luke 22:42). Paul encourages us to persevere, *"After you have suffered for a little while, the God of all grace, who called you to His eternal glory in Christ, will Himself perfect, confirm, strengthen and establish you"* (1 Pet. 5:10). And David reminds us God is faithful and our only refuge in the midst of the pain.

> My soul, wait in silence for God only, For my hope is from Him. He only is my rock and my salvation, My stronghold; I shall not be shaken. On God my salvation and my glory rest; The rock of my strength, my refuge is in God. Trust in Him at all times, O people; Pour out your heart before Him; God is a refuge for us. Selah. (Ps. 62:5-8)

Through Paul, I am reminded that God's grace is sufficient for me, for power is perfected in weakness. So, I say with Paul, *"Most gladly, therefore, I will rather boast about my weaknesses, so that the power of Christ may dwell in me"* (2 Cor 12:9). I will continue to transparently and truthfully share my pain, heartbreak, longing, and struggles because that is my reality. But most importantly, I will continue to transparently share because each time I share is an opportunity to testify how His grace meets me there and sustains me.

My pain, heartbreak, longing, and struggles are a means to point other hurting people to Him, I will not squander those very costly redemptive opportunities in the name of stoicism.

I love Sarah with a deep and abiding love, I will long for her until the day we are gloriously reunited. My heart will always ache for her. I will not hide that or pretend otherwise, I will not be stoic. I will boast about my brokenness because it is that very brokenness that drives me to my knees daily with a desperate longing for my God and my Savior. It is the sharing of that brokenness that enables me to connect with wounded people around me and encourage them to cleave to the Rock with me. I will strive to faithfully serve Him all the days of my life, and He has given me permission and encouragement that I will be rewarded as I persevere, even with, or perhaps especially with a tear-streaked face.

> He who goes to and fro weeping, carrying his bag of seed, Shall indeed come again with a shout of joy, bringing his sheaves with him. (Ps. 126:6)

"There is no charm equal to tenderness of heart."
—JANE AUSTEN

"A STRANGER WITH THEE"

MAY 21, 2018

"Hear my prayer, O LORD, and give ear to my cry; Do not be silent at my tears; For I am a stranger with Thee, A sojourner like all my fathers."
Psalm 39:12

This month has been tremendously painful. Senior Prom, Mother's Day, graduation festivities, and the constant yet staggering unavoidable awareness that this is the last month of our first year without Sarah. That dreaded date is upon us, just around the corner.

In my last post, I resolved to be transparent, not stoic. I must confess though, each day I struggle more and more to be transparent. The reverberating call to "move on" continues to ring in my ears, despite my best attempts to throw it off. I know the precious band of supporters who remain close to our family is undoubtedly weary of our struggles as well. If I continue to be transparent, how much longer can they bear up before they, too, withdraw to a safer distance? Through those thoughts, fear of abandonment and alienation creeps in.

Giving way to this fear, I have inadvertently allowed myself to create a walled fortress of silence. Choosing to be silent about the pain and struggles of my soul can protect me from the harsh judgment and words of those who lack understanding. But even more tempting, my silence can safeguard against unintentionally driving away those who yet remain with us.

Outwardly my silence allows me to appear normal and to blend back in where I once felt I belonged, but inwardly it fails to thwart the alienation I dread. My silence comes at the expense of transparency and authenticity, and in so doing actually amplifies the aloneness it was supposed to prevent.

> I was mute and silent, I refrained even from good, And my sorrow grew worse. (Ps. 39:2)

I've been meditating on Psalm 39 for a couple of weeks now. The struggles and cries of David's heart in this Psalm are very much mine as well. Aside from relating to David's observation of his silence intensifying his sorrow, I also deeply relate to David's longing for God to hear his cry, and not be silent at his tears. On initial reading, I thought David was saying in verse 12 that God was like a stranger to him. However, as I continued to study and meditate I learned he was affirming the opposite.

> Hear my prayer, O LORD, and give ear to my cry; Do not be silent at my tears; For I am a stranger with Thee, A sojourner like all my fathers. (Ps. 39:12)

"I am a stranger with Thee." Lord, You and I, we are strangers together. This phrase points back to what God himself spoke in Leviticus, *"for you are but aliens and sojourners with Me"* (Lev. 25:23).

Divinely inspired, David connected his suffering and longing for God's attention to the fact that we are strangers and sojourners with God Himself. Likewise, this prompts me to ponder the correlation between God's silently allowing my pain and tears to persist with my role as a sojourner. Perhaps He allows the pain, struggles and sorrow to remain indefinitely to remind us that this is not our home. Perhaps

"A STRANGER WITH THEE"

they are thorns left to remind us we are sojourners with Him, and we are only passing through.

> I am a stranger in the earth; Do not hide Your commandments from me. My soul is crushed with longing After Your ordinances at all times. (Ps. 119:19-20)

> O God, You are my God; I shall seek You earnestly; My soul thirsts for You, my flesh yearns for You, In a dry and weary land where there is no water. (Ps. 63:1)

Would my soul be crushed with longing after his ordinances if walking righteously in this life came easily or at little cost? Would I truly understand what it is for my soul to thirst for Him and my flesh to yearn for Him as in a dry and weary land if I never actually journeyed through a desolate and parched land? With certainty, this pain and sorrow cause me to gasp for Him as for the very air my lungs require to survive.

> Behold, You have made my days as handbreadths, And my lifetime as nothing in Your sight; Surely every man at his best is a mere breath. Selah. Surely every man walks about as a phantom; Surely they make an uproar for nothing; He amasses riches and does not know who will gather them. And now, Lord, for what do I wait? My hope is in You. (Ps. 39:5-7)

We do not belong here, this world is not our home. This life is but a single breath, and it is for Him alone that we wait. As I wait for Him, I will continue to surrender to His use of my sorrows and struggles as refining flames to burn away the dross of my sinful nature. I will persevere, purposefully utilizing the pain and tears as catalysts to lift my eyes from both past and present to fix my focus on joining all of creation in groaning with great urgency for what is yet to come.

> For we know that the whole creation groans and suffers the pains of childbirth together until now. And not only this, but also we ourselves, having the first fruits of the Spirit, even we ourselves groan within ourselves, waiting eagerly for our adoption as sons, the redemption of our body. For in hope we have been saved, but hope that is seen is not hope; for who hopes for what he already sees? But if we hope for what we do not see, with perseverance we wait eagerly for it. (Rom. 8:22-25)

As His Word has testified to me, I will testify to others that the persisting pain and barrage of struggles this world holds are not evidence of God's abandonment or His being a stranger to us. They are evidence that we are but sojourners in a land in which we do not belong. I am so thankful for the unfolding of God's Word that faithfully encourages weary and wounded hearts.

We may be alienated, but we are not alone. We are strangers WITH Him. We are aliens WITH Him. We are sojourners WITH Him. So, press on with perseverance weary homeward-bound travelers. Let's fix our eyes together on Him who is with us. He hems us in, both behind and before, and He will usher us safely home (Psalm 139:5; John 14:3). Come, Lord Jesus.

> All these died in faith, without receiving the promises, but having seen them and having welcomed them from a distance, and having confessed that they were strangers and exiles on the earth. For those who say such things make it clear that they are seeking a country of their own. And indeed if they had been thinking of that country from which they went out, they would have had opportunity to return. But as it is, they desire a better country, that is, a heavenly one. Therefore God is not ashamed to be called their God; for He has prepared a city for them. (Heb. 11:13-16)

THE SECOND YEAR IS HARDER?

JUNE 1, 2018

Not many weeks after Sarah's death, another bereaved parent shared that the second year is harder than the first. I vividly remember the horror of that statement washing over me in the moments that followed.

At that point, I was still struggling to sleep more than an hour or two at a time. When I did manage to drift off to sleep, I would invariably be violently jolted awake by the thoughts that the bus had crashed and Sarah was killed. I would have to painstakingly walk myself through the details that confirmed its truth. Reminding myself repeatedly that she was not safely asleep in her bed, but she was actually gone.

This new idea that I would hurt more deeply than I had in those horrific preceding moments, hours, days and weeks was devastatingly discouraging. I remember sitting on the bed with Scott afterward, weeping as if from the very tips of my toes, and declaring with certainty in between sobs, "If the pain of losing her gets worse than this, I can't bear it."

Since then I have seen countless posts and comments by bereaved parents indicating the second year is harder than the first. Some even go on to say each year gets progressively harder indefinitely. These thoughts have been like a looming dark cloud that has finally arrived as I find myself a matter of days away from concluding the first year of my life without Sarah, and face to face with the dreaded second year.

After much wrestling within myself, I am sharing some of my views of the first year along with some of my expectations for the year ahead. I intend to revisit this topic next year to see how my perspective may have changed and what if any new insights I may have gleaned over the second year.

I have some reluctance to share my thoughts on this because I recognize the uniqueness of each person's pain and grief, and I am fearful of being wrongly perceived as arguing with or attempting to refute the experiences of other wounded parents. That is not my intent at all. I have deep, tender love and compassion for my fellow brokenhearted sojourners, and would never do anything intentionally to wound or discourage them, or to discount their experiences.

On the other hand, my intention in writing about our journey from the beginning has been to encourage those who will unfortunately journey behind us. Because I found it so profoundly discouraging to entertain the idea that my already overwhelming pain was going to continue to intensify or compound over the coming years—and I now believe that is not going to be our experience—I think it is a topic worthy of thoughtful consideration. If I am right in my prediction that there is a chance that the second year is not necessarily harder for everyone then I want to offer that hope.

Scott and I grieve differently, but we both find ourselves believing that the second year of grieving Sarah's departure can not possibly be worse than the first year we have just endured.

We know the coming year will bring new aspects and challenges possibly coupled with new pain, but at the same time, other aspects will be slightly less raw than they have been this first year. We do not expect our pain to be diminished this year. We know we will not be healed. Our constant longing for our child will not somehow miraculously disappear despite her continued absence. We expect this year, like the first, will hold countless hours, days, and nights of weeping and indescribable aching in our hearts. But we are equally convinced regarding grieving Sarah's absence, that the dark path before us holds no agony deeper or darker than the excruciating path already behind us.

The explanation I see most frequently for the second year being harder than the first is that you are numb the first year but the second year the numbness wears off and the weight of reality sets in. I do not doubt that the parents who share this are speaking the truth about their experience, but I have not felt that full numbness since the first week. Because the pain of those days was so very intense, for me it doesn't feel accurate to refer to it as numbness at all.

I remember very clearly the gut-wrenching sensation of leaving Atlanta in a jet, knowing I was leaving one of my four precious daughters behind. I can still vividly recall the agony of my soul as I wrote my daughter's obituary alone in the wee hours of the morning. I remember the excruciating pain of walking down what seemed like an ever-lengthening aisle toward the casket at the front of the church with my beloved daughter in it, my first time seeing her since I watched her get on that bus four days before. I remember watching that same casket being lowered into the ground and questioning if I would ever be able to breathe again.

I remember sitting on the sofa day after day, peering into her room expecting and longing to see her walk around that corner any second. I was not numb to those devastating experiences, I felt every twinge and piercing pain. And that's just a few snippets of the first week.

The days, weeks, and months of the first year have progressively revealed just how deep, wide, and gaping the hole of Sarah's absence is. We are acutely aware of how radically altered our family is because of her departure, and we have been for months. It's an incapacitating thought to think the depth of pain we have consistently felt and continue to feel in staggering waves this first year is an anesthetized version of what is yet to come.

Thankfully I do not believe that to be true for us. We are not numb. Though the frequency and intensity of the waves of pain vary, the overall depth of our pain has not plunged any deeper for several months now. I genuinely believe we reached the bottom of this dark valley some time ago and the second year will be a continuation of this same painful deep valley path. Certainly, the landscape and obstacles may continue to change along the way, but I do not believe the pain of her absence will plunge deeper yet.

I can't leave the topic of emotional numbness in the first year without at least mentioning the possibility of a correlation with medications. It is not uncommon for those taking antidepressant medications to experience a feeling of emotional "numbness" called emotional blunting. Some studies have shown half of the people being treated with antidepressants reported emotional blunting. I share that simply to offer another factor for consideration. Medication versus no medication may be a significant variable affecting our perceptions of our first-year experiences and how they compare to subsequent years.

I am so thankful for the testimonies shared by wounded parents who have traveled before us. Testimonies of countless examples of God's grace amid devastation. Testimonies that speak hope in the midst of this dark valley. Though our experiences and journeys are each uniquely different, there is tremendous comfort in knowing we truly understand one another's deep brokenness in the absence of our children.

I don't believe the second year will be harder than the first year for us, but I won't be surprised at all if it's just as hard. We approach the coming year with the experience of His sustaining grace being sufficient for the first year and knowing it will be sufficient for the second as well. Based on the truth of His Word and encouraged by the testimonies of those who have gone before us, we know He will enable us to persevere. I hope to report to you next year that what we believed was true, and the second year was not harder for us. But if I'm wrong and the second year is harder, I will truthfully share that next year. And should that be the case, I trust I will be able to share how His sufficient grace met us there.

And He has said to me, "My grace is sufficient for you, for power is perfected in weakness." Most gladly, therefore, I will rather boast about my weaknesses, so that the power of Christ may dwell in me. Therefore I am well content with weaknesses, with insults, with distresses, with persecutions, with difficulties, for Christ's sake; for when I am weak, then I am strong. (2 Cor. 12:9-10)

rivers & roads, rivers & roads, rivers till I reach you

SOUL MELTING SORROW

JUNE 16, 2018

"My soul melts away for sorrow; strengthen me according to your word!"
Psalm 119:28 ESV

As I was meditating on Psalm 119 recently, verse 28 resonated deeply within my heart. We have no way of knowing with certainty the specific source of the Psalmist's sorrow in this text. Though some speculate about the specifics, I wonder if perhaps the source was divinely concealed to allow each of us to more easily relate and apply the wisdom contained to our unique griefs and sorrows.

The Psalmist describes the effect of his deep grief and sorrow as causing his soul to both cling to the dust and melt away within Him (vv. 26-28). It is his response to this crushing sorrow that ministered to my wounded soul. He doesn't plead with God to remedy the source of the sorrow or remove the sorrow itself, he instead asks God to strengthen him. His request in response to his crippling sorrow seems to indicate he has no expectation of its removal. He has accepted his soul melting sorrow is ongoing and he knows the only answer is the strength to bear up under it.

SOUL MELTING SORROW

SOME SORROWS WON'T GO AWAY.

Some sorrows won't go away. For those who don't know the weight of life-altering sorrow, this is an uncomfortable thought. Some refuse to accept it as truth, and in their ignorance will chide the wounded around them saying they simply need to "move on" or "let go" of their sorrow. In the context of child loss, I'm not certain what people mean exactly when they say we must move on or let go. The very reason the pain and great sorrow exist is because I am moving forward in life without my child. I am still getting out of bed each day and prayerfully striving to live a fruitful life, but in the midst of that, each day bears the deep sting of living this life without Sarah.

Accepting that the pain and sorrow will persist does not equate to giving up, defeat, failure, or hopelessness, and it certainly is not sin. Recognizing that in this life we are permanently marked by grief makes us completely aware of our utter dependence on God. Like the Psalmist, we realize we are incapable of one more breath, one more step, one more task, one more interaction, or one more conversation apart from His gracious sustaining provision of strength to endure and persevere.

The recognition of the permanence of our brokenness causes us to cry out with absolute desperation, *"Strengthen me according to your word!"*

I believe the Psalmist was talking about a weight of sorrow of this magnitude when he prayed for strength rather than healing or deliverance. Some soul melting sorrows won't go away. For these sorrows, the answer is not continually pleading for healing or removal of the sorrow. The answer is the prayer the Psalmist prayed, *"Strengthen me according to your word."* Strength to endure and persevere is the answer.

HE IS THE SOURCE OF OUR STRENGTH.

Throughout the Old and New Testaments, He tells us time and time again that He will strengthen us, and that He alone is the source of our strength to endure and persevere. We cry out to Him for strength because He promises to strengthen us.

> Do not fear, for I am with you; Do not anxiously look about you, for I am your God. I will strengthen you, surely I will help you, Surely I will uphold you with My righteous right hand. (Isa. 41:10)

> Now may our Lord Jesus Christ Himself and God our Father, who has loved us and given us eternal comfort and good hope by grace, comfort and strengthen your hearts in every good work and word. (2 Thess. 2:16-17)

> But the Lord is faithful, and He will strengthen and protect you from the evil [one.] (2 Thess. 3:3)

HE STRENGTHENS US THROUGH HIS WORD.

Knowledge and understanding of His character and the revelations and promises of His Word play an integral role in strengthening us. It is imperative that we humbly and prayerfully dig into the Word of God to be equipped to endure and persevere, steadfast and immovable. The entirety of Psalm 119 is the Psalmist's repeated declaration of His desperation for and dependence upon the Word of God as an anchor for his soul in both good times and bad.

> My soul is crushed with longing After Your ordinances at all times (v. 20)... This is my comfort in my affliction, That Your word has revived me (v. 50)... I have remembered Your ordinances from of old, O LORD, And comfort myself (v. 52)...If Your law had not been my delight, Then I would have perished in my affliction. I will never forget Your precepts, For by them You have revived me. I am Yours, save me; For I have sought Your precepts (vv. 92-94)... I opened my mouth wide and panted, For I longed for Your commandments (v. 131)... Your testimonies are righteous forever; Give me understanding

that I may live (v. 144)… My soul keeps Your testimonies, And I love them exceedingly (v. 167).

Over the past year His Word has sustained and strengthened me in countless ways, many recorded here in this book, but below are just a few ways presently most prominent in my mind.

I am strengthened by knowing pain, sorrow and grief are to be expected.

I am strengthened in my sorrow by the reminders in His Word that my pain and grief are to be expected in this fallen world. We are repeatedly implored to endure, persevere, and be steadfast, all of which would be unnecessary if believers were to be free of pain, trials, tribulation, and suffering. On the contrary, we are clearly warned that we will endure all of these.

What a detriment we are to new believers and wounded believers specifically if we somehow teach or imply to them that a life of faith will be one of health, wealth, and prosperity. In so doing we render them rootless. I am reminded of the danger of this in the parable of the seed. Christ says of the seed on the rocky ground, *"the ones who, when they hear the word, immediately receive it with joy. And they have no root in themselves, but endure for a while; then, when tribulation or persecution arises on account of the word, immediately they fall away"* (Mark 4:16b-17).

> Indeed, all who desire to live godly in Christ Jesus will be persecuted. (2 Tim. 3:12)

> But we have this treasure in earthen vessels, so that the surpassing greatness of the power will be of God and not from ourselves; [we are] afflicted in every way, but not crushed; perplexed, but not despairing; persecuted, but not forsaken; struck down, but not destroyed; always carrying about in the body the dying of Jesus, so that the life of Jesus also may be manifested in our body. (2 Cor. 4:7-10)

> To this present hour we are both hungry and thirsty, and are poorly clothed, and are roughly treated, and are homeless; and we toil, working with our own hands; when we are reviled, we bless; when we are persecuted, we endure; when we are slandered, we try to conciliate; we have become as the scum of the world, the dregs of all things, [even] until now. (1 Cor. 4:11-13)

I AM STRENGTHENED BY KNOWING JESUS UNDERSTANDS AND INTERCEDES FOR ME.

We have a Great High Priest who truly knows our every pain, temptation, and struggle. When no one else can possibly know or understand, He does. He was tempted in all things as we are and yet did not sin, and now our gracious, compassionate Savior lives to intercede for us.

> For we do not have a high priest who cannot sympathize with our weaknesses, but One who has been tempted in all things as [we are, yet] without sin. Therefore let us draw near with confidence to the throne of grace, so that we may receive mercy and find grace to help in time of need. (Heb. 4:15-16)

> but Jesus, on the other hand, because He continues forever, holds His priesthood permanently. Therefore He is able also to save forever those who draw near to God through Him, since He always lives to make intercession for them. (Heb. 7:24-25)

I AM STRENGTHENED BY KNOWING JOY AND SORROW CAN AND DO COEXIST.

Some have the flawed idea that the ongoing presence of pain and sorrow eliminates the possibility of joy and peace, and prevents gratitude, praise, and worship. I am strengthened by God's Word which clearly testifies otherwise. The apostle Paul is the one who, inspired by the Holy Spirit, wrote to the church at Phillipi, *"Rejoice in the Lord always; again I will say, rejoice"* (Phil. 4:4). And yet Paul also states in his letter to the Romans, *"I am telling the truth in Christ, I am not lying, my conscience testifies with me in the Holy Spirit, that I have great sorrow and unceasing grief in my heart"* (Rom. 9:1-2). Joy and Sorrow coexist. Peace, joy, contentment, praise, and worship can all exist simultaneously amid relentless pain and sorrow.

> Beloved, do not be surprised at the fiery ordeal among you, which comes upon you for your testing, as though some strange thing were happening to you; but to the degree that you share the sufferings of Christ, keep on rejoicing, so that also at the revelation of His glory you may rejoice with exultation. (1 Pet. 4:12-13)

I AM STRENGTHENED BY THE HOPE OF ETERNITY.

I am strengthened by the hope of eternity. Not only am I strengthened by the hope of eternity itself, I am strengthened by knowing it is good and right to long for eternity. We are repeatedly reminded in Scripture that this life is but a wisp, a vapor, a flower here today and gone tomorrow. We can confidently lift our eyes from our temporal pain and struggles to fix them on the hope of eternity. In so doing we are strengthened to live urgently, expectantly, and fruitfully in anticipation of His coming.

> For to me, to live is Christ and to die is gain. But if [I am] to live [on] in the flesh, this [will mean] fruitful labor for me; and I do not know which to choose. But I am hard-pressed from both [directions,] having the desire to depart and be with Christ, for [that] is very much better; yet to remain on in the flesh is more necessary for your sake. Convinced of this, I know that I will remain and continue with you all for your progress and joy in the faith (Phil. 1:21-25)

> Therefore be patient, brethren, until the coming of the Lord. The farmer waits for the precious produce of the soil, being patient about it, until it gets the early and late rains. You too be patient;

strengthen your hearts, for the coming of the Lord is near. (James 5:7-8)

I AM STRENGTHENED BY THE TRANSPARENT TESTIMONIES OF PERSEVERING SAINTS IN SCRIPTURE.

I am regularly and profoundly impacted and strengthened by the countless candid testimonies of those who have gone before us in Scripture. Job, David, Jeremiah, Peter, and Paul, among others, have been great witnesses to me, encouraging and strengthening me to persevere through this valley.

Some sorrows won't go away, but He who is faithful will graciously strengthen us to persevere through His indwelling Spirit and the power of His Word. *"For whatever was written in earlier times was written for our instruction, so that through perseverance and the encouragement of the Scriptures we might have hope. Now may the God who gives perseverance and encouragement grant you to be of the same mind with one another according to Christ Jesus, so that with one accord you may with one voice glorify the God and Father of our Lord Jesus Christ"* (Rom. 15:4-6).

> Therefore, having been justified by faith, we have peace with God through our Lord Jesus Christ, through whom also we have obtained our introduction by faith into this grace in which we stand; and we exult in hope of the glory of God. And not only this, but we also exult in our tribulations, knowing that tribulation brings about perseverance; and perseverance, proven character; and proven character, hope; and hope does not disappoint, because the love of God has been poured out within our hearts through the Holy Spirit who was given to us. (Rom. 5:1-5)

REMEMBER MY CHAINS

JULY 13, 2018

"I, Paul, write this greeting with my own hand. Remember my chains. Grace be with you." Colossians 4:18 ESV

Our family recently had the tremendous blessing of going on a mission trip to Botswana. The clear focus of the mission and the confidence that we were in the center of God's will in being there was refreshing to my soul. Coming home, where the specifics of His will and purpose for me in this season are not nearly as clear, was extremely difficult.

Three days after we arrived home Scott and I celebrated our twenty-fifth wedding anniversary. The day began and ended with tears. We have been refined through the flames of shared soul crushing sorrow, as a result, our marriage has never been stronger and our love has never been purer.

But "celebrating" that special date only served to amplify the gaping hole in our family and the aching in our hearts. As we reminisced about our wedding day expectations and anniversaries of years gone by we were reminded once again that for the remainder of this life, we will bear the weight of the chains of separation and grief and a desperate longing for eternity.

As I teetered on the brink of despair, the Lord led me to Colossians. I've spent all week studying and meditating there, He specifically spoke to me through Colossians 1:9-12:

> For this reason also, since the day we heard [of it,] we have not ceased to pray for you and to ask that you may be filled with the knowledge of His will in all spiritual wisdom and understanding, so that you will walk in a manner worthy of the Lord, to please [Him] in all respects, bearing fruit in every good work and increasing in the knowledge of God; strengthened with all power, according to His glorious might, for the attaining of all steadfastness and patience; joyously giving thanks to the Father, who has qualified us to share in the inheritance of the saints in Light.

My impassioned prayer from this passage has been that He will fill me *"with the knowledge of His will in all spiritual wisdom and understanding."* I hunger and thirst, desperate for this filling recognizing it alone equips me *"so that"* I can do all that I need to do, long to do, and am called to do for the remainder of my days.

FILL ME WITH THE KNOWLEDGE OF YOUR WILL IN ALL SPIRITUAL WISDOM AND UNDERSTANDING...

- so that I will walk in a manner worthy of You
- so that I will please You in all respects
- so that I will bear fruit in every good work
- so that I will increase in the knowledge of You
- so that I will be strengthened with all power, according to Your glorious might
- so that I will attain all steadfastness and patience
- so that I will joyously give thanks to You, who have qualified me to share in the inheritance of the saints in Light.

As I meditated on this passage once again today, I read on to the conclusion of the letter. The final verse, verse 18, captivated me: *"I, Paul, write this greeting with my own hand. Remember my chains. Grace be with you."*

So, a scribe had most likely recorded all of the preceding verses, but for this final greeting, Paul takes the parchment and pen in chained hands to conclude. Of all that He could conclude with, he says *"Remember my chains."*

Commitments and activities that were balanced with ease before Sarah left can be extremely taxing now, particularly when it feels like I am expected to do them as though nothing has changed. I desire to press on, to persevere, to finish well, but I am acutely aware of the reality and ramifications of my chains.

I feel the weight of the chains of the fallenness of this world that resulted in the death of my child. I feel the weight of the chains of the pulsing pain of separation. I feel the weight of the chains of brokenness that have scarred and altered every individual and relationship in our family.

As life and expectations press in hard I find myself frequently longing to say: *"Remember my chains."* Hence Paul's parting words to the Colossians resonate deeply in my heart.

Before reminding the believers at Colossae about his chains, Paul had just passionately contended for the purification and perseverance of their faith. Remembering that he is contending for them and praying for them without ceasing while in bondage gives an even greater sense of urgency and weight to his exhortations (Col. 1:9). His example challenges me to pray more fervently, and once again reminds me that bondage does not prevent fruitful ministry.

> For I want you to know how great a struggle I have for you and for those at Laodicea and for all who have not seen me face to face, that their hearts may be encouraged, being knit together in love, to reach all the riches of full assurance of understanding and the knowledge of God's mystery, which is Christ, in whom are hidden all the treasures of wisdom and knowledge. (Col. 2:1-3 ESV)

Remembering his chains keeps us aware that we as believers can and will suffer. Some will suffer bound by chains that can be seen, while others will suffer beneath the weight of those that can not be seen. Either way, we are reminded as Peter said, that we should not be surprised as though something strange were happening when fiery ordeals befall us.

> Beloved, do not be surprised at the fiery ordeal among you, which comes upon you for your testing, as though some strange thing were happening to you; but to the degree that you share the sufferings of Christ, keep on rejoicing, so that also at the revelation of His glory you may rejoice with exultation. (1 Pet. 4:12-13)

Proponents of the prosperity gospel would have us believe that every chain is broken in the here and now, and that if we pray hard enough and long enough and have enough faith God will always grant earthly deliverance. Paul's chains and eventual execution testify otherwise.

Some chains will endure until we depart or Christ returns. The fallenness, chains, and bondage of this earth fuel our groaning with all of creation, longing for eternity and the promised liberation and restoration that will only come through Christ's return.

> For we know that the whole creation has been groaning together in the pains of childbirth until now. And not only the creation, but we ourselves, who have the firstfruits of the Spirit, groan inwardly as we wait eagerly for adoption as sons, the redemption of our bodies. (Rom. 8:22-23 ESV)

Lastly, I am deeply encouraged by Paul pointing out his chains and encouraging others to remember them. He was not divinely immune to their weight. He did not pretend they did not exist or were without consequence. Instead, he acknowledged their presence. He was not seeking pity or complaining, but simply acknowledging his earthly limitation.

I believe his reminder was at least twofold, both encouragement and request. He knew his dogged perseverance in spite of his chains would encourage others in bondage to persevere. But, I also believe he was acknowledging the hardship of his chains as a reminder and request for prayers to be offered up on his behalf.

> You also must help us by prayer, so that many will give thanks on our behalf for the blessing granted us through the prayers of many. (2 Cor. 1:11 ESV)

The Father of Lies would have us believe we are to silently bear up under our chains, to pretend their weight does not weary or impede us in any way. Paul's testimony encourages otherwise. We are free to acknowledge the chains, to share their reality knowing that God can use that testimony to encourage others in chains. We also acknowledge them because we are called to help one another through prayer. The only way for that to happen is for us to be truthful about our chains.

As I ponder this I am reminded of the countless times our family has been told by brothers and sisters in Christ that they were lifting us in prayer over the past year. We know the prayers of the many have been powerful and effective in enabling us to stand and persevere. We have not and do not take them for granted and once again offer deep heartfelt gratitude along with the parting words and prayerful blessing of Paul, *"Grace be with you."*

NOT ashamed

HOPE FIXED COMPLETELY

JULY 30, 2018

"Commit your way to the LORD, Trust also in Him, and He will do it. He will bring forth your righteousness as the light And your judgment as the noonday. Rest in the LORD and wait patiently for Him; Do not fret because of him who prospers in his way, Because of the man who carries out wicked schemes." Psalm 37:5-7

The wickedness of this world can be wearisome and daunting. So often my heart aches and I am anguished in spirit as I helplessly watch the righteous man suffer, the scheming man prosper, and wickedness prevail. As time and trials press on, I am increasingly grateful for the promises of Scripture that give hope in the midst of every seemingly hopeless situation.

Over the past year, I've read 1 Peter and 2 Peter countless times. I would probably have naturally been drawn to them in my grief because of the wealth of hope they contain, but they also have a special sweetness for me personally. They were the last passages Sarah was meditating on and journaled about finding both comfort and challenge in.

HOPE FIXED COMPLETELY

> Therefore, prepare your minds for action, keep sober [in spirit,] fix your hope completely on the grace to be brought to you at the revelation of Jesus Christ. (1 Pet. 1:13)

As I was spending time in 1 Peter once again recently, I noticed a phrasing I had previously failed to appreciate. The latter part of 1 Peter 1:13 says, *"Fix your hope completely on the grace to be brought to you at the revelation of Jesus Christ."* Completely, not some, not partially, not mostly, but *completely*. Translations vary slightly, but most render it either "fully" or "completely," and some as "without wavering" and "perfectly, completely."

So, I am to fix my hope perfectly, completely, fully, without wavering on this grace I do not fully possess yet. The grace that will be brought to me at the revelation of Jesus Christ. I am so very thankful for this timely reminder, this wonderful word of encouragement. We all need hope, but when you are broken and wounded you recognize your desperation for it.

Worldly thought and personal desires may tempt us to fix our hope, at least partially, on a variety of temporal goals, such as healing, justice, vindication, restoration of broken relationships, and so on. Though these are good things to desire, 1 Peter 1:13 makes it exceedingly clear that there is only one thing on which we can and should fix our hope: *"the grace to be brought to [us] at the revelation of Jesus Christ."*

This hope is the confident anticipation of the culmination of all the promises to be delivered at the coming of Christ. Promised blessings to be granted by grace through faith in the Lord Jesus Christ (Eph. 2:8-9). The context of the passage in 1 Peter 1 clarifies the most prominent blessings of this grace to be brought: life beyond death, an imperishable inheritance reserved for us in heaven, and the salvation of our souls.

Life Beyond Death

> Blessed be the God and Father of our Lord Jesus Christ, who according to His great mercy has caused us to be born again to a living

> hope through the resurrection of Jesus Christ from the dead (1 Pet. 1:3)

By God's grace through Christ Jesus, I have the hope of life beyond death. Christ's atonement and resurrection broke the chains of sin and death. No longer eternally separated from our Holy God by sin, through the precious blood of Jesus, we look forward to intimately dwelling with Him for eternity. And not only Him, through His abundant grace we have the blessed hope of dwelling eternally with all of our brothers and sisters (and children) in Christ; never to be separated by death or impacted by sin again.

> My sheep hear My voice, and I know them, and they follow Me; and I give eternal life to them, and they will never perish; and no one will snatch them out of My hand. "My Father, who has given [them] to Me, is greater than all; and no one is able to snatch [them] out of the Father's hand. (John 10:27-29)

AN IMPERISHABLE INHERITANCE IN HEAVEN

> to [obtain] an inheritance [which is] imperishable and undefiled and will not fade away, reserved in heaven for you (1 Pet. 1:4)

As we plod along in a fallen world filled with injustice, we must remember our inheritance or reward is not here. Our inheritance is in heaven. Certainly, God graciously provides for us here, and we may enjoy many good gifts from above, but everything here will fade away and perish. Regardless of our circumstances on earth, good or bad, Christ's followers have a certain hope of an inheritance reserved for us in heaven by God. If it is reserved *"for us"* then we, too, are going there. A wonderful reminder that we are but sojourners passing through. This world is not our home, we have a glorious eternal destination yet before us.

> Do not store up for yourselves treasures on earth, where moth and rust destroy, and where thieves break in and steal. But store up for yourselves treasures in heaven, where neither moth nor rust destroys, and where thieves do not break in or steal; for where your treasure is, there your heart will be also. (Matt. 6:19-21)

The Salvation of Our Souls

> [for you] who are protected by the power of God through faith for a salvation ready to be revealed in the last time. (1 Pet. 1:5)

His grace is so rich and abundant. Not only did He provide salvation through Christ, but through faith He will protect our souls and complete the work of salvation in us, by His power (Phil 1:6). Through faith in Him, the God of the universe will continually sustain, equip, and empower us to persevere by His incomprehensibly infinite power. He Himself is protecting us by His power to finally and completely receive the grace of salvation to be revealed at the revelation of Jesus Christ. Hallelujah, Praise the Lord!

> and though you have not seen Him, you love Him, and though you do not see Him now, but believe in Him, you greatly rejoice with joy inexpressible and full of glory, obtaining as the outcome of your faith the salvation of your souls. (1 Pet. 1:8-9)

Hope for Suffering

> In this you greatly rejoice, even though now for a little while, if necessary, you have been distressed by various trials, so that the proof of your faith, [being] more precious than gold which is perishable, even though tested by fire, may be found to result in praise and glory and honor at the revelation of Jesus Christ (1 Pet. 1:6-7)

It is this hope alone that enables us, even while suffering, to *"greatly rejoice with joy inexpressible and full of glory"* (1 Pet. 1:8). If I am obedient to fix my hope *"completely on the grace to be brought to [me] at the revelation of Jesus Christ,"* then absolutely none of my hope can be fixed on temporal outcomes such as healing, justice, vindication, restoration of broken relationships, or any number of other options.

Though I long for such outcomes and will prayerfully work toward them where appropriate, I find great encouragement in knowing that hope properly fixed can not and will not be disappointed, diminished, or lost in their temporal absence.

In this fallen world, the righteous will continue to suffer, lying and scheming men will continue to prosper, and wickedness will continue to prevail. But our hope, fixed on eternity and held by the sovereign God of the universe, gloriously transcends the fallenness of this world. Hold onto faith, fellow wounded sojourner. As we cry out to Him, *"Lord, I believe, help my unbelief,"* by His infinite power He will strengthen us to stand and persevere. He will powerfully enable us to *"greatly rejoice with joy inexpressible and full of glory"* as we praise Him for this hope *"we have as an anchor of the soul, a [hope] both sure and steadfast"* (Heb. 6:19).

For this reason I too, having heard of the faith in the Lord Jesus which [exists] among you and your love for all the saints, do not cease giving thanks for you, while making mention [of you] in my prayers; that the God of our Lord Jesus Christ, the Father of glory, may give to you a spirit of wisdom and of revelation in the knowledge of Him. [I pray that] the eyes of your heart may be enlightened, so that you will know what is the hope of His calling, what are the riches of the glory of His inheritance in the saints, and what is the surpassing greatness of His power toward us who believe. [These are] in accordance with the working of the strength of His might which He brought about in Christ, when He raised Him from the dead and seated Him at His right hand in the heavenly [places,] (Eph. 1:15-23)

WHY I WON'T SAY "CHOOSE JOY"

AUGUST 15, 2018

"Whoever sings songs to a heavy heart is like one who takes off a garment on a cold day, and like vinegar on soda." Proverbs 25:20 ESV

Some precious friends who also know the horrific sting of child loss were recently sent a post on social media outlining how they must choose joy and not sorrow. My heart ached for them as I read it. The reality is this sweet family has done a remarkable job of demonstrating faith, perseverance, and joy in the midst of deep loss. I have no doubt the sender was well-meaning and motivated by love, but it was obvious the post was written by one who lacks the understanding and wisdom gleaned from the depths of sorrow and loss that these dear friends intimately know.

There may be times in life when the mantra "choose joy" might be fitting and appropriate, particularly when spoken inwardly as a challenge to oneself. However, when dealing with deeply wounded, grieving, or struggling people, those two words may do more harm than good.

SAYING "CHOOSE JOY" IMPLIES THEY ARE NOT "CHOOSING JOY."

It's been fourteen months since Sarah left and I have made progress in learning how to carry the weight of sorrow. But some days are still of the magnitude of the very first days: staggering, take you to your knees, struggle to breathe days. A few days ago I had one of those days. No major trigger or cause, I just felt the full weight of missing my little girl.

I longed to be sharing in the excitement of her beginning college, to celebrate the next round of milestones with all her peers and their parents. My heart and eyes were overflowing with sorrow intermittently all day. If you had seen me that day, you could have reasonably yet wrongly concluded I lack joy.

If you aren't intimately walking alongside a broken person daily it is impossible to accurately assess the presence or absence of joy in their lives. If they happen to reveal or share the weight of sorrow in their heart, it is not an indication that their heart is void of joy. Likewise, if they share the joy of their heart, that does not indicate their heart is now free of grief and sorrow. Even if you are confident in your assessment that a broken person is lacking joy, I beg of you to reconsider advising them to "choose joy."

SAYING "CHOOSE JOY" IMPLIES JOY AND SORROW ARE MUTUALLY EXCLUSIVE.

> But it is still my consolation, And I rejoice in unsparing pain, That I have not denied the words of the Holy One. (Job 6:10)

The exhortation to "choose joy" is rooted in truth but lacking context. It fails to acknowledge the proper biblical context which consistently shows sorrow or distress and joy or rejoicing existing simultaneously in the lives of believers. Saying "choose joy" implies that joy and sorrow are mutually exclusive, that one must choose either joy or sorrow, one or the other. Therefore, if you are experiencing sorrow you must be failing to choose joy.

No right-minded person would ever choose to feel sorrow or bear grief. For most, if not all, it is inescapably thrust upon us. Sarah will not come back and my sorrow will not go away this side of heaven. If sorrow and joy are mutually exclusive I can never have joy. Praise God, that is not true. Joy and sorrow are NOT mutually exclusive. Joy and sorrow coexist.

Saying "choose joy" conveys you believe sorrow is no longer appropriate.

I am weary with my sighing; Every night I make my bed swim, I dissolve my couch with my tears. (Ps. 6:6)

If a deeply wounded person shares the details of their sorrow with me and my response to them is "choose joy," I risk conveying to them that I believe their pain and sorrow are no longer appropriate. It may be perceived as indicating that I believe it is time for them to move on from their sorrow; that they should no longer feel it. Should they receive it that way they will likely no longer feel safe to be transparent with me about their sorrow. Thus potentially further isolating them in their pain and sorrow.

Saying "choose joy" is not actionable advice.

Be gracious to me, O LORD, for I [am] pining away; Heal me, O LORD, for my bones are dismayed. (Ps. 6:2)

In the midst of their brokenness and sorrow a challenge to "choose joy" is little more than an exhortation to "pull yourself up by your bootstraps." While it sounds slightly more spiritual or religious, there is very little difference between saying "choose joy" and saying "don't worry, be happy."

How do you choose joy? If my soul is overwhelmed with grief, would I not prefer to feel joy if I knew how? How do I make it happen? Where does joy come from when your heart is completely shattered and the life you knew is no more?

I won't say "Choose joy," but I will weep with them.

> Rejoice with those who rejoice, weep with those who weep. (Rom. 12:15 ESV)

Weep with those who weep. Such simple instruction but so profoundly impactful. We were sent so many thoughtful gifts, cards, and letters, and the vast majority were precious, encouraging, and meaningful. I in no way want to diminish their value, but the greatest gift we have been given over the past year is the tears of those who have wept with us.

Just a couple of weeks ago I met someone whom I had not previously met. He shared with me that he had prayed for us and wept on our behalf in the days and weeks following Sarah's death. As he shared, his eyes once again brimmed with tears. My heart was instantly knit to his, as was Scott's when I shared with him. His tears and sharing of our pain were a comforting balm for our sorrowful hearts.

I won't say "Choose joy," but I will walk with them.

> Bear one another's burdens, and so fulfill the law of Christ. (Gal. 6:2 ESV)

> ...encourage the fainthearted, help the weak, be patient with everyone. (1 Thess. 5:14)

There is no end for some sorrows on this earth. It is not a sin for sorrow to linger. With that in mind, through the power and love of the indwelling Holy Spirit, I will continue to walk with my wounded friends. As the Holy Spirit leads I will share comfort from the comfort He has given me (2 Cor. 1:3-4). I will prayerfully *"put on a heart of compassion, kindness, humility, gentleness and patience*" to bear with the broken and sorrowful around me (Col. 3:12).

I won't say "Choose joy,"
but I will pray for them to have Hope.

> Now may the God of hope fill you with all joy and peace in believing, so that you will abound in hope by the power of the Holy Spirit. (Rom. 15:13)

I believe Scripture makes it clear that our joy and our hope are inextricably linked. There is no joy apart from hope. If we are truly struggling to experience joy, then our hope is likely fractured or failing as well. If we fix our hope completely and properly, our joy will soon be "fixed" as well.

God fills us with joy, it is the fruit of the Spirit (Gal. 5:22). We can not simply muster it up, or will it into existence. Rather, as we crucify our flesh and fix our hope completely on the grace to be brought to us at the revelation of Jesus Christ, the Holy Spirit Himself will produce in us the joy God commands us to have (1 Pet. 1).

What a breathtakingly powerful encouragement it is that the God of hope will fill us with all joy and peace as we choose to believe in Him and thus we will abound in hope! Beautiful confirmation that it is not something we must muster, but that it is by the power of the Holy Spirit (Rom. 15:13). Hallelujah, Praise the Lord!

And I will pray for them to be empowered to greatly rejoice
with joy inexpressible and full of glory!

If you, my precious brother or sister, find yourself feeling crushed beneath the weight of sorrow today, I pray for you as I pray for myself, and as Paul prayed for the Ephesians (vv. 1:16-21):

- that our Father may give us the Spirit of wisdom and of revelation in the knowledge of him

- that the eyes of our hearts may be enlightened
- that we may know what is the hope to which He has called us
- that we may know what are the riches of His glorious inheritance in the saints
- that we may know the immeasurable greatness of His power toward us who believe
- that we may know all of this according to the working of His great might that He worked in Christ when He raised him from the dead and seated Him at His right hand in the heavenly places
- that even in our deepest sorrow, we may be empowered through the working of the Holy Spirit, and through the glorious hope of His grace yet to be delivered, to greatly rejoice with joy inexpressible and full of glory! (1 Pet. 1:8, 13)

Life appears to me too short to be spent nursing animosity or registering wrongs.

— CHARLOTTE BRONTË

THE HYPOCRISY OF GRIEF

SEPTEMBER 4, 2018

Scott and Sarah loved quoting movie lines to each other. A large portion of their quotes came from *The Princess Bride* and *Elf*. Pretty much every day as she was telling him goodbye or goodnight she would tell him, "Have fun storming the castle!"[1] To which he would reply, "I hope you find your dad!"[2]

Recently as Scott and I were on a walk through the neighborhood, we were discussing a painful secondary issue we are dealing with related to Sarah's death. Tears had been flowing only moments before when a neighbor we hadn't met yet crossed our path and greeted us with "Hello, how are you?" to which I instantly replied, "Fine, thank you. How are you?"

As soon as they had passed, Scott turned to me with a smirk and perfectly reenacted the "Liar!" scene from *The Princess Bride.*[1] His impressive reenactment provided a much-needed hearty laugh for both of us, but at the same time superficially reflected a deeper struggle that has been weighing heavily on my heart.

For months now I've wrestled with the idea of hypocrisy in grief, and more specifically—my potential hypocrisy in my grief. If I, with dry eyes, profess my hope in Christ and yet regularly cry myself to sleep because of the aching in my heart, am I a hypocrite? If most people only see me in the moments of light when I have a firm grip on the hope I profess, and not in the dark of the night when I am crying out, "Lord I believe, help my unbelief!" does that make me a hypocrite?

According to Merriam-Webster, "the word hypocrite ultimately came into English from the Greek word hypokrites, which means 'an actor' or 'a stage player.' The Greek word itself is a compound noun: it's made up of two Greek words that literally translate as 'an interpreter from underneath.' That bizarre compound makes more sense when you know that the actors in ancient Greek theater wore large masks to mark which character they were playing, and so they interpreted the story from underneath their masks."[3]

Merriam-Webster also defines a hypocrite as one "who acts in contradiction to his or her stated beliefs or feelings."[4] A biblical understanding of hypocrisy is similar, having to do with an inconsistency between the heart and behavior. But what happens when there is tension between one's beliefs and one's feelings? Is it hypocrisy to act in accordance with one when it seems in opposition to the other?

What I have found myself referring to as the "hypocrisy of grief" is my acting in accordance with my beliefs despite my feelings. My beliefs and actions are aligned but frequently seem contradictory to my feelings. For example, when I am worn and weary I may not feel hopeful, but I choose hope, believe hope, and profess hope. If I profess with my mouth the hope that I believe in my mind but am struggling to feel in my heart, is that hypocrisy?

The translation of *"hypokrites"* by Merriam-Webster, *"an interpreter from underneath* [a mask]" deeply resonates with me. The mask I wear is a reflection of the hope I possess. My hope is real and true, and my soul is anchored by the truth upon which my hope is fixed (1 Pet. 1:13; Heb. 6:19). The mask is much simpler than I am, though. It frequently smiles and says nothing of the pain while the streams of tears are still wet on my cheeks. Behind the mask is an indescribably complex reality of intermingled oppressive sorrow, prevailing peace, piercing pain, eternal hope, desperate longing, and abiding joy.

The mask is not untruth, but it is only a portion of the truth. It is representative of what I believe, the confidence of the hope I possess and profess, but it is not the totality of me. It fails to reflect the daily complexity of the mingling of my hope with the sorrow, pain, and longing that remain. Knowing the mask is not knowing me.

Months ago when I first felt the tension of the hypocrisy of grief, I made a case for it as I wrote "Faking Fine in the Midst of Grief?"[5] Six months later I am still convinced of all that I wrote then, but with the passage of time I have learned there is a deep loneliness that comes with "interpreting from underneath the mask."

I believe many, if not most of us, have an intrinsic longing to be known, to be understood and related to. I definitely do. I crave authentic relationships where trust, transparency, and honesty are the standard. I believe I have always been an open book. I am the same everywhere and if you know me, you know the real me. That is until Sarah went home and I found myself by necessity hurled into being "an interpreter from underneath a mask."

Anytime I am blessed with time and an appropriate opportunity to engage in deeper discussion that moves beyond the mask, I am grateful. But those times are infrequent. As I've recently found myself regularly longing for more opportunities for others to see beyond the mask, the Lord has gently reminded me that I am shifting my focus from Him in desiring others to do what He alone can. I am longing to be completely understood, to have my heart known, but He alone is the knower of hearts (Acts 1:24).

However, I am comforted by realizing my longing to be known, to be transparent and authentic, actually reveals that my perceived "hypocrisy of grief" is not truly hypocrisy. The mask is simply a necessary filter, not a shroud of deception.

And many of those feelings, the pain, sorrow, and longing, that sometimes seem contradictory to the peace, joy, and hope of my beliefs are not actually contradictory. They are my *"groaning inwardly."* They are my grief over the fallenness and brokenness of this world, and my burdened longing for eternity (2 Cor. 5:4; Rom. 8:23). Both of which are in agreement with and rooted in the biblical truths and hope I profess.

> For while we are still in this tent, we groan, being burdened–not that we would be unclothed, but that we would be further clothed, so that what is mortal may be swallowed up by life. (2 Cor. 5:4 ESV)

> And not only the creation, but we ourselves, who have the firstfruits of the Spirit, groan inwardly as we wait eagerly for adoption as sons, the redemption of our bodies. (Rom. 8:23 ESV)

Should my feelings actually be in contradiction to my biblical beliefs, acting in accordance with those beliefs in spite of the contradictory feelings is not hypocrisy. It is part of the crucifixion of my flesh, the denial of self and daily taking up of my cross to follow Him (Gal. 5:24; Luke 9:23). Feelings are deceptive, and the heart is deceptive, hence the call to circumcise it (Deu. 10:16). The sometimes painful process of humbly and sincerely choosing surrendered faith and obedience to Him instead of indulging our feelings is part of that crucifixion or circumcision. As I purposefully meditate on His truths and continue to act in obedience, my feelings will eventually come into alignment as well.

> Finally, brothers, whatever is true, whatever is honorable, whatever is just, whatever is pure, whatever is lovely, whatever is commendable, if there is any excellence, if there is anything worthy of praise, think about these things. What you have learned and received and heard and seen in me–practice these things, and the God of peace will be with you. (Phil. 4:8-9 ESV)

If you, too, struggle with feeling alone and unknown in what sometimes feels like a chasm between a painful present reality and the hope of our glorious promised future, hang on. Cling with me to the promises of His Word that affirm we are not alone or unknown. Neither are we hypocrites when we profess our hope in the midst of our ongoing brokenness, even when that hope is professed between tearfully whispered prayers of "Lord I believe, help my unbelief."

We are intimately known, deeply loved, and powerfully held by the omnipotent, faithful, righteous, and loving God of the universe. And so we press on knowing that this same God, our God, has promised that He who began the good work in us will bring it to completion in *"just a little while."* (Phil. 1:6, 3:12-24; Heb. 10:37).

Come, Lord Jesus!

> O LORD, you have searched me and known me! You know when I sit down and when I rise up; you discern my thoughts from afar. You search out my path and my lying down and are acquainted with all my ways. Even before a word is on my tongue, behold, O LORD, you know it altogether. You hem me in, behind and before, and lay your hand upon me. Such knowledge is too wonderful for me; it is high; I cannot attain it. Where shall I go from your Spirit? Or where shall I flee from your presence? If I ascend to heaven, you are there! If I make my bed in Sheol, you are there! If I take the wings of the morning and dwell in the uttermost parts of the sea, even there your hand shall lead me, and your right hand shall hold me. If I say, "Surely the darkness shall cover me, and the light about me be night," even the darkness is not dark to you; the night is bright as the day, for darkness is as light with you. (Ps. 139:1-12 ESV)

---

1. *The Princess Bride.* Directed by Rob Reiner, Twentieth Century Fox, 1987.
2. *Elf.* Directed by Jon Favreau, New Line Cinema, 2003.
3. "The origin of 'Hypocrite.'" *Merriam-Webster Dictionary,* merriam-webster.com/wordplay/hypocrite-meaning-origin. Accessed 4 Sep. 2018.
4. "Hypocrite, N. (2)." *Merriam-Webster Dictionary,* merriam-webster.com/dictionary/hypocrite. Accessed 4 Sept. 2018.
5. see "Faking Fine in the Midst of Grief?" pp. 141-144.

WALKING IN DARKNESS

SEPTEMBER 24, 2018

The darkness of circumstances surrounding our family is so oppressive that it frequently seems there is no light in sight. Recently I once again spent substantial time in the Psalms crying out to God, but was still feeling crushed by the darkness pressing in around us. I pleaded with God to meet me in His Word, and in His gracious and compassionate faithfulness, He did. He led me to shift my attention from the Psalms to Isaiah where He has since repeatedly encouraged me.

As I read Isaiah chapter 50, verse 10 instantly resonated deeply within my weary and heavy-laden heart. In this text, the Lord is addressing His faithful servants, those who fear Him and obey Him. But most notably the Lord is specifically addressing His faithful servant who *"walks in darkness and has no light."*

> Who is among you that fears the LORD, That obeys the voice of His servant, That walks in darkness and has no light? Let him trust in the name of the LORD and rely on his God. (Isa. 50:10)

Faithful and obedient servants are not exempt from experiencing darkness and lack of light. What tremendous encouragement that He forewarned us that His faithful servants may be required to walk in the darkness of distress and suffering with no light of hope for temporal deliverance. If I am fearing and obeying Him and yet find myself in the darkness without light, I need not be surprised nor afraid that I have lost my way or left the path He has marked out for me.

> Beloved, do not be surprised at the fiery ordeal among you, which comes upon you for your testing, as though some strange thing were happening to you (1 Pet. 4:12)

The darkness and lack of light may be ongoing. I am profoundly encouraged by Isaiah 50:10 because it is a charge to the servant who *"walks in darkness."* The servant is not enduring a fleeting moment of darkness, a single event or incident, but an ongoing period or season of darkness. The servant is journeying in darkness with no light.

This is God's acknowledgment of and charge for the faithful servant who, like Job, is experiencing deep distress, trial upon trial, and sorrow upon sorrow with no end in sight.

> As an example, brethren, of suffering and patience, take the prophets who spoke in the name of the Lord. We count those blessed who endured. You have heard of the endurance of Job and have seen the outcome of the Lord's dealings, that the Lord is full of compassion and [is] merciful. (James 5:10-11)

God sees us walking in darkness. Isaiah 50:10 is encouraging because it is a clear reminder that God's eye remains on His servant who is walking in darkness with no light. No matter how dark our valley is, He is never unaware of our plight. Though we may find ourselves unable to see Him through the shroud of darkness that envelops us, we are never out of sight or unseen by Him.

> If I say, "Surely the darkness shall cover me, and the light about me be night," even the darkness is not dark to you; the night is bright as the day, for darkness is as light with you. (Ps. 139:11-12 ESV)

God's simple instruction: *"Let him trust in the name of the LORD and rely on his God."* I love how clearly and concisely God instructs the weary servant walking in darkness. I see His graciousness and love in the simplicity of the wording of His requirement for His servant–*trust in who I am and rely on Me.*

Trust in the name of the LORD.

We are to trust in the name of the LORD, in who He is. How vital that we continually meditate on and hide His Word in our hearts. He has chosen to reveal Himself to us through His Word. As we spend time with Him through His Word He allows and enables us to understand and know Him. Through this understanding and knowledge, we are equipped to confidently trust in His name.

> but let him who boasts boast of this, that he understands and knows Me, that I am the LORD who exercises lovingkindness, justice and righteousness on earth; for I delight in these things," declares the LORD. (Jer. 9:24)

> Behold, God is my salvation, I will trust and not be afraid; For the LORD GOD is my strength and song, And He has become my salvation. (Isa. 12:2)

> Trust in Him at all times, O people; Pour out your heart before Him; God is a refuge for us. Selah. (Ps. 62:8)

> The name of the LORD is a strong tower; The righteous runs into it and is safe. (Prov. 18:10)

It is to trust, not to anything more. No attempts to stifle tears are required. There is no sin in sorrow. The emotions which we feel to God in bright days are not appropriate at such times. There are seasons in every life when all that we can say is, "Truly this is a grief, and I will bear it."[1]

— ALEXANDER MACLAREN

Rely on your God.

We are also to rely on our God. The context provided in the verses preceding Isaiah 50:10 demonstrates the faithfulness of God as our helper, defender, and sustainer. Because of who He is, and through His provision of sustaining strength and power we can *"set our faces like flint"* in confident reliance upon Him.

> For the Lord GOD helps Me, Therefore, I am not disgraced; Therefore, I have set My face like flint, And I know that I will not be ashamed. (Isa. 50:7)

Whatever the source of our distress we have the assurance that it is temporal in nature. Both earthly and spiritual adversaries are like garments that will soon wear out and be eaten by moths. But we rely upon our eternal God who has promised and secured for us, through the blood of Jesus, our eternal hope. We may or may not see the light of temporal deliverance, but we trust in Him and confidently rely upon Him knowing the glorious light of eternal deliverance is coming *"in just a little while"* (Heb. 10:37).

> For we were so utterly burdened beyond our strength that we despaired of life itself. Indeed, we felt that we had received the sentence of death. But that was to make us rely not on ourselves but on God who raises the dead. He delivered us from such a deadly peril, and he will deliver us. On him we have set our hope that he will deliver us again. (2 Cor. 1:9-10 ESV)

Look, sirs! If you do not rely upon God in the dark, it would seem as if, after all, you did not trust God, but were trusting to the light, or were relying on your own eyesight. Too often we think we believe, but all the while we are miles off from believing. Unless we trust in God alone, and in God wholly, we do not trust Him at all. Faith is the opposite of sight. When a man sees he has no need of faith. Blessed is he to whom God Himself is all the light he needs.[2]

— CHARLES SPURGEON

Do not contrive to create your own light.

Immediately following His command to trust in His name and rely on Him, the Lord issues a stern warning against attempting to create your own light in the darkness.

> Behold, all you who kindle a fire, Who encircle yourselves with firebrands, Walk in the light of your fire And among the brands you have set ablaze. This you will have from My hand: You will lie down in torment. (Isa. 50:11)

In the midst of the darkness, we must not give in to the temptation to create our own light, to make our own way of deliverance. I am not to set my focus on attempting to dispel the darkness, to eradicate or replace the source of my distress or suffering. Instead, I am clearly instructed to simply *"trust in the name of the LORD and rely on [my] God"* as I continue to obediently *"walk in darkness and have no light."*

> It is in the occupation of heart and mind with Jesus that joy and peace come. To make them our direct aim is the way not to attain them. Though now there seems a long wintry interval between seed time and harvest, yet "in due season we shall reap if we faint not."[1]

— ALEXANDER MACLAREN

The faithful prophet, Jeremiah, shares a beautiful testimony of this in Lamentations. In the darkness Jeremiah meditated on who God is, He trusted in His name and relied upon Him.

> He has driven me and made me walk In darkness and not in light. ... In dark places He has made me dwell, Like those who have long been dead. ... This I recall to my mind, Therefore I have hope. The LORD'S lovingkindnesses indeed never cease, For His compassions never fail. [They] are new every morning; Great is Your faithfulness. "The LORD is my portion," says my soul, "Therefore I have hope in Him." The LORD is good to those who wait for Him, To the person who seeks Him. [It is] good that he waits silently For the salvation of the LORD. (Lam. 3:2, 6, 21-26)

The Everlasting Light is coming.

Our God sees us walking in darkness, and out of His vast tender lovingkindness and compassion, He has called us to trust in His name and rely on Him. As we do, He will guide our every step through the darkness of the midnight hour until the dawning of that glorious morning when, praise God, we will bask in His everlasting light never to sorrow again. Come, Lord Jesus!

> The sun will no more be your light by day, nor the brightness of the moon shine on you, for the LORD will be your everlasting light, and your God will be your glory. Your sun will never set again, and your moon will wane no more; the LORD will be your everlasting light, and your days of sorrow will end. (Isa. 60:19-20 NIV)

---

1. Maclaren, Alexander. "A Call to Faith (Isaiah 50:10)." *Blue Letter Bible,* 17 Feb. 2022, blueletterbible.org/comm/maclaren_alexander/expositions-of-holy-scripture/isaiah/a-call-to-faith.cfm.
2. Spurgeon, C.H. "The Child Of Light Walking In Darkness." *Spurgeon's Sermons Volume 33: 1887 - Christian Classics Ethereal Library,* ccel.org/ccel/spurgeon/sermons33.xlviii.html.

THE VOICE OF THE LORD IN THE STORM

OCTOBER 10, 2018

> "The voice of the LORD is upon the waters; The God of glory thunders, The LORD is over many waters. The voice of the LORD is powerful, The voice of the LORD is majestic." Psalm 29:3-4

"The voice of the LORD is upon the waters; The God of glory thunders." Profoundly meaningful words as I have just returned from walking alongside the ocean in the midst of the tropical storm conditions preceding Hurricane Michael. Both the sounds and sights of the wind and the powerful stirring of the waves were breathtakingly awe-inspiring.

> Those who go down to the sea in ships, Who do business on great waters; They have seen the works of the LORD, And His wonders in the deep. For He spoke and raised up a stormy wind, Which lifted up the waves of the sea. They rose up to the heavens, they went down to the depths; Their soul melted away in [their] misery. (Ps. 107:23-26)

As Scott and I walked next to the ocean beneath billowing dark clouds echoing back the thunderous sounds of the crashing surf I found it strangely comforting. It was as if my eyes were suddenly beholding the storm that has encompassed us for the past sixteen months.

I could see the raging ocean with the massive waves that have repeatedly threatened to drown us and still continue to batter us. No longer just feeling the darkness of the storm, I was seeing it as the ominous dark clouds above completely obscured the light and warmth of the sun.

As I have continued to walk in the darkness of our storm, and more recently in silence yet again, I have found myself increasingly desperate to hear God's voice. In prayer I have echoed the words of the Psalmists, the prophets, and Job, longing to hear from Him, for Him to turn His face to me and speak to me. I am longing for Him, not for something from Him, not a specific word or action, just simply for Him and His voice. I am willing to hear whatever He wants to speak; I just need Him to speak.

I recognize saying that makes some people uncomfortable, though, myself included. We are so very blessed to have God's inspired and revealed Word in Scripture, but just reading it is not the same as hearing Him speak that very same Word to my heart. I hear Him as I bask in His Word and He turns and exposes the truths of His Word, speaking them to my very soul. In those holy moments, He speaks truth through the power of His indwelling Holy Spirit; He teaches me through the unfolding of His Word in such a way that it transforms my heart for His glory and my good.

When He speaks His living Word to my heart, it washes over me in a profoundly impactful way; a way that encourages me, convicts me, strengthens me, and equips me. I hear His voice in those moments and I am changed.

> As the deer pants for the water brooks, So my soul pants for You, O God. My soul thirsts for God, for the living God; When shall I come and appear before God? My tears have been my food day and night, While [they] say to me all day long, "Where is your God? (Ps. 42:1-3)

But sometimes I don't hear His voice. Sometimes I am left in silence. I am desperately devouring His Word, longing for Him to speak and yet hearing nothing. Certainly, I can extract wisdom from His Word and glean applicable truth, but that is not the same as the comfort of His voice speaking His truth directly into this weary and tattered heart. Such has been my plight in recent weeks. Yet another period of Him teaching me to wait patiently and longingly and to persevere in hungering and thirsting for Him.

As we continued our walk on the beach eastward toward the storm, something beautiful happened. For a few seconds, the dark clouds were pierced by blinding rays of light, it was a spectacular sight to behold. My heart and mind were instantly flooded with Scripture reminding me of God's faithfulness in the storm: His promise to never leave us nor forsake us, His promise that He sees us and we can not escape His sight, and His promise to redeem all things and make all things new (Isa. 43:1- 2; Heb. 13:5-6; Ps. 139; Rev. 21:5).

When I got back to the condominium I pulled out one of Sarah's journals and flipped to the entry closest to the current date to use it as a guide for my time in Scripture that morning. I hadn't read her journals in quite a while but brought them to the beach in hopes they might be of some comfort. Following her reading plan for October 10, 2016, I read 2 Thessalonians 1, Joel 1-2, and Psalms 29 and 30.

I was encouraged by 2 Thessalonians 1 as I was reminded in verses 6 and 7 that God promises relief for the afflicted *"when the Lord Jesus will be revealed from heaven with His mighty angels in flaming fire."* As I read Joel 1-2, I was greatly encouraged by the reminders of God's compassion and abounding lovingkindness, the promise now fulfilled to pour out His Holy Spirit, and His promise of deliverance for His people who cry out to Him.

But when I flipped to Psalm 29 and saw the editor's title for the Psalm, *"The Voice of the Lord in the Storm,"* I was captivated. As I slowly read each verse meditating on the meaning of each, my heart began to race in anticipation. He was speaking and I could hear Him.

"The voice of the LORD is upon the waters; The God of glory thunders." The entire Psalm is about the voice of the Lord, the voice I have been desperately longing to hear. I read verse after verse expectantly and

with increasing awe as I was reminded of who He is. With the visions and sounds of the storm still fresh in my mind, I worshipped Him in those moments.

Then He spoke verse 11 to my heart, pouring it over me as a comforting balm, *"The LORD will give strength to His people; The LORD will bless His people with peace."*

From the very day Sarah left until today, Scott and I have consistently prayed asking the Lord for two specific things: strength to persevere and peace to endure. Recently in my weariness, I felt both were waning. Using a piercing light in a dark storm and the journal of my sweet Sarah, He answered my cry to hear His voice. He spoke His perfect Word to my weary heart, the exact Word I needed to hear at the exact moment.

If you find yourself in a storm today, I pray Psalm 29 encourages you as well. I pray you, too, will hear His voice testify through His Word and His indwelling Holy Spirit that He will strengthen you to persevere and grant you peace to endure. He may not divert the storm, He never promised He would.

But the omnipotent God of the universe who powerfully stirs the seas with His voice is He who has promised to strengthen, sustain, and preserve us. He is infinitely faithful and He can be trusted. All praise, glory, and honor to Him alone, because He alone is worthy.

I close with the beautiful exposition of Psalm 29:11 by Charles Spurgeon. Read and be blessed and encouraged.

> "Power was displayed in the hurricane whose course this Psalm so grandly pictures; and now, in the cool calm after the storm, that power is promised to be the strength of the chosen. He who wings the unerring bolt, will give to his redeemed the wings of eagles; he who shakes the earth with his voice, will terrify the enemies of his saints, and give his children peace. Why are we weak when we have divine strength to flee to? Why are we troubled when the Lord's own peace is ours? Jesus the mighty God is our peace–what a blessing is this today! What a blessing it will be to us in that day of the Lord which will be in darkness and not light to the ungodly! Dear reader, is not this a noble

Psalm to be sung in stormy weather? Can you sing amid the thunder? Will you be able to sing when the last thunders are let loose, and Jesus judges quick and dead? If you are a believer, the last verse is your heritage, and surely that will set you singing."[1]

— CHARLES SPURGEON

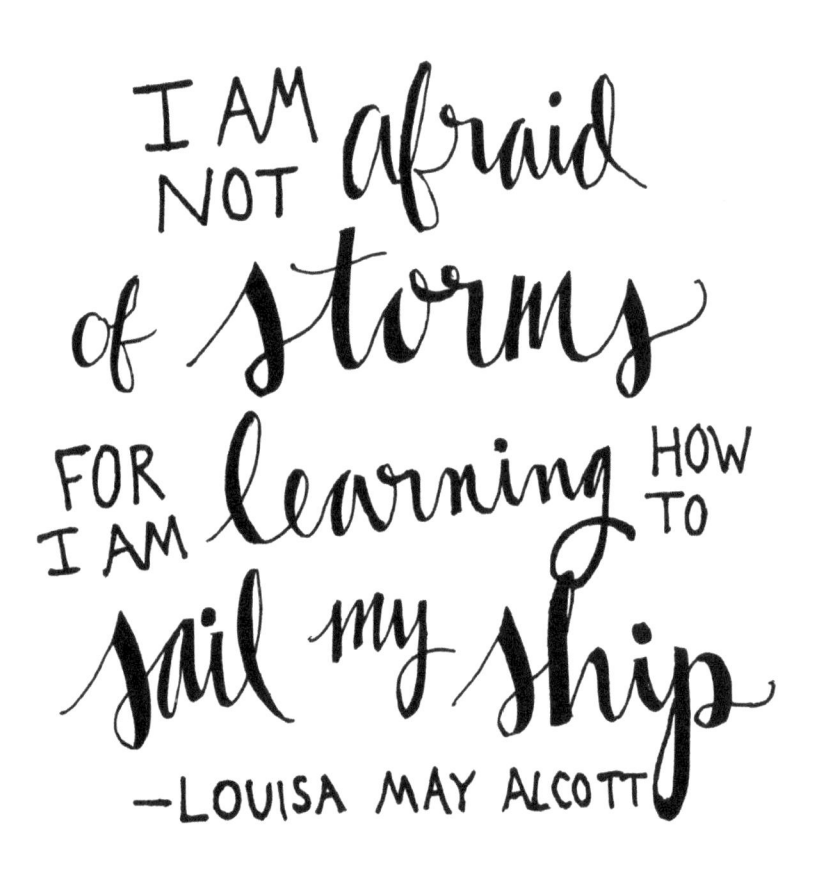

I AM NOT afraid of storms FOR I AM learning HOW TO sail my ship

—LOUISA MAY ALCOTT

---

1. Spurgeon, Charles. "Psalm 29." *Blue Letter Bible*, 5 Dec 2016, blueletterbible.org/Comm/spurgeon_charles/tod/ps029.cfm.

ABANDONMENT IN GRIEF

OCTOBER 27, 2018

"My heart throbs, my strength fails me; And the light of my eyes, even that has gone from me. My loved ones and my friends stand aloof from my plague; And my kinsmen stand afar off." Psalm 38:10-11

In the midst of deep grief, opportunities for feelings of abandonment abound. As time wears on those opportunities only multiply. As I have interacted with many others also walking this painful path I have come to realize experiencing feelings of abandonment in one or more relationships is more likely the norm than the exception.

For months now I have been praying for wisdom to understand a proper heart response to such abandonment. I've had countless conversations with others who have experienced it, but have found very few biblical resources acknowledging and addressing it.

I'm thankful it is not absent in God's Word, though. We are not the first to struggle with being or feeling abandoned amid deep grief, and we will not be the last. God's Word faithfully addresses it and illumines our responsibility in the midst of it.

David and Job both felt the sting of abandonment in deep grief. Jesus Christ Himself felt the sting of abandonment in deep grief.

Many others in Scripture cried out to God in their isolation and desperation, and by the grace of God, their prayers are recorded as testimony and encouragement for all who may journey that painful path behind them.

Types of Abandonment

Meditating on the account of Job, I realized he experienced several forms of abandonment in his suffering. In his despair, he proclaimed the following in Job 19:13-19:

- "He has removed my brothers far from me"
- "my acquaintances are completely estranged from me"
- "My relatives have failed"
- "my intimate friends have forgotten me"
- "All my associates abhor me"
- "those I love have turned against me."

I have felt the pangs of some of these experiences. Perhaps you, too, can relate to one or more of Job's abandonment experiences. If so, I hope the following will be of encouragement.

We may not be purposefully abandoned.

Three of Job's friends traveled from their homes *"to sympathize with him and comfort him"* (Job 2:11). We are told in Job 2:12-13, *"When they lifted up their eyes at a distance and did not recognize him, they raised their voices and wept. And each of them tore his robe and they threw dust over their heads toward the sky. Then they sat down on the ground with him for seven days and seven nights with no one speaking a word to him, for they saw that [his] pain was very great."*

Scripture gives no indication that Job's friend's intentions were anything but pure when they came to comfort Job in the beginning. Unfortunately, they began speaking on the eighth day and ended up

ABANDONMENT IN GRIEF

speaking wrongly about both Job and God, leading to Job's lament about his abandonment in Job 19.

Likewise, we know beyond any shadow of a doubt that Jesus' inner circle, Peter, James, and John, deeply loved Him. And yet, it is they who abandoned Him during His deepest grief.

> And He took with Him Peter and James and John, and began to be very distressed and troubled. And He said to them, "My soul is deeply grieved to the point of death; remain here and keep watch." And He went a little beyond [them,] and fell to the ground and [began] to pray that if it were possible, the hour might pass Him by. And He was saying, "Abba! Father! All things are possible for You; remove this cup from Me; yet not what I will, but what You will." And He came and found them sleeping, and said to Peter, "Simon, are you asleep? Could you not keep watch for one hour?" (Mark 14:33-37)

I don't believe either set of friends, Job's or Jesus', purposefully abandoned their grieving friend. I believe they were each compelled to come alongside their hurting friend and yet each failed differently. They had hearts to be present but human frailty led to their failure, just as Jesus warned in the garden, *"The spirit is willing, but the flesh is weak"* (Mark 14:38).

I suspect the same is true for many modern-day friends who fail to come alongside their grieving friends. Feelings of abandonment may come from friends like Job's friends who show up and say all the wrong things. Or they may be from friends like Jesus' friends who after being told He was *"deeply grieved to the point of death,"* seem completely unaware of the depth of His anguish and grief and drift off to sleep instead. Whichever the case, if we are feeling abandoned it is helpful to realize that we have most likely not been purposefully abandoned.

WE ARE NOT ABANDONED.

Before I go any further I must declare a vital truth with boldness.

No matter how alone or abandoned we may feel, we are not abandoned.

Despite their physical presence, the friends of Jesus were not present with Him in His suffering. Those He asked to stay awake to pray for Him abandoned Him to sleep through His deepest anguish. Not once, not twice, but three times He had to awaken them as they slumbered through His agony. Immediately after He awakened them the third time, He was seized and we are told in response, *"They all left Him and fled"* (Mark 14:50).

Jesus knows earthly abandonment. He knows the sting of human aloneness. What tremendous comfort it is that He who now lives to intercede for us is the One abandoned, *"despised, and forsaken of men, a man of sorrows and acquainted with grief"* (Isa. 53:3).

> Therefore, since we have a great high priest who has passed through the heavens, Jesus the Son of God, let us hold fast our confession. For we do not have a high priest who cannot sympathize with our weaknesses, but One who has been tempted in all things as [we are, yet] without sin. Therefore let us draw near with confidence to the throne of grace, so that we may receive mercy and find grace to help in time of need. (Heb. 4:14-16)

Jesus Christ was willingly abandoned, tortured, crucified, and killed to pay our sin debt. He then rose from death to life and reigns as our great High Priest. Because He, our great High Priest, *"always lives to make intercession for us,"* we will never be abandoned or alone.

He who knows and empathizes with the deepest, indescribable, and un-utterable pains of my heart is continually interceding for me. Even if all others should fail and fall away, He will remain faithful still. We will never be completely abandoned, and we will never, under any circumstance, be abandoned by the One who matters most of all.

How do I respond to abandonment?

It is a tremendous comfort that Jesus understands the sting of both deep grief and abandonment, and that He will never abandon us. But the sting of abandonment by earthly companions remains real nonetheless, so how are we to respond?

Job endured relentless accusations and offenses from his friends as they rebuked him for the sin they wrongly presumed to be in his life. At the end of the account of Job, God rebukes the friends of Job for not speaking what was right about Him as Job had. He then tells them to make an offering and have Job pray for them, and that He would accept Job's prayer on their behalf (Job 42:6-7).

> the LORD turned the captivity of Job, when he prayed for his friends... (Job 42:10 KJV)

The Lord has spoken powerfully to my heart through this verse, *"the LORD turned the captivity of Job, when he prayed for his friends..."* It's important to note that prior to this Job had already *"repented in dust and ashes."* (Job 42:6). But it was when he prayed for his friends—the friends who had inflicted so much unnecessary hurt during his suffering—that the Lord *"turned his captivity,"* or released him from the oppression he had been suffering, and restored his well being.

Scripture goes on to say, *"Then all his brothers and all his sisters and all who had known him before came to him, and they ate bread with him in his house; and they consoled him and comforted him for all the adversities that the LORD had brought on him..."* (Job 42:11).

Job welcomed all those who had previously abandoned him in his suffering back into his home, and they consoled and comforted him.

Forgiveness Following Repentance

Part of my hesitation in broaching this subject is that I might be perceived as advocating a requirement for forgiveness in the absence of repentance. For those already deeply wounded through heavy grief or suffering that would be yet another heavy burden to place on their weary backs. My personal conviction is that would also be an inappropriate extrabiblical burden requiring of them more than Scripture itself requires. For more on biblical repentance and forgiveness, I highly recommend the book *Unpacking Forgiveness* by Chris Brauns.[1]

The Book of Job cannot be used to support requiring forgiveness in the absence of repentance. Though it does not explicitly state Job's friends and family sought forgiveness from him, we see evidence of the three primary friends repenting through their making the offering required by God and requesting or accepting Job's intercession on their behalf.

The family and friends that had previously abandoned him all returned bearing gifts for him and seeking to comfort and console him. This return would also be reflective of repentance or "turning" from their previous actions of any wrongdoing or abandonment.

Forgiveness is very clearly biblically mandated in the presence of repentance (Luke 17:3-4). Job responded in righteousness as he prayed for his three friends and welcomed them, his other friends, and his family back into his home.

Grace, Grace, God's Grace

Where wounds are deep and raw it is God's grace alone that grants us the willingness, strength, and power to choose to look beyond those wounds. Through His divine power, I can lift my eyes from focusing on the pain of those wounds to instead focus on His eternal purposes. As I meditate on who He is and on eternity, my focus will shift to that which brings Him the greatest glory and honor.

> To this end we always pray for you, that our God may make you worthy of his calling and may fulfill every resolve for good and every work of faith by his power, so that the name of our Lord Jesus may be glorified in you, and you in him, according to the grace of our God and the Lord Jesus Christ. (2 Thess. 1:11-12 ESV)

What great encouragement that we are given the example of Job doing exactly that. After God confronted Job with the majesty of who He is, Job recognized how his temporal tragedies paled in comparison. As Job's eyes were fixed on the eternal God of the universe he was strengthened to forgive his three friends and let go of the deep pains of false accusations, betrayal, and abandonment by them, his family, and other friends.

God is glorified through repentance, forgiveness, and reconciliation within the body of Christ. God is glorified as His love abounds in us and is extended to one another. And praise be to Him that it is His grace, His strength, His power, and His love in us that enables us to love those who have wounded us through abandonment.

Turned Captivity, Comfort and Consoling

Job's humbly praying for his friends is directly linked in Scripture to his *"turned captivity"* and the restoration of his fortunes and well-being. Scripture also says those who had previously abandoned Job, *"consoled him and comforted him"* upon their return.

While we absolutely should not fix our hope or our focus on liberation from temporal captivity, comfort, or consoling, we would be foolish to overlook these connections.

If I refuse to forgive where necessary and receive back those who have previously abandoned me, I may well forego some degree of liberation from temporal captivity, or consoling and comforting that God is making available through my acceptance of returning friends.

In short, my failure to trust Him enough to walk in obedience in this regard will not only dishonor Him but may also result in missed personal blessings.

Longing to Come Out as Pure Gold

> Behold, we consider those blessed who remained steadfast. You have heard of the steadfastness of Job, and you have seen the purpose of the Lord, how the Lord is compassionate and merciful. (James 5:11 ESV)

Though Job did not fully understand all that was happening in the heavens throughout his ordeal, he recognized his suffering as a trial or test. I believe the final testing of Job was of his willingness to intercede on behalf of those friends who had so terribly wronged him and to receive back into fellowship those who had previously abandoned him.

In the midst of his suffering Job was able to shift his focus back to eternity, confidently proclaiming God had not lost sight of him, and in the end, He would bring him forth sanctified and purified as pure gold.

> He knows the way I take; [When] He has tried me, I shall come forth as gold (Job 23:10)

May our wounds of abandonment be redemptively used as a sanctifying flame. May we be marked by willing surrender to allow the God of peace to sanctify us completely. May we overflow with His grace and love toward one another in such a way that the world may know we are His (John 13:35). May we continually have our hope fixed completely on the grace to be brought to us at the revelation of Jesus Christ (1 Pet. 1:13). And may that hope fuel our passion to be kept blameless at His coming so that we, too, may come forth as pure gold.

> Now may the God of peace himself sanctify you completely, and may your whole spirit and soul and body be kept blameless at the coming of our Lord Jesus Christ. (1 Thess. 5:23 ESV)

---

1. Brauns, Chris. *Unpacking Forgiveness: Biblical Answers for Complex Questions and Deep Wounds.* Crossway, 2008.

BE OF GOOD COURAGE

NOVEMBER 14, 2018

*L*ast week was exceedingly discouraging. We were notified that we will be required to walk through a trial we had been praying to be spared from.[1] The weight of the impending holidays was already upon us: Thanksgiving, Sarah's birthday, and then Christmas. A painful series of "seconds without Sarah" about to fall like a line of dominoes, and now we add this additional heavy trial behind those. As we were still staggering from the news of the trial, our adversary saw our dismay and opportunistically pounced with a barrage of smaller emotionally depleting schemes (2 Cor. 2:11).

Weary, warworn, and greatly discouraged I opened the Word to bask in it. 2 Corinthians 5 was the next chapter in my daily reading. I've meditated on it multiple times since the crash, and I found comfort in it once again.

> For we know that if the earthly tent which is our house is torn down, we have a building from God, a house not made with hands, eternal in the heavens. For indeed in this [house] we groan, longing to be clothed with our dwelling from heaven, inasmuch as we, having put it on, will not be found naked. For indeed while we are in this tent, we groan,

being burdened, because we do not want to be unclothed but to be clothed, so that what is mortal will be swallowed up by life. (vv. 1-4)

Prior to Sarah's departure, I did not fully relate to the groaning Paul speaks of. But now I deeply understand as my soul continually groans with longing. I long to be liberated from my own sin and fallenness, from the painful impacts and consequences of the sins of others, and from the fallenness of the world about us. Oh, how I desperately long to be swallowed up by life.

In retrospect, I had previously been so captivated by verses 1-4 that I had failed to absorb the verses that follow. This week was different, though. Against the backdrop of my discouragement, I was immediately struck by the statement that we are *"of good courage"* repeated twice in verses 5-8.

> Now He who prepared us for this very purpose is God, who gave to us the Spirit as a pledge. Therefore, being always of good courage, and knowing that while we are at home in the body we are absent from the Lord– for we walk by faith, not by sight– we are of good courage, I say, and prefer rather to be absent from the body and to be at home with the Lord.

BE OF GOOD COURAGE:
GOD HAS PREPARED US FOR THIS VERY PURPOSE.

> Now He who prepared us for this very purpose is God, who gave to us the Spirit as a pledge. (2 Cor. 5:5)

We are strengthened to be of good courage by knowing God has prepared us for this very purpose: to be *"clothed with our dwelling from heaven."* God has prepared us to wait expectantly for eternity. It is good and right to groan with longing to be liberated from the temporal and clothed with the eternal. This longing for eternity is not a sinful lack of contentment, but an appropriate longing for the fulfillment of the promises of grace He has prepared for us.

God has also prepared us through His gift of the Holy Spirit as a pledge. Through the teaching of the indwelling Holy Spirit, we are strengthened to be of good courage. The presence of the Holy Spirit is a precious foretaste of abiding in His presence. Now, we hear His voice, but one day, *"in just a little while,"* we shall behold our Savior and God face to face (Heb. 10:37; Rev. 22:3-4).

> But the Helper, the Holy Spirit, whom the Father will send in My name, He will teach you all things, and bring to your remembrance all that I said to you. (John 14:26)

BE OF GOOD COURAGE: WE WALK BY FAITH, NOT BY SIGHT.

> Therefore, being always of good courage, and knowing that while we are at home in the body we are absent from the Lord– for we walk by faith, not by sight (2 Cor. 5:6-7)

I can't see God's hand in this specific trial. I can't see how He will deliver, vindicate, sustain, and heal in the coming months. But I am strengthened to be of good courage by Paul's reminder that we walk by faith and not by sight. I can't see how He will do it, but I know that He who has promised is faithful, and in His time He will accomplish all He has promised.

The same Greek word *tharreō*, translated as "good courage" in 2 Corinthians 5, is translated as "confidently" in Hebrews 13:6. Because He has promised He will never leave me nor forsake me, I am of good courage to say with Paul: *"The Lord is my Helper, I will not fear; what can man do to me?"*

> ... for he has said, "I will never leave you nor forsake you." So we can confidently say, "The Lord is my helper; I will not fear; what can man do to me? (Heb. 13:5b-6 ESV)

Be of Good Courage: This is not our Home.

> we are of good courage, I say, and prefer rather to be absent from the body and to be at home with the Lord. (2 Cor. 5:8)

I am so thankful we are repeatedly reminded throughout Scripture that this world is not our home. We are strengthened to be of good courage in the midst of our temporal suffering by the reminder that our preference as believers is to be absent from the body and to be at home with the Lord. In recognizing the brevity of this temporal life, we are strengthened with good courage to live the remainder of our days urgently and fruitfully for Him.

> For to me, to live is Christ and to die is gain. But if [I am] to live [on] in the flesh, this [will mean] fruitful labor for me; and I do not know which to choose. But I am hard-pressed from both [directions,] having the desire to depart and be with Christ, for [that] is very much better; yet to remain on in the flesh is more necessary for your sake. Convinced of this, I know that I will remain and continue with you all for your progress and joy in the faith (Phil. 1:21-25)

Be of Good Courage: Our sole ambition is to please Him.

> Therefore we also have as our ambition, whether at home or absent, to be pleasing to Him. (2 Cor. 5:9)

What tremendous encouragement I found in this reminder that my sole ambition is to be pleasing to Him. In my discouragement, I had allowed my attention to shift to pleasing men. I was wrongly allowing their approval and disapproval to affect my courage. Reading this verse the Holy Spirit brought to memory Paul's words to the Galatians, *"For am I now seeking the favor of men, or of God? Or am I striving to please men? If I were still trying to please men, I would not be a bond-servant of Christ."* (Gal. 1:10).

BE OF GOOD COURAGE

> Suffer hardship with [me,] as a good soldier of Christ Jesus. No soldier in active service entangles himself in the affairs of everyday life, so that he may please the one who enlisted him as a soldier. (2 Tim. 2:3-4)

Such blessed encouragement to be reminded the only One whom I am striving to please is the very One who sees and knows my heart. He is *"compassionate and gracious, Slow to anger and abounding in lovingkindness. ... For He Himself knows our frame; He is mindful that we are but dust"* (Ps. 103:8, 14).

I am so thankful for God's faithfulness to speak through His Word. With compassionate lovingkindness, He spoke to my discouraged heart not once, but twice—*"Be of good courage."* He gently reminded me that He has prepared me for eternity, to be *"swallowed up by life,"* and to fix my hope completely on that.

Though I can not see the way before me, I am of good courage as I am reminded I am walking by faith and not by sight. Above all, I praise God that this is not my home and my only responsibility, my sole ambition, is to please Him and no other. Hallelujah! Come, Lord Jesus!

> These things I have spoken to you, so that in Me you may have peace. In the world you have tribulation, but take courage; I have overcome the world. (John 16:33)

> So do not throw away your confidence; it will be richly rewarded. You need to persevere so that when you have done the will of God, you will receive what he has promised. For, 'In just a little while, he who is coming will come and will not delay.' And, 'But my righteous one will live by faith. And I take no pleasure in the one who shrinks back.' But we do not belong to those who shrink back and are destroyed, but to those who have faith and are saved. (Heb. 10:35-39 NIV)

---

1. We had prayed for seventeen months that the bus driver would accept responsibility and rightly plead guilty to the state's misdemeanor vehicular homicide charge but were notified he still had not, so it was scheduled to go to trial in early January.

DO I REALLY BELIEVE?

DECEMBER 8, 2018

Eighteen months ago today my sweet Sarah left. As I've anticipated this day over the past couple of weeks my thoughts have repeatedly drifted to Sarah as a chunky little eighteen-month-old. What a treasure trove of joyful memories those first eighteen months were. They stand so painfully stark in contrast to these first eighteen months.

When my heart is longing for my child, the recognition that it could be decades before I see her and hold her again is staggering. When all the many facets of grief collide with the unique challenges and trials of the day I can easily slide into despair, questioning how I can possibly do this one more day, let alone for decades more.

While reading Luke recently I was immediately convicted. Luke 1:45 says, *"And blessed [is] she who believed that there would be a fulfillment of what had been spoken to her by the Lord."* Like an arrow through my heart, I was pierced by a question—"Do I really believe?" I am confident the Bible is God's Word, infallible and inerrant. I believe each word of Scripture to be inspired by the Lord, but am I actually believing each truth contained?

I believe His Word to be true as a whole, but am I actively

believing there will be a fulfillment of everything that has been spoken by the Lord?

> For this reason also, since the day we heard [of it,] we have not ceased to pray for you and to ask that you may be filled with the knowledge of His will in all spiritual wisdom and understanding, so that you will walk in a manner worthy of the Lord, to please [Him] in all respects, bearing fruit in every good work and increasing in the knowledge of God; strengthened with all power, according to His glorious might, for the attaining of all steadfastness and patience; joyously giving thanks to the Father, who has qualified us to share in the inheritance of the saints in Light. (Col. 1:9-12)

I had just journaled Colossians 1:9-12 and meditated on it when I was confronted with Luke 1:45. I was instantly convicted I had failed to truly believe the availability of all that is spoken of in the prayer of Colossians 1. I was not believing, trusting, or resting in the truth that my God, the God of the universe Himself, would do for me all that He inspired Paul to pray for the believers at Colossae.

I was not resting in the belief that he would fill me *"with the knowledge of His will in all spiritual wisdom and understanding."* I was not fully believing that through His filling He would continually enable me to walk this treacherously painful path *"in a manner worthy of Him."* In my weariness and sorrow, I was struggling to persevere, frequently feeling it impossible to press on to *"please [Him] in all respects, bearing fruit in every good work, and increasing in the knowledge of Him."*

What struck me most significantly though was the realization that I was failing to believe that through my God I can be *"strengthened with all power, according to His glorious might."* The most beautiful part of this particular passage to me is understanding the purpose for which He strengthens me with all power according to His glorious might. The purpose of attaining the very qualities I need most. We are *"strengthened with all power, according to His glorious might, for the attaining of all steadfastness and patience."* Steadfastness and patience, not magnificent displays of might or works, but *"for the attaining of all steadfastness and patience."*

> but thanks be to God, who gives us the victory through our Lord Jesus Christ. Therefore, my beloved brethren, be steadfast, immovable, always abounding in the work of the Lord, knowing that your toil is not [in] vain in the Lord. (1 Cor. 15:57-58)

The steadfastness and patience that come through Him are exactly what I need to face and live fruitfully through the days and decades ahead. If I believe Him, through His glorious might I can be steadfast, immovable, firm, unwavering, and constant. If I believe Him I can be strengthened with all power for the attaining of patience to wait continually and expectantly upon Him.

> Now may the God of hope fill you with all joy and peace in believing, so that you will abound in hope by the power of the Holy Spirit. (Rom. 15:13)

As I believe Him and His every Word throughout Scripture, I can not help but *"joyously give thanks to the Father, who has qualified us to share in the inheritance of the saints in Light."* It is *"in believing"* that the *"God of hope will fill us with all joy and peace, so that we will abound in hope by the power of the Holy Spirit"* (Rom. 15:13).

> and though you have not seen Him, you love Him, and though you do not see Him now, but believe in Him, you greatly rejoice with joy inexpressible and full of glory, obtaining as the outcome of your faith the salvation of your souls. (1 Pet. 1:8-9)

And so, confidently believing He will answer and strengthen me with all power according to His glorious might, I echo the cry of a grieved father from long ago, *"I do believe; help my unbelief"* (Mark 9:24).

STEADFAST

DECEMBER 23, 2018

"Therefore, my beloved brethren, be steadfast, immovable, always abounding in the work of the Lord, knowing that your toil is not [in] vain in the Lord."
1 Corinthians 15:58

The month of December has been so very challenging for this weary heart. The rawness that accompanies Sarah's birthday and the Christmas season has provided ample opportunity for heartache and despair. On more than one occasion I have tearfully questioned if I can or will persevere.

In the midst of my pain and discouragement, the Lord has repeatedly drawn my eye to the word "steadfast" in Scripture. Merriam-Webster Dictionary defines steadfast as being "firmly fixed in place, IMMOVABLE, not subject to change, firm in belief, determination, or adherence."[1]

CALLED TO STEADFASTNESS

We are repeatedly implored in Scripture to be steadfast. King David cried out to God longing for steadfastness in Psalm 51:10, *"Create in me a clean heart, O God, And renew a steadfast spirit within me."*

The prophet Isaiah, through the inspiration of God, wrote *"The steadfast of mind You will keep in perfect peace, Because he trusts in You"* (Isa. 26:3).

The Apostle Paul, inspired by God in his letter to the Corinthians, implored all believers everywhere to *"be steadfast, immovable, always abounding in the work of the Lord, knowing that your toil is not [in] vain in the Lord"* (1 Cor. 15:58).

Paul similarly exhorted the Colossians, *"If indeed you continue in the faith firmly established and steadfast, and not moved away from the hope of the gospel that you have heard, which was proclaimed in all creation under heaven, and of which I, Paul, was made a minister"* (Col. 1:23).

The Foundation of Our Steadfastness

As I meditated on each of the passages and their context I was suddenly struck by the foundation of steadfastness in each passage. Each reference connects our steadfastness to the hope of eternity found in salvation through Jesus Christ.

When David cried out to God to cleanse him from all unrighteousness, to create a pure heart and renew a steadfast spirit within him, he immediately followed by connecting that steadfastness to abiding in the presence of God and the joy of salvation:

> Create in me a clean heart, O God, And renew a steadfast spirit within me. Do not cast me away from Your presence And do not take Your Holy Spirit from me. Restore to me the joy of Your salvation And sustain me with a willing spirit. (Ps. 51:10-12)

Isaiah's proclamation, *"The steadfast of mind You will keep in perfect peace, Because he trusts in You,"* is within the context of, and directly linked to the hope of eternity promised to the children of God:

> The LORD of hosts will prepare a lavish banquet for all peoples on this mountain; A banquet of aged wine, choice pieces with marrow, [And] refined, aged wine. And on this mountain He will swallow up

the covering which is over all peoples, Even the veil which is stretched over all nations. He will swallow up death for all time, And the Lord GOD will wipe tears away from all faces, And He will remove the reproach of His people from all the earth; For the LORD has spoken. And it will be said in that day, "Behold, this is our God for whom we have waited that He might save us. This is the LORD for whom we have waited; Let us rejoice and be glad in His salvation." (Isa. 25:6-9)

Paul's exhortation in Corinthians to *"be steadfast, immovable, always abounding in the work of the Lord,"* is the concluding exhortation to an entire chapter devoted to a precise explanation of the gospel and a bold defense of the hope of the resurrection:

in a moment, in the twinkling of an eye, at the last trumpet; for the trumpet will sound, and the dead will be raised imperishable, and we will be changed. For this perishable must put on the imperishable, and this mortal must put on immortality. But when this perishable will have put on the imperishable, and this mortal will have put on immortality, then will come about the saying that is written, "DEATH IS SWALLOWED UP in victory. "O DEATH, WHERE IS YOUR VICTORY? O DEATH, WHERE IS YOUR STING?" The sting of death is sin, and the power of sin is the law; but thanks be to God, who gives us the victory through our Lord Jesus Christ. Therefore, my beloved brethren, be steadfast, immovable, always abounding in the work of the Lord, knowing that your toil is not [in] vain in the Lord. (1 Cor. 15:52-58)

In his letter to the Colossians, the Apostle Paul once again connects our steadfastness to the hope of eternity through Christ's reconciliation of all things to Himself. Paul challenges the Colossians and us to persevere in steadfastness compelled by the desire to be presented before Him, holy and blameless and beyond reproach:

And although you were formerly alienated and hostile in mind, [engaged] in evil deeds, yet He has now reconciled you in His fleshly body through death, in order to present you before Him holy and blameless and beyond reproach– if indeed you continue in the faith firmly established and steadfast, and not moved away from the hope of the gospel that you have heard, which was proclaimed in all creation under heaven, and of which I, Paul, was made a minister. (Col.1:21-23)

The Source of Our Steadfastness

We are called to be steadfast, and the foundation of our steadfastness is directly linked to the sure and certain hope of eternity. But where does the strength required for steadfastness come from? Praise God, we are not told to simply "muster it up" or to "pull ourselves up by our bootstraps." Just as God graciously reveals the foundation of our steadfastness he also graciously reveals its source.

King David knew it was through God's power alone that he could and would be strengthened to be steadfast. He acknowledged this when he requested of God not only a steadfast spirit but a willing spirit as well:

> Create in me a clean heart, O God, And renew a steadfast spirit within me. Do not cast me away from Your presence And do not take Your Holy Spirit from me. Restore to me the joy of Your salvation And sustain me with a willing spirit. (Ps. 51:10-12)

Isaiah also points to the power of God in sustaining steadfastness. According to Isaiah, as we trust in God, He will keep us in perfect peace. Through His perfect peace, we are kept, strengthened, and enabled to persevere in steadfastness:

> The steadfast of mind You will keep in perfect peace, Because he trusts in You. (Isa. 26:3)

Finally, in his prayer for the Colossians, the apostle Paul boldly proclaims the source of our steadfastness:

For this reason also, since the day we heard [of it,] we have not ceased to pray for you and to ask that you may be... strengthened with all power, according to His glorious might, for the attaining of all steadfastness and patience... (Col. 1:9a, 11)

Steadfast in Him

I am so very thankful that Scripture makes it clear the foundation of our steadfastness is the promise of the resurrection and the glorious hope of eternity. This earth holds no goal or reward worthy of persevering through all our present and future pain and suffering, but heaven does.

Both the foundation of our steadfastness and the means for achieving it are graciously and freely given by Him. He Himself will strengthen us *"with all power, according to His glorious might, for the attaining of all steadfastness and patience"* (Col. 1:11).

Entirely by Him and through Him, we can be strengthened to remain *"steadfast, immovable, always abounding in the work of the Lord, knowing that [our] toil is not in vain in the Lord."* By Him, we can *"joyously give thanks,"* and be kept *"in perfect peace."* One glorious day, *"in just a little while"* we will boldly proclaim with all the saints, *"DEATH IS SWALLOWED UP in victory. "O DEATH, WHERE IS YOUR VICTORY? O DEATH, WHERE IS YOUR STING?"* (Heb. 10:37; 1 Cor. 15:54-55, 58).

Praise God, Hallelujah, in that glorious day *"He will swallow up death for all time, And the Lord GOD will wipe tears away from all faces, And He will remove the reproach of His people from all the earth; For the LORD has spoken. And it will be said in that day, 'Behold, this is our God for whom we have waited that He might save us. This is the LORD for whom we have waited; Let us rejoice and be glad in His salvation"* (Isa. 25:8-9).

---

1. "Steadfast, *Adj.* (1-2)." *Meriam-Webster Dictionary.* merriam-webster.com/dictionary/steadfast. Accessed 23 Dec. 2018.

THE LINES HAVE FALLEN FOR ME

JANUARY 14, 2019

*I*n the days and weeks after Sarah's death music ministered deeply to my shattered heart. Recognizing my vulnerability, I chose to only listen to music that was firmly rooted in Scripture. One of the albums I listened to with regularity early on was Shane & Shane's album, "Psalms II." Predictably, each song on the album is based on a Psalm. It became one of my favorite albums, but every time I would listen there was one lyric I found myself unable to sing. It was a lyric from the song "Psalm 16," *"The lines have fallen for me in pleasant places,"* straight from verse 6 of Psalm 16.[1]

The boundary lines for my life prior to June 8, 2017, had absolutely fallen in pleasant places. But this new life with this soul-deep, endless aching is far from pleasant. The dismantling of our family as we knew it and the instant evaporation of the life and future that had been at our fingertips only moments before are in no way "lines falling in pleasant places." For weeks each time that lyric was sung, I was silent.

As I was having my quiet time this morning, the next Psalm to read and meditate on was Psalm 16. To my surprise, I realized as I read it that I am now able to praise the Lord in agreement with David in proclaiming, *"The lines have fallen to me in pleasant places."*

I deeply loved and appreciated the pleasant and beautiful life I had here prior to June 8, 2017. Because of June 8, 2017, the remainder of my days here will be marked with soul-deep pain and longing for eternity.

Over the past nineteen months, the Lord has been gently and gradually ratcheting my eyes upward. I realize now that all of my days prior to June 8, 2017, should have been marked by this same soul-deep longing for eternity as well.

Prior to June 8, 2017, I intellectually embraced the fact that my hope and inheritance are in eternity. I understood that my hope was to be fixed completely on the grace to be brought to us at the revelation of Jesus Christ (1 Pet. 1:13). I intellectually knew that I was just a sojourner here (Ps. 39:12). But I confess I more deeply desired and loved my life here. Had Jesus stood before me to carry me home, I likely would have said, "Not yet, Lord, I have things here yet to do, children to see married, grandchildren to meet…" In doing so I would have chosen the temporal over the eternal.

> I will bless the LORD who has counseled me; Indeed, my mind instructs me in the night. I have set the LORD continually before me; Because He is at my right hand, I will not be shaken. (Ps. 16:7-8)

My elevating of the temporal over the eternal rendered me unable to sing with David (and Shane & Shane), *"The lines have fallen for me in pleasant places."* It took the Lord's faithful and gentle ratcheting of my eyes upward over the past nineteen months for me to rejoice in my soul this morning as I read those Words.

The beautiful blessings and the agonizing losses of this life are not the pleasant places marked by the lines fallen for me, they are not my inheritance. The lines that *"have fallen for me in pleasant places"* are the lines that were drawn for me in the precious blood of Jesus. The lines *"fallen for me in pleasant places"* mark out an inheritance for me that is indeed more pleasant than I can think or imagine.

but just as it is written, "THINGS WHICH EYE HAS NOT SEEN AND EAR HAS NOT HEARD, AND [which] HAVE NOT ENTERED THE HEART OF MAN, ALL THAT GOD HAS PREPARED FOR THOSE WHO LOVE HIM. (1 Cor. 2:9)

Praise Him that through His grace we who believe can all confidently proclaim, *"The lines have fallen to me in pleasant places; Indeed, my heritage is beautiful to me."* He is both our inheritance and the holder of our inheritance. *"In just a little while"* we will step into eternity with Him and all who have loved Him and preceded us (Heb. 10:37). May this glorious truth spur us on in urgent surrender for the remainder of our journey.

Come, Lord Jesus!

For this reason also, since the day we heard [of it,] we have not ceased to pray for you and to ask that you may be filled with the knowledge of His will in all spiritual wisdom and understanding, so that you will walk in a manner worthy of the Lord, to please [Him] in all respects, bearing fruit in every good work and increasing in the knowledge of God; strengthened with all power, according to His glorious might, for the attaining of all steadfastness and patience; joyously giving thanks to the Father, who has qualified us to share in the inheritance of the saints in Light. (Col. 1:9-12)

---

1. Shane & Shane. "Pslam 16." *Pslams II.* Wellhouse Records LL, 2015. CD.

LONELY AND AFFLICTED

FEBRUARY 6, 2019

"Turn to me and be gracious to me, For I am lonely and afflicted."
Psalm 25:16

As I meditated on Psalm 25 recently, verse 16 resonated within my heart. It struck me that David lamented his loneliness to the Lord, but more notably that his lament of loneliness preceded his lament of affliction. He goes on to describe the severity of his affliction and doing so only increases the significance of his mentioning the sorrow of his loneliness first.

> The troubles of my heart are enlarged; Bring me out of my distresses. Look upon my affliction and my trouble, And forgive all my sins. Look upon my enemies, for they are many, And they hate me with violent hatred. (Ps. 25:17-19)

The path of child loss for most is an indescribably lonely one. It is multifaceted beyond comprehension and is almost always accompanied by significant secondary and tertiary struggles. Even those who are blessed with a strong inner circle of support must trudge through many aspects of their sorrow alone. Try as we may, we can never articulate the indescribable ache of our hearts in a way that fully ushers others into its presence. It is a sacred pain whose depths must ultimately be confronted and traversed alone.

Perhaps all great pains isolate like this, being truly known and understood only by the afflicted one. The very affliction that isolates us then compounds its painful impact by the loneliness it creates. David experienced this so much so that in the midst of his many afflictions he first laments his loneliness.

I'm so thankful for the transparent heart cries and prayers of David, the other Psalmists, and the prophets. Their laments are an encouraging reminder that many before us have navigated the treacherous path of loneliness and affliction. Most importantly they leave us inspired guidance for how we can successfully navigate it as well.

TRUST HIM

David begins Psalm 25 by expressing his absolute trust in God, *"To You, O LORD, I lift up my soul. O my God, in You I trust..."* Do I trust Him? When my world has fallen apart and I am left sitting alone amidst the ashes, will I choose to trust Him? Throughout Scripture, He is calling us to trust Him regardless of our circumstances. When we are lonely and afflicted our first choice must be to trust Him.

> Who is among you that fears the LORD, That obeys the voice of His servant, That walks in darkness and has no light? Let him trust in the name of the LORD and rely on his God. (Isa. 50:10)

He has revealed His character to us through His Word. When I find myself walking in darkness with no light I can confidently trust Him because He has revealed He alone is worthy of that trust. Though I may not understand the circumstances He has allowed in my life, I can trust Him in the midst of them knowing that my Sovereign God, the Lord God Almighty, is continually exercising lovingkindness, justice, and righteousness because He delights in those things.

but let him who boasts boast of this, that he understands and knows Me, that I am the LORD who exercises lovingkindness, justice and righteousness on earth; for I delight in these things," declares the LORD. (Jer. 9:24)

Wait for Him

The second action David takes in response to his loneliness and affliction is to wait upon the Lord. David said three separate times in Psalm 25 that he waits for the Lord. Throughout this Psalm, David demonstrates expectant waiting. He is trusting in God's character and promises, and waiting for Him to act in accordance with them.

David is not passively waiting, but actively waiting upon God. He demonstrates this when he says, *"My eyes are continually toward the LORD, For He will pluck my feet out of the net"* (v.15). David cried out to God to vindicate, teach, lead, forgive, and instruct, and he waited expectantly for Him to do each of those things (vv. 2, 4, 5, 7-8).

> Indeed, none of those who wait for You will be ashamed... Lead me in Your truth and teach me, For You are the God of my salvation; For You I wait all the day... Let integrity and uprightness preserve me, For I wait for You. (Ps. 25:3, 5, 21)

Obey Him

In his loneliness and affliction, David continues to obey the Lord. He is trusting and waiting upon the Lord to lead Him, and as the Lord leads, David strives to obediently follow.

> Good and upright is the LORD; Therefore He instructs sinners in the way. He leads the humble in justice, And He teaches the humble His way. All the paths of the LORD are lovingkindness and truth To those who keep His covenant and His testimonies. For Your name's sake, O LORD, Pardon my iniquity, for it is great. Who is the man who fears the LORD? He will instruct him in the way he should choose. ... Let

integrity and uprightness preserve me, For I wait for You. (Ps. 25:8-12, 21)

I find it of great comfort that He not only leads and guides us in the way we should go, but it is also He who strengthens us to trust Him, wait for Him, and walk in the way in which He leads. With great thankfulness, I praise God that I am strengthened according to His glorious might to walk in obedience.

Make me understand the way of Your precepts, So I will meditate on Your wonders. My soul weeps because of grief; Strengthen me according to Your word. Remove the false way from me, And graciously grant me Your law. (Ps. 119:27-29)

Rest in His Forgiveness

Within David's declaration of reliance upon God, he acknowledges his failings and trusts in God to forgive his iniquities. The adversary delights to use the despair of loneliness and deep affliction to taunt us that we have erred beyond the bounds of God's forgiveness; that we are now abandoned and forsaken.

Praise God that Psalm 25 reminds us that forgiveness is available according to the character of God, not the perceived degree of our sinfulness. His infinite compassion and lovingkindness exceed the wickedness of our greatest iniquity, and out of their overflow, He pardons us.

Remember, O LORD, Your compassion and Your lovingkindnesses, For they have been from of old. Do not remember the sins of my youth or my transgressions; According to Your lovingkindness remember me, For Your goodness' sake, O LORD. Good and upright is the LORD; Therefore He instructs sinners in the way. ... For Your name's sake, O LORD, Pardon my iniquity, for it is great. (Ps. 25:6-8, 11)

Remember You Are Not Alone

Though David laments his loneliness in Psalm 25, he is lamenting it *to* God. Through his lament, the intimacy of his relationship with God is beautifully displayed. He knows God and he is confident God knows him and sees him in his loneliness and affliction.

> Lead me in Your truth and teach me, For You are the God of my salvation; For You I wait all the day. ... Guard my soul and deliver me; Do not let me be ashamed, for I take refuge in You. (Ps. 25:5, 20)

In addition to the availability of the same knowledge of God that David enjoyed, we can also have the confidence of having and knowing Jesus Christ as the great high priest who lives to continually intercede for us.

> but Jesus, on the other hand, because He continues forever, holds His priesthood permanently. Therefore He is able also to save forever those who draw near to God through Him, since He always lives to make intercession for them. (Heb. 7:24-25)

We know that Christ was tempted in all things just as we are, yet without sin (Heb. 4:15). Scripture even records specifically his experiencing aloneness in the midst of deepest affliction. Christ testified that during that time He was alone yet not alone because the Father was with Him (John 16:32).

> Behold, an hour is coming, and has [already] come, for you to be scattered, each to his own [home,] and to leave Me alone; and [yet] I am not alone, because the Father is with Me. (John 16:32)

We may feel or actually be alone here, but we are never truly alone. We have a Father who sees, knows, and deeply loves us out of the infinite overflow of His goodness and lovingkindness. We have a Savior who has experienced and knows the deep pain of loneliness and affliction and He is continually interceding on our behalf. Praise God, though we may be lonely, we are not alone.

Comfort Others

> Redeem Israel, O God, Out of all his troubles. (Ps. 25:22)

David concluded Psalm 25 by interceding for Israel, longing for the blessings of God's promises and provision to extend to others. Similarly, in 2 Corinthians 1, we are instructed to consider others and to comfort them with the comfort we have been given.

> Blessed [be] the God and Father of our Lord Jesus Christ, the Father of mercies and God of all comfort, who comforts us in all our affliction so that we will be able to comfort those who are in any affliction with the comfort with which we ourselves are comforted by God. (2 Cor. 1:3-4)

God intends to use both our spiritual gifts and our testimonies for the building up of His church. In the midst of our loneliness and affliction, we must fight the strong temptation to withdraw and isolate.

Through His strength, we can and should obediently seek to share with others the comfort He has given us. In so doing we will not only have the joy of obedience but also the blessing of seeing Him use and redeem our pain for His glory and the good of His children.

> For to me, to live is Christ and to die is gain. But if [I am] to live [on] in the flesh, this [will mean] fruitful labor for me...(Phil. 1:21-22)

Persevere dear lonely and afflicted sojourner. Confidently trust Him, expectantly wait for Him, urgently obey Him, peacefully rest in His forgiveness, thankfully celebrate His abiding presence, and tenderly comfort others with the comfort you have been given. *"For,*

'In just a little while, he who is coming will come and will not delay'" (Heb. 10:37).

He who testifies to these things says, "Yes, I am coming quickly." Amen. Come, Lord Jesus. (Rev 22:20)

Amen, Come, Lord Jesus.

> the steadfast LOVE of the Lord never ceases His mercies never come to an end; they are NEW every morning. great is your faithfulness
> —LAMENTATIONS 3:22-23

SERVE LIKE _____

FEBRUARY 13, 2019

"You also became imitators of us and of the Lord, having received the word in much tribulation with the joy of the Holy Spirit, so that you became an example to all the believers in Macedonia and in Achaia."
1 Thessalonians 1:6-7

I'm not sure where exactly #servelikesarah originated after the crash. One of Sarah's sisters looked on social media the day after the crash and showed us that it had not only been created but was already rapidly spreading. It blessed each of our hearts to see our sweet Sarah being honored and remembered in such a way.

The flurry of #servelikesarah posts continued through the first few months after Sarah's death. As one would expect, those posts then became less and less frequent, and eventually only occasional. In the week preceding the one-year anniversary of Sarah's death, there was once again a surge in people remembering her and sharing #servelikesarah.

The week after the anniversary of Sarah's death I saw criticism voiced publicly saying "It should be #servelikejesus, not #servelikesarah." Reading that criticism was like a twisting of the dagger already lodged in my heart. I was already wrestling with the painful realization that my precious child would soon be forgotten by the world around me. A rebuke in that moment for my child being remembered and honored on that particular day was doubly painful.

What pained my heart even more, though, was that I was not confident that the criticism was unfounded. My heart sank at the thought that perhaps it was wrong of us to support drawing attention to and publicly celebrating Sarah's life and testimony in a variety of ways, including #servelikesarah. But after the week of the anniversary, the hashtag quickly faded from sight, and with it, my focus to resolve whether or not we were actually wrong to use it.

I just started studying 1 Thessalonians this week. This morning as I read I was instantly reminded of that painful criticism and simultaneously filled with joy. Scripture clearly testifies it is not and was not wrong to remember and celebrate Sarah's beautiful testimony in any way, including #servelikesarah.

> You [*all the believers in Thessalonica*] also became imitators of us [*Paul, Silvanus and Timothy*] and of the Lord, having received the word in much tribulation with the joy of the Holy Spirit, so that you [*all the believers in Thessalonica*] became an example to all the believers in Macedonia and in Achaia. (1 Thess. 1:6-7) [*emphasis mine*]

Paul commended the believers at Thessalonica for becoming imitators of the faithful example of his companions and him, and of the Lord. He then commended them for becoming a faithful example in the same way for the believers in Macedonia and Achaia to follow. Similarly, the author of Hebrews references at least eighteen individuals as examples of faith, challenging us to consider their examples and do likewise (Heb. 11). The message is clear: imitate and serve like the faithful who have gone and go before you.

> Brothers, join in imitating me, and keep your eyes on those who walk according to the example you have in us. (Phil. 3:17 ESV)

Sarah was spurred on in her walk with the Lord by the testimonies of many faithful believers. Three who immediately come to mind are Corrie Ten Boom, Jim Elliot, and Anita Dittman. Their faithful testimonies and powerful examples encouraged her to trust in God's faithfulness to strengthen, sustain, and use ordinary, sinful yet repentant men and women.

> Now when they saw the boldness of Peter and John, and perceived that they were uneducated, common men, they were astonished. And they recognized that they had been with Jesus. (Act 4:13 ESV)

Sarah's testimony is inspiring because it is a beautiful demonstration of the power of God in using a shy, ordinary seventeen-year-old girl who fully surrendered to Him. Sarah's testimony is comprised of both her humble surrender and obedience to God *and* God's faithfulness to her. We continue to be in awe of how God used her and honored her as He hurled her testimony around the globe, glorifying Himself through her, just as He did through all the believers at Thessalonica.

> For the word of the Lord has sounded forth from you, not only in Macedonia and Achaia, but also in every place your faith toward God has gone forth, so that we have no need to say anything. (1 Thess. 1:8)

Faithful believers, those who long to *"know Him and the power of His resurrection and the fellowship of His sufferings, being conformed to His death,"* are worthy of imitation (Phil. 3:10). As I pondered the impact and importance of faithful servants of Christ who serve as examples, Colossians 1:24 came to mind.

> Now I rejoice in my sufferings for your sake, and in my flesh I do my share on behalf of His body, which is the church, in filling up what is lacking in Christ's afflictions. (Col.1:24)

Our supreme example is Christ, but God in His grace has also granted through His church to provide earthly examples of His sustaining power and faithfulness. Throughout history He has been strengthening believers to stand firm in faith for the gospel of Jesus Christ, spurring one another on in obedience and faithfulness to Him. And until the church is removed God will continue to raise up such believers, believers worthy of imitation.

Praise God for the many believers in our lives worthy of imitation. We can and should joyfully celebrate their testimonies of faith as they inspire us to walk in like manner. He is daily beckoning each of us to be one of these faithful believers. May we each respond through humble surrender and obedience so that we, too, may glorify Him and be examples worthy of imitation.

EASTER IN THE SHADOW

APRIL 23, 2019

"He brought them out of darkness and the shadow of death, and burst their bonds apart." Psalm 107:14 ESV

We haven't used the girls' childhood Easter baskets since Sarah left. I asked Katelyn, Kristen, and Sophie last year if they wanted to use them and they said they didn't care. I chose to believe them and to use gift bags instead to spare my heart from the sting of having to create another option for Sarah's basket. Saturday night as I was preparing Easter gift bags for them I went to the basement to get tissue paper, carefully counting out two sheets for each bag. When I got back upstairs to complete the bags, I realized I had eight sheets. I had once again subconsciously reverted to counting in multiples of four instead of only three. The realization brought with it a tidal wave of grief.

This is our second Easter without Sarah. Twenty-two months without her. To be exact, Easter Sunday made 683 days. And yet my heart still struggles to fully grasp that she is not and will not be here.

As we walked into church on Easter morning someone looked at us and kindly commented on the "beautiful ladies." I was instantly transported back to every Easter before Sarah left, vividly remembering the joy of walking in and hearing all the sweet compliments about "all the Harmening ladies." As we walked further we began seeing all of the families reunited and complete to celebrate and worship together. I didn't even make it to the pew before the tears spilled out.

The atmosphere of worship was rightly celebratory, but in the midst of the celebration my spirit was groaning within me. I struggled the entire service to contain the tears, for the most part to no avail. At first, I felt guilt for my inability to stifle the deep sorrow that was involuntarily bubbling out. I am inexpressibly grateful for and fervently cling to the tremendous hope I have because of Easter Sunday. I wanted to joyfully celebrate in those moments, but instead, my spirit was longing for something more.

Christ arose and His resurrection and the fact that He lives are absolutely the source of my hope. But it is not where my hope is fixed. My hope is fixed on what is yet to be because He lives: a beautiful dawning yet to come. My hope is fixed *"fully on the grace that will be brought to [all who believe] at the revelation of Jesus* Christ" (1 Pet. 1:13). My hope is fixed on His imminent return, on the day when *"the sun of righteousness will rise with healing in its wings; and [we] will go forth and skip about like calves from the stall"* (Mal. 4:2). My spirit groans for the day when *"God shall wipe away all tears from [our] eyes; and there shall be no more death, neither sorrow, nor crying, neither shall there be any more pain: for the former things are passed away"* (Rev. 21:4).

Christ's resurrection powerfully transforms this life through the hope of the next. If we somehow view the resurrection only in terms of its impact on this present life apart from eternity we are missing the greatest blessing. *"If in Christ we have hope in this life only, we are of all people most to be pitied"* (1 Cor. 15:19). It is the eternal impact of the resurrection that we celebrate. Because Christ secured eternity for those who believe, we are able to say with Paul, *"we do not lose heart, but though our outer man is decaying, yet our inner man is being renewed day by day. For momentary, light affliction is producing for us an eternal weight of glory far beyond all comparison, while we look not at the things which are seen, but at the things which are not seen; for the things which are* seen are temporal, but the things which are not seen are eternal" (2 Cor. 4:16-18)

Until Christ returns I will celebrate Easter in the shadow of death. For the remainder of this temporal life, I will treasure memories of precious past Easters with our complete family, while simultaneously bearing the persisting painful sting of my child's daily absence. Death was defeated at the resurrection but it has yet to be destroyed: *"The last enemy to be destroyed is death"* (1 Cor. 15:26). So each day and every Easter I will celebrate the resurrection morning of my Lord, but to an equal or greater degree I will groan with longing for the dawn yet to come *"when this perishable will have put on the imperishable, and this mortal will have put on immortality, [and] then will come about the saying that is written, "DEATH IS SWALLOWED UP in victory"* (1 Cor. 15:54).

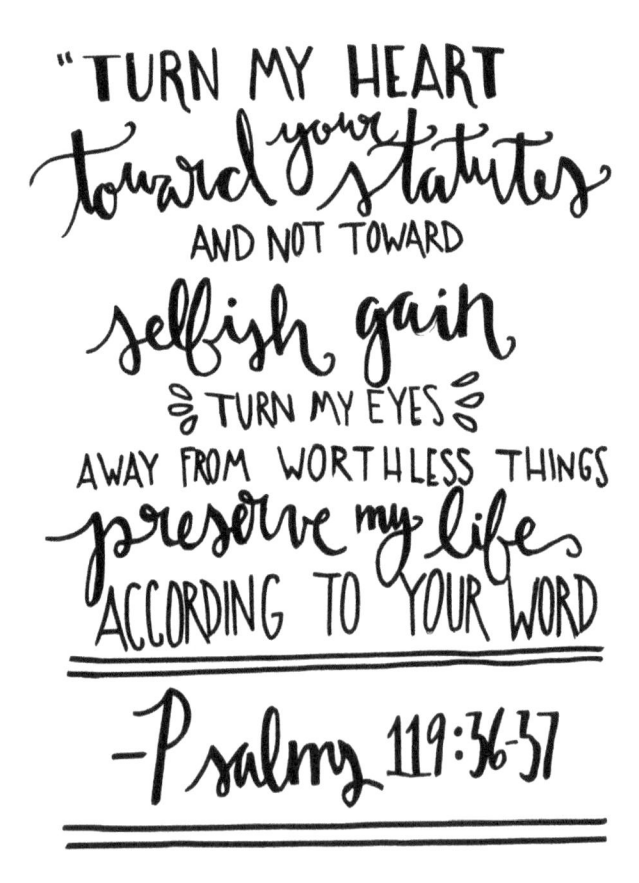

> "TURN MY HEART toward your statutes AND NOT TOWARD selfish gain TURN MY EYES AWAY FROM WORTHLESS THINGS preserve my life ACCORDING TO YOUR WORD
> —Psalms 119:36-37

SUNSHINE CHRISTIANITY & FORBIDDEN LAMENT

MAY 10, 2019

"I have sunk in deep mire, and there is no foothold; I have come into deep waters, and a flood overflows me. I am weary with my crying; my throat is parched; My eyes fail while I wait for my God." Psalm 69:2-3

Scott has had the misfortune of being chided a couple of times recently for answering the question, "How are you?" in a way that didn't reflect the joy the person asking expected. As a result, we have a running joke that someday he will answer with his best Jack Nicholson impression, "You can't handle the truth!"[1]

The truth is many people refuse to handle the truth. Particularly the truth that sometimes suffering does not miraculously resolve, and some sorrows will linger until Christ returns or we go home.

A while ago, I came across the phrase "sunshine Christianity" in an article about the prosperity gospel movement. I wish I could find the article that referenced it to give proper credit, but I can't. The phrase stuck with me though, as a clever encapsulation of a phenomenon I am becoming increasingly aware of.

Sunshine Christianity makes no distinction between happiness and joy and sets them as both the goal and mark of Christianity. We are to be guided by the pursuit of joy, constantly striving for and consciously choosing that which makes us happy. That same happiness is then the mark and measure of our faith. Bolstered by a belief that God will not allow prolonged suffering, it sets time limits on brokenness and sorrow and will not tolerate their lingering. The broken and sorrowful are admonished to "choose joy," with the clear implication that any expression other than a joyous one reflects failed faith. Sunshine Christianity wrongly presumes sorrow and struggle must be eradicated and replaced with happiness. It fails to realize our capacity for joy in the midst of sorrow.

Tragically, Sunshine Christianity effectively eliminates a tremendously valuable component of worship displayed throughout Scripture. It banishes lament. The laments contained in Scripture are profound and powerful examples of faith. They have been used mightily by God throughout the centuries to inspire and spur on countless weary and warworn saints. Christ Himself modeled lament in the presence of His disciples as He cried out to God the Father in the garden of Gethsemane.

The laments in Scripture typically include three main components. They begin with a detailed account of the sorrows of the lamenter followed by an acknowledgment of the character and nature of God and conclude with a declaration of trust in and praise to God.

> When I wept in my soul with fasting, It became my reproach. When I made sackcloth my clothing, I became a byword to them. Those who sit in the gate talk about me, And I [am] the song of the drunkards. But as for me, my prayer is to You, O LORD, at an acceptable time; O God, in the greatness of Your lovingkindness, Answer me with Your saving truth. ... Answer me, O LORD, for Your lovingkindness is good; According to the greatness of Your compassion, turn to me, ... But I am afflicted and in pain; May Your salvation, O God, set me [securely] on high. I will praise the name of God with song And magnify Him with thanksgiving. And it will please the LORD better than an ox [Or] a young bull with horns and hoofs. The humble have seen [it and] are glad; You who seek God, let your heart revive. (Ps. 69:10-13, 16, 29-32)

The detailed expression of sorrow and distress at the beginning of the lament is no less appropriate or God-honoring than the expression of trust or praise at the conclusion. On the contrary, the expression of trust and praise to God at the conclusion is actually magnified by the degree of sorrow and distress presented at the beginning.

Through sharing our struggles, sorrow, distress, anguish, and heartache we are best able to testify to God's sufficient grace, lovingkindness, mercy, and sustaining power. Sharing struggles not only allows us to shoulder one another's burdens, but it also allows us to glorify God together as we see His hand in preserving and sustaining through trial and tribulation.

Sunshine Christianity wrongly robs us of this experience, but perhaps that is by design. Perhaps Sunshine Christianity is a double-edged sword precisely designed and wielded by the adversary to both shame the sorrowful into silence and isolation, and simultaneously prevent the magnification of God's glory through silencing their transparent testimonies of lament.

A song of lament will echo in my heart and mind until Christ comes or I go home. My sorrow at Sarah's absence and my longing for my Savior, heaven, and her will not cease in this life. The fact that they remain is testimony of my faith in God's promise of our glorious future prepared in heaven by Him (Heb. 11:36).

Songs of lament flowing from shattered hearts are like beacons in the night for the wounded masses of this fallen world. Just as God powerfully uses the laments contained in Scripture, He will use our transparent testimonies of lament as well. Through honestly sharing our sorrows we have the opportunity to *comfort others with the comfort we have been given*; pointing them to the sure and certain hope freely given to all who will believe, and the glorious reminder that we are but sojourners here for *"just a little while"* longer (Heb. 10:37).

Come, Lord Jesus.

---

1. *A Few Good Men*. Directed by Rob Reiner, Castle Rock Entertainment, 1992.

CHILD LOSS: THE SECOND YEAR

≪∅≫

JUNE 8, 2019

"Grace and peace be multiplied to you in the knowledge of God and of Jesus our Lord; seeing that His divine power has granted to us everything pertaining to life and godliness, through the true knowledge of Him who called us by His own glory and excellence. For by these He has granted to us His precious and magnificent promises, so that by them you may become partakers of [the] divine nature, having escaped the corruption that is in the world by lust." 2 Peter 1:2-4

As I sit down to write this it remains incomprehensible that it has been two years since Scott and I touched, held, talked with, or laughed with our sweet Sarah. It is even more incomprehensible that we are now entering our third year without her: the third Father's Day, the third round of family birthdays, the third Thanksgiving, the third Christmas, the third New Year, the third Easter, the third Mother's Day, and so on. Not to mention all of the in-between dates and days that hold similar or worse stings. In so many ways it seems it was just yesterday when she left, but the aching in our hearts and arms testifies to the reality of our missing and longing for her each of the 17,520 hours of the past 730 days.

Last year I approached the one-year mark with great dread, fearful

CHILD LOSS: THE SECOND YEAR

of what the second year would hold. I wrote about it and promised to report back at the end of the second year to share Scott's and my experience.[1] I am sharing primarily for those who are walking behind us on this painful path. Most of the resources and stories I read last year shared the view that the second year is worse or harder, so I am sharing our experience as an alternate view.

For us, the second year was not worse or harder than the first. Over the course of the second year, some aspects became less raw. Some new struggles and challenges related to Sarah's death emerged, other preexisting ones were intensified, while still others were diminished or resolved. The second year for us was not worse or harder, but it wasn't dramatically easier either. Scott regularly says it is probably best described simply as "different."

In the pages that follow I've attempted to share our experience with some of the issues most prominent in our minds that we or other bereaved parents have mentioned struggling with in the absence of our children. I'm sure there are many other struggles I have failed to include but hopefully sharing our experience with these few will be of some encouragement or help to those following behind us.

THE WEIGHT OF SORROW

The weight of sorrow in response to Sarah's absence remains the same after two years. The pain of the void she left and our longing for her have not diminished in any way. However, over the past two years, God has been consistently strengthening us to bear it with increasing grace and peace.

I am reminded of Peter's admonition in 2 Peter 1, one of the very passages Sarah was meditating on while on the bus just before she went home. We have experienced the truth of this passage as grace and peace have been, and continue to be, multiplied to us as we have fixed our focus on the *"true knowledge"* of God and Christ and on His promises. As we have focused daily on the reality of our eternal hope in Christ, He has been faithful to powerfully sustain us.

Just as Peter wrote, God has used the joy of the hope set before us to strengthen us to bear up under this present sorrow with "multiplying grace and peace." We do not believe He will remove the painful weight of Sarah's absence on this side of heaven. But with grateful hearts, we are confident He will continue to *"strengthen us with all power, according to His glorious might, for the attaining of all steadfastness and patience* enabling us to *wait eagerly with perseverance"* for His glorious return and our subsequent reunion with sweet Sarah (Col. 1:11; Rom. 8:25).

Rawness

There were so many experiences in the first year that were cripplingly painful. Many of the most painful were the random firsts that catch you off guard and that few would think of outside of having lost a child themselves. For example, the excruciating sting of the first days and weeks of eating dinner at our table for six without her, or at a restaurant having to request a table for five instead of six.

At the conclusion of the second year, I still cringe when I have to deduct one from the number of our family, but it doesn't consistently wreak the same emotional havoc it initially did. The same is true for many of the other things that were physically gut-wrenching the first year. I still feel the sting and ache, but being more acquainted with them and what intensifies them, I am usually able to mentally prepare and press through them now.

Sleep

Throughout the first year sleep was extremely challenging. When I managed to sleep, waking up was indescribably painful as I would have to systematically process through the reality of Sarah's departure. There are no words to adequately describe the agony of those moments.

At the close of the second year I still routinely have those mornings (or middle of the nights) where the reality hits me like a sledgehammer knocking the breath from my lungs, but it is no longer every single time I wake. Sleep remains a challenge, but it has definitely improved, and nighttime now no longer holds the same daunting degree of dread it did in the first year.

Holidays and Special Dates

As we approached each of the second-year holidays and significant dates without Sarah, I found courage in knowing that God had graciously carried us through all of the same dates and events the first year. By remembering and learning from the first year's holidays and dates, most of the second-year ones were better navigated.

The pain was similar to the firsts on each of the dates, but making wise choices about commitments during those times made them more manageable, Easter being the exception. Easter was extremely difficult, but in retrospect, I realize I naively thought it would not be difficult and, as a result, failed to adequately anticipate and prepare for all of the aspects that were actually extremely difficult.

Public Places and Conversations

Throughout the past two years, I have learned better how to handle awkward public situations and conversations. I feel particularly liberated having finally accepted that it is okay for me to limit how much information I give in answering questions in casual conversation. For example, I am now comfortable answering that I have four children and then immediately redirecting the conversation without explaining that Sarah is not here.

Initially, I felt I had to explain, but I no longer feel the need to volunteer that in passing conversation unless there is a specific reason or prompting to do so. Certain places are still more challenging than others, but they no longer consistently cause the same level of stress they did the first year.

Recognizing Limitations

Learning to recognize and accept my brokenness and resulting limitations and vulnerabilities has been tremendously beneficial in the second year. Bearing them in mind I have learned to be extremely prayerful about plans and commitments. This has also helped me to learn to set more realistic expectations for myself than I probably did the first year.

Learning to recognize not just my limitations, but those of each member of our remaining family has been extremely helpful to safeguard us from overextending or overcommitting in a way that strains our family unnecessarily. This is still a work in progress, at times we still get overextended, but we learn from it when we do, and purpose to proactively guard against it in the future.

Nuclear Family

Soon after Sarah left we, her remaining family, made the tragic realization that we were all grieving not only the absence of Sarah but the loss of who we were as her nuclear family. None of us are who we were before Sarah left. As a result, our family is no longer the same family we were before Sarah left.

The first weeks and months were extremely difficult as we had to willingly let go of who we were both as individuals and as a family. We had to allow room for each of us to change and who we are as a family to reflect those changes. The first year held most of the major challenges in this process.

For me, the first year was filled with uncertainty and to some degree fear about the emotional and spiritual well-being of our remaining children as we attempted to guide them in the midst of our own brokenness. The second year I would describe as feeling much more secure in this regard. We have relearned each other for the most part. We have settled into and accepted the changes that were thrust upon us with Sarah's departure, though we still routinely feel the pangs of the loss of the family we were.

Friendships

One of the challenges I've seen most frequently referenced as causing pain in the second year of child loss is the distancing or walking away of the inner circle friends who consistently walked alongside the grieving parents the first year. There were friends we were saddened to see back away after Sarah left, but for us that occurred primarily in the first year. When I run into them I feel a twinge of pain in being reminded of their absence, but in general, it stings less than it did the first year.

We were tremendously blessed by and are extremely appreciative of the many who graciously gave us "cups of cold water" in the first year and even into the second year, but there was not a specific group of individuals who consistently walked with us day by day. While there was a sadness to that, in retrospect I see how God used it for our good. The lack of a specific core group of individuals consistently ministering to us kept our focus and dependence clearly upon God instead of others.

Having said that, I am in no way advocating pulling away from wounded and grieving friends, Scripture is clear to the contrary. I share only to testify how God used our particular circumstances for our good.

Loneliness

Loneliness has been one of two significant struggles for me (outside of the primary struggle of missing and longing for Sarah). I felt it the first year, but it intensified in the second year. It's not the loneliness of simply desiring human interaction, though. Instead, it's the loneliness of longing to be truly known and understood coupled with the realization that being truly known and understood isn't nearly as attainable as it once was.

That loneliness has intensified in the second year as acquaintances have more readily shared their beliefs about what we should and should not be experiencing in response to Sarah's absence. Misconceived opinions expressed about how and how long we should or should not grieve Sarah's absence are painful reminders of how difficult it is for others who have not experienced the loss of a child to accurately comprehend the magnitude of the impact. The individuals who critically express such things reveal they are currently incapable of knowing and understanding us. In response to such encounters, I find myself increasingly guarded and reluctant to engage transparently in person, which only compounds the loneliness.

That loneliness is unintentionally compounded yet again as Sarah is rarely mentioned by others. In the first year, people regularly brought her up to us, acknowledging both her and the sorrow of her absence. Unfortunately, that has changed significantly in the second year. We deeply miss her being remembered and mentioned by others, but at the same time we understand that others' lives will naturally go on without her and she will be thought of less and less by them. There is no anger or expectation that they should remember her. There is just a deep loneliness in her being forgotten while, for us, she continues to be the same integral member of our family she always has been.

We became part of a While We're Waiting support group for bereaved parents halfway through the second year and it has helped combat the loneliness.[2] We only meet once a month, but those couple of hours a month are among my favorites. Being with others who know and understand the profound pain and challenges of child loss and yet are continuing to strive to live hope-filled fruitful lives is like an oasis in the desert.

Weariness

Weariness is the second significant struggle I have had through the second year. I wrestled with whether or not it should be listed separately from loneliness because, for me, loneliness is a major contributing factor to weariness. Nevertheless, I will attempt to note other contributing factors here.

In addition to loneliness, the progressive realization of the potential length of this journey breeds weariness. In the first year, we were so focused on simply surviving as a family that I didn't allow myself to think about how long and lonely this path could be. My mantra for the first year was "Just do the next right thing." In the second year, it has been more difficult to abide by that mantra because of responsibilities and commitments that have required us to look ahead.

Being forced to drop my gaze from eternity to look down the path of this earthly journey is the equivalent of looking down a long desert path you have to walk with only a single cup of water in hand. My flesh screams it can't be done, my heart grows faint within me and I feel so very weary. I know His mercies are new every morning and they will be like streams of refreshing water all along that desert path, but daily convincing my aching heart of that truth has been a challenge during the second year.

The second year both Scott and I realized we are particularly subject to weariness when the majority of our time is being dominated by mundane tasks. We both wrestle to muster the energy and motivation to repeatedly do the yardwork and housework. It all seems so meaningless and inconsequential now. To combat this weariness we have learned it is essential that we are always purposeful to have something eternally significant going on as well; spending time with our remaining children, investing in others, sharing Sarah's testimony and ours, leading or teaching in small groups, and so on.

With Paul, we proclaim, *"For to me, to live is Christ and to die is gain. But if I am to live on in the flesh, this will mean fruitful labor for me; and I do not know which to choose. But I am hard-pressed from both directions, having the desire to depart and be with Christ, for that is very much better"* (Phil. 1:21-23).

Secondary Crises

Unfortunately, the death of a child does not shield us from additional concurrent hardships and struggles. I feel I must not conclude without acknowledging the role of secondary crises in our grief journeys as they can be significant factors impacting and influencing the specifics of our greatest struggles.

Scott was one of two primary witnesses to the crash that took Sarah's life. The prosecutor's office informed him he would be the primary witness should the bus driver, a fellow church member, choose not to accept responsibility thereby forcing their misdemeanor vehicular homicide case to trial. Scott was filled with dread and physically sickened at the thought of having to recount all that he witnessed that day. Unfortunately, two months after the crash, in our only in-person conversation with the driver, he indicated he was not accepting responsibility and that he and his attorney were hiring a team to reconstruct and disprove the state's and Scott's account of what happened. For the majority of the first two years, this secondary crisis played a profound role in painfully compounding our struggles in multiple ways. Throughout that time we felt led to not speak publicly about the driver, his decisions, or our interactions with him; we remain confident we were being obedient to the Lord's leading in that choice, but that obedience was inexpressibly costly.

I share that to transparently point out that my two greatest struggles of loneliness and weariness have likely been as much or more a byproduct of our secondary crisis than of Sarah's death specifically. For those journeying behind us, please don't be discouraged by my sharing those specific struggles, and don't assume you will experience them in the same way. Though we share the core commonality of the devastation of child loss, the experiences and circumstances surrounding our losses are unique, bringing with them unique challenges and struggles for each of us.

Conclusion

If you are following behind us on the excruciating path of child loss, I am so thankful to be able to offer you honest hope that your second year of this journey may not be harder or worse than your first year. If I could have you take away one truth from our experience it would be that God uses the joy of the hope set before us to strengthen us to bear up under this present sorrow with multiplying grace and peace.

If you haven't already, you will likely soon hear it implied or directly stated that joy should have replaced your sorrow by now. I humbly yet boldly disagree. There is no sin in our lingering sorrow, nor does our lingering sorrow prohibit our present or future joy.

He has promised that *"He will wipe away every tear from [our] eyes, and death shall be no more, neither shall there be mourning, nor crying, nor pain anymore, for the former things have passed away"* (Rev. 21:4). This promise has not yet been fulfilled, but praise God, with certainty there is coming a day when it will be.

He knows the sting of death and He weeps with us, and one day He is coming to wipe every tear away (John 11:33-35; Rev. 7:17). These are among the many precious and magnificent promises of His Word that allow grace and peace to be multiplied to us.

Though I do not know you by name, as I type this I am praying over you that God's truths that have so richly encouraged and comforted me over the past two years will encourage and comfort you as well. I pray that you will choose to run to Him daily as your stronghold and refuge. I pray that His living Word will resonate in your heart and soul as you seek Him through it. I pray that grace and peace will be multiplied to you in the true knowledge of God and of Jesus our Lord. I pray that He will give you glimpses of how He is redeeming even this most painful of trials for your good and His glory. And lastly, I pray that you will be strengthened with all power according to His glorious might to live fruitfully and wait expectantly, *"For, 'In just a little while, He who is coming will come and will not delay'"* (Heb. 10:37).

> I pray that the eyes of your heart may be enlightened, so that you will know what is the hope of His calling, what are the riches of the glory of His inheritance in the saints, and what is the surpassing greatness of His power toward us who believe. These are in accordance with the working of the strength of His might which He brought about in

Christ, when He raised Him from the dead and seated Him at His right hand in the heavenly places. (Eph.1:18-20)

> WHEREVER *you are* IS MY *home,* MY ONLY HOME
>
> — Charlotte Brontë —

---

1. see "The Second Year is Harder?" pp. 177-181.
2. While We're Waiting, Faith Based Retreats and Support Groups for Bereaved Parents, whilewerewaiting.org

RESPONDING TO ABANDONMENT

JULY 16, 2019

The devastating path of child loss can be an indescribably lonely one. For many if not most bereaved parents, their deep loneliness is compounded by varying degrees of abandonment. We have been no exception to that common experience.

If you are struggling through the compounding pain of abandonment in the midst of your grief, I am transparently sharing this part of my journey for you. I am so sorry you are experiencing the painful sting of watching those you thought would walk through your grief hand in hand with you, back away from you instead. It is my prayer that, at the appropriate time, the Scripture I share here will encourage you just as it has encouraged me.

Shortly after we passed the two-year mark of life without our precious Sarah, I began studying 1 John. I was almost immediately deeply conflicted by the challenging exhortation of selfless love repeatedly expressed throughout 1 John.

> The one who says he is in the Light and [yet] hates his brother is in the darkness until now. The one who loves his brother abides in the Light and there is no cause for stumbling in him. But the one who hates his brother is in the darkness and walks in the darkness, and does not

know where he is going because the darkness has blinded his eyes. (vv. 2:9-11)

By this the children of God and the children of the devil are obvious: anyone who does not practice righteousness is not of God, nor the one who does not love his brother. (v. 3:10)

We know that we have passed out of death into life, because we love the brethren. He who does not love abides in death. (v. 3:14)

We know love by this, that He laid down His life for us; and we ought to lay down our lives for the brethren. (v. 3:16)

Beloved, let us love one another, for love is from God; and everyone who loves is born of God and knows God. The one who does not love does not know God, for God is love. (vv. 4:7-8)

Hour after hour and day after day as I studied through 1 John, I wrestled with the Lord and my sorrows. Initially, I believed, argued, and attempted to justify that I was only apathetic toward those who had abandoned us in our grief, I didn't "hate" them. The Lord who knows my heart would not allow my excuses, though. As piercing conviction broke through my resistance I was forced to admit that, though I did not hate them, I was undeniably not desiring to love them. In truth, I was not apathetic at all—I had been and still was deeply hurt by their unexpected abandonment.

Perhaps recognizing my lack of desire to love them was enlightening, but it in no way marked a victory. My flesh was waging war against the call to righteousness in 1 John. After all, they walked away from us, avoided us, and continue to avoid us. It certainly seems they don't love us, so surely we are exempt from the command to love them. Before those words were even fully formed or spoken in my mind the Holy Spirit within me was testifying to their falsehood, and yet I continued to wrestle.

In the midst of wrestling through 1 John, I began studying and preparing to teach a lesson on Peter's denial of Christ. Over that week, I read and reread the accounts of the Last Supper, Peter's denial, the crucifixion, the resurrection, and Christ's interaction with the disciples following the resurrection in Matthew, Mark, Luke, and parts of John.

Sunday morning, before I was to teach the lesson on Peter's denial, our pastor preached a sermon from John 13. As he read aloud the account of Jesus washing the disciples' feet, the Holy Spirit began powerfully speaking to my heart. My heart and mind were flooded with all I had been studying in 1 John and each of the gospel accounts that week.

As Jesus humbled Himself and compassionately washed the feet of His disciples, He did it already knowing that each and every one of them was going to fall away and abandon Him (Mark 14:27). He knew Judas would betray Him (Mat. 26:21). When He was *"grieved to the point of death,"* James, John and Peter would somehow fail to recognize the gravity of those moments and would sleep, even though Christ in His anguish had told them to keep watch and pray (Mark 14:34-38). Peter would deny even knowing Him as He looked on silently as "the Lamb" ready to be slaughtered (Luke 22:61). And yet, our precious Lord and Savior washed their feet, and *"He loved them to the end"* (John 13:1).

After Jesus washed their feet He gave them and us this command:

> If I then, the Lord and the Teacher, washed your feet, you also ought to wash one another's feet. "For I gave you an example that you also should do as I did to you. Truly, truly, I say to you, a slave is not greater than his master, nor [is] one who is sent greater than the one who sent him. If you know these things, you are blessed if you do them." (John 13:14-17)

He who was abandoned by His disciples and closest friends while His soul was *"deeply grieved, to the point of death"* intimately understands the anguish of our abandonment (Matt. 26:38). He compassionately empathizes and weeps with us (John 11:33-35). He always lives to intercede for us (Heb. 7:25). And it is He who has commanded us, *"A new commandment I give to you, that you love one another: just as I have loved you, you also are to love one another"* (John 13:34).

Just as He has loved us.

While we were yet sinners, Christ died for us (Rom. 5:8).

All of this swirled through my heart and mind as our pastor read these Words of Christ, *"For I gave you an example that you also should do as I did to you. Truly, truly, I say to you, a slave is not greater than his master, nor [is] one who is sent greater than the one who sent him. If you know these things, you are blessed if you do them."*

In those sacred moments the Lord in His power through the leading of His Holy Spirit and the conviction of His Word created within me the desire to love those who had abandoned us. I am compelled by His love and filled with longing to be pleasing to Him. He who said, *"If you know these things, you are blessed if you do them"* is absolutely faithful. The blessedness of drawing nearer to Him through obedience far outweighs any cost of obedience.

Recognizing I am utterly dependent on Him for the power to walk in obedience, I am daily praying that He will *"sustain me with a willing spirit"* to be a surrendered and obedient vessel for His love to flow through (Ps. 51:12). I am praying for His love in me to readily flow not only to those who have loved us well but also to those who have abandoned us, so that whenever and however He calls me to *"wash their feet,"* I will willingly do just as He did: humbly, joyfully, and without hesitation—*loving them to the end.*

> Since you have in obedience to the truth purified your souls for a sincere love of the brethren, fervently love one another from the heart, for you have been born again not of seed which is perishable but imperishable, [that is,] through the living and enduring word of God. (1 Pet. 1:22-23)

FELLOW PARTAKERS

AUGUST 1, 2019

I came to Revelation last week as I was working my way through the New Testament portion of my quiet time. I've studied through Revelation multiple times, but not since Sarah left. Initially, when I realized Revelation was next, I hesitantly flipped back to Matthew to start my New Testament reading over again. But as I stared at the title page of Matthew I felt unsettled and a strong prompting to go back to Revelation to complete my journey through the New Testament instead. I flipped back to Revelation and prayerfully began reading.

> The revelation of Jesus Christ, which God gave him to show to his servants the things that must soon take place... Blessed is the one who reads aloud the words of this prophecy, and blessed are those who hear, and who keep what is written in it, for the time is near. (Rev. 1:1a, 3 ESV)

I'm so thankful I heeded the prompting to turn back and immerse myself in the truths of Revelation. Just as verse 3 promises, I've already been so very blessed and encouraged by meditating on the many rich truths of chapter one alone over the past week and a half.

In my previous readings, I'm certain I failed to appreciate the richness of verse 9. Rereading it now, though, with the lingering weight of sorrow in Sarah's absence, and the acute awareness of the brokenness and fallenness of this world, I was captivated by the significance of the verse.

We are regularly bombarded by the implied or overtly spoken message, tainted by the prosperity gospel, that this life will be one of ease and blessing if we choose to follow Christ. In the midst of suffering and sorrow, it is tremendously encouraging each and every time Scripture confirms that message as a lie. Such is the case with Revelation 1:9. John Wesley noted the significance this verse and the book of Revelation as a whole holds for suffering saints when he wrote of it, "It was given to a banished man; and men in affliction understand and relish it most."[1]

> I, John, your brother and fellow partaker in the tribulation and kingdom and perseverance which are in Jesus… (Rev. 1:9)

John, in this verse, confirms that we who are servants of Jesus Christ are fellow partakers in three specific aspects: fellow partakers in tribulation in Jesus Christ, fellow partakers in the kingdom in Jesus Christ, and fellow partakers in the perseverance that is in Jesus Christ.

Fellow Partakers in Tribulation

> These things I have spoken to you, so that in Me you may have peace. In the world you have tribulation, but take courage; I have overcome the world. (John 16:33)

God is so gracious to repeatedly warn and encourage us throughout His Word that *"all who desire to live a godly life in Christ Jesus will be persecuted"* (2 Tim. 3:12). Indeed this was true for John who goes on to say in verse 9 that he *"was on the island called Patmos on account of the word of God and the testimony of Jesus."* Following Christ did not lead

John to health, wealth, and prosperity, it led him to tribulation. John's obedience and service to Christ in proclaiming the Word of God led him to the desolate prison island of Patmos. And his words to us in verse 9 are in agreement with the rest of Scripture that indicates we, too, will be partakers in tribulation and suffering in Jesus Christ.

> Rejoice in hope, be patient in tribulation, be constant in prayer. (Rom. 12:12 ESV)

The apostle John's reminder is precious encouragement in a Christian culture where insidiously infiltrated prosperity theology regularly implies that tribulation and hardship are indicators we have failed to rightly follow Christ. Certainly, sin and failure to follow Christ can and will eventually lead to painful consequences or discipline, but Scripture is replete with examples of righteous saints, in addition to John, enduring tribulation, suffering, and martyrdom in the midst of faithfully following Him. And so their examples along with God's precious promises are written for us that we may have peace in our tribulation.

> Who will separate us from the love of Christ? Will tribulation, or distress, or persecution, or famine, or nakedness, or peril, or sword? Just as it is written, "FOR YOUR SAKE WE ARE BEING PUT TO DEATH ALL DAY LONG; WE WERE CONSIDERED AS SHEEP TO BE SLAUGHTERED." But in all these things we overwhelmingly conquer through Him who loved us. For I am convinced that neither death, nor life, nor angels, nor principalities, nor things present, nor things to come, nor powers, nor height, nor depth, nor any other created thing, will be able to separate us from the love of God, which is in Christ Jesus our Lord. (Rom. 8:35-39)

Fellow Partakers in the Kingdom

> ... To Him who loves us and released us from our sins by His blood—
> and He has made us [to be] a kingdom, priests to His God and Father...
> (Rev. 1:5-6)

We are fellow partakers in the kingdom in Jesus. Our partnership in the kingdom is present tense. The message given through John in verses 5-6 echoes the message given through Peter in 1 Peter 2:9-10, *"But you are a chosen race, a royal priesthood, a holy nation, a people for his own possession, that you may proclaim the excellencies of him who called you out of darkness into his marvelous light. Once you were not a people, but now you are God's people; once you had not received mercy, but now you have received mercy."* Through the precious blood of Jesus Christ, we are freed from the bondage of sin and death and united with Him, partakers in His kingdom.

> For He rescued us from the domain of darkness, and transferred us to the kingdom of His beloved Son, in whom we have redemption, the forgiveness of sins. (Col. 1:13-14)

> He who has the Son has the life; he who does not have the Son of God does not have the life. These things I have written to you who believe in the name of the Son of God, so that you may know that you have eternal life. (1 John 5:12-13)

His Word grants peace in the midst of tribulation by allowing us to confidently know that we are present partakers of His kingdom now through faith in Jesus Christ. Peter goes on to clarify in 1 Peter 2:11 that as partakers of this kingdom in Jesus we are now *"sojourners and exiles"* on earth. As sojourners and exiles our hope is not fixed on anything earthly, but is instead fixed completely *on the grace to brought to us at the revelation of Jesus Christ* (1 Pet. 1:13).

As partakers in His kingdom, we have the sure and certain hope of His imminent return when *"The kingdom of the world shall become the kingdom of our Lord and of his Christ, and He shall reign forever and ever"*

(Rev. 11:15). And so we groan with longing as we expectantly watch for Him who is *"coming with the clouds"* (Rev. 1:7).

> For we know that if the earthly tent which is our house is torn down, we have a building from God, a house not made with hands, eternal in the heavens. For indeed in this [house] we groan, longing to be clothed with our dwelling from heaven (2 Cor. 5:1-2)

Fellow Partakers in Perseverance

> For in hope we have been saved, but hope that is seen is not hope; for who hopes for what he [already] sees? But if we hope for what we do not see, with perseverance we wait eagerly for it. (Rom. 8:24-25)

We who are servants of Jesus Christ are fellow partakers in perseverance (also translated as patient endurance) in Jesus Christ. The knowledge that we are or will be partakers in tribulation in Him, and the hope of the knowledge that we are partakers in the kingdom in Him work together to bring about our partaking of the perseverance that is also found in Him. This is the visible working out of the prayer of Colossians 1:9-11.

> ...that you may be filled with the knowledge of His will in all spiritual wisdom and understanding, so that you will walk in a manner worthy of the Lord, to please [Him] in all respects, bearing fruit in every good work and increasing in the knowledge of God; strengthened with all power, according to His glorious might, for the attaining of all steadfastness and patience...

God, through His Word, graciously grants us knowledge and understanding that cause us to desire to persevere in obedience to Him, even in tribulation. What indescribable hope and joy are ours in knowing He Himself will graciously and compassionately strengthen us in our frailty with all power according to His glorious might specifically to enable us to patiently endure, steadfast and immovable.

Therefore, we *"must not throw away our confidence, for* [we] *have need of endurance, so that when* [we] *have done the will of God,* [we] *may receive what was promised. 'FOR YET IN A VERY LITTLE WHILE, HE WHO IS COMING WILL COME, AND WILL NOT DELAY. BUT MY RIGHTEOUS ONE SHALL LIVE BY FAITH; AND IF HE SHRINKS BACK, MY SOUL HAS NO PLEASURE IN HIM.' But we are not of those who shrink back to destruction, but of those who have faith to the preserving of the soul"* (Heb. 10:36-39).

For whatever was written in earlier times was written for our instruction, so that through perseverance and the encouragement of the Scriptures we might have hope. Now may the God who gives perseverance and encouragement grant you to be of the same mind with one another according to Christ Jesus, so that with one accord you may with one voice glorify the God and Father of our Lord Jesus Christ. (Rom. 15:4-6)

> And now, dear children, continue in him, so that when he appears we may be confident & unashamed before him at his coming.
> —1 John 2:28

---

1. Wesley, John. "Revelation 1:9." *Wesley's Explanatory Notes.* StudyLight.org, studylight.org/commentaries/eng/wen/revelation-1.html.

JUST KEEP TRYING

AUGUST 21, 2019

> *"Do you not know that those who run in a race all run, but [only] one receives the prize? Run in such a way that you may win."*
> 1 Corinthians 9:24

*B*efore Sarah was killed the path before me was so clearly illuminated I felt as though I could almost see over the horizon to the finish line. Life was bright and, in general, discerning what was pleasing to the Lord came with some degree of ease. The well-lit path enabled me to freely strive to *run the race in such a way that I might win.*

On June 8, 2017, in an instant, we were hurled from that bright sunny path to this treacherous path through the dark valley of the shadow of death. Satan sought to sift us through the taking of Sarah's physical life and the turmoil that ensued. I longed to continue running, but suddenly discerning the way of righteousness in the midst of the darkness was so very difficult.

> Who is among you that fears the LORD, That obeys the voice of His servant, That walks in darkness and has no light? Let him trust in the name of the LORD and rely on his God. (Isa. 50:10)

Since the day Sarah left I have been desperate to navigate this dark valley in obedience to Him, desperate to run in a manner pleasing to Him. I thought the path would once again become easier to discern with time. But days have turned to weeks, weeks have turned to months, and inconceivably, months have now turned to two years, and it still remains extremely difficult to discern each step of the path marked out for me.

I long to run again, but instead, I am continuing to inch along the shadowy path before me. I have a burning urgency to be used by Him for His name's sake. Yet, I find myself continually crawling along, blinking and groping in the darkness only discerning one step at a time, and repeatedly forced to wait between each step for discernment to find the next.

God has been faithful to illumine each next step, but my slow pace and difficulty discerning the way of righteousness through this dark winding valley recently culminated in discouragement. I used to be able to run, it used to be easy to see, and it used to be easy to discern what was next; having to pray, study, and try so very hard to discern His will for every little step began to feel much like failure.

Thankfully, as He eventually always does, in His lovingkindness and compassion He recently spoke directly to my discouraged heart through His Word. Ever so tenderly, He spoke through a passage He had impressed powerfully on Sarah's heart as well.

> for you were formerly darkness, but now you are Light in the Lord; walk as children of Light … trying to learn what is pleasing to the Lord. (Eph. 5:8, 10)

Sarah repeatedly journaled prayers that God would enable her to "walk as a child of light." I have meditated on Ephesians 5:8 multiple times since she left, but only just now in my discouragement did verse 10 come into focus—*"trying to learn what is pleasing to the Lord."*

"Trying to Learn." The Children of Light are those who are *"trying to learn what is pleasing to the Lord."* What blessed encouragement that it doesn't say those who always know what is pleasing to the Lord, or those who quickly know what is pleasing to the Lord. But instead, He says those who are *"trying to learn,"* implying those who are continually trying to learn.

The Greek word translated in the NASB as "trying to learn" is *dokimazō.* Other translations render it "carefully determining", "proving", "trying to discern" and "testing." The *Outline of Biblical Usage* lists its usage as "to test, examine, prove, scrutinise," and "to recognise as genuine after examination."[1] It carries the idea of examining and testing as with metals.

Our *"trying to learn,"* our longing and effort to discern what is pleasing to Him is in itself pleasing to Him. Certainly, as He reveals His will we should run in it, but in the seasons where we must wait for Him to illumine the next step, our *"trying to learn"* as we wait upon Him is pleasing to Him.

> For You do not delight in sacrifice, otherwise I would give it; You are not pleased with burnt offering. The sacrifices of God are a broken spirit; A broken and a contrite heart, O God, You will not despise. (Ps. 51:16-17)

What a precious reminder that it is not about the acts of obedience themselves but about the heart that desires and strives to walk in them. I can't run this part of my path without running ahead of His guiding and leading. This part of my journey is one of learning to expectantly yet patiently stand firm, wait, and walk as He leads—one step at a time. My obedience to do just that is no less pleasing to Him than my obediently running when I am called to run.

> Put on the full armor of God, so that you will be able to stand firm against the schemes of the devil. ... Therefore, take up the full armor of God, so that you will be able to resist in the evil day, and having done everything, to stand firm. (Eph. 6:11, 13)

Wherever you find yourself on your journey today, I pray you find encouragement to just keep trying. Whether you are in the deepest depth of the valley with your mouth in the dust or running the race with gusto along a well-lit path, be encouraged that His call for us remains the same (Lam. 3:29; 1 Cor. 9:24). Whatever our posture and pace may be, He is pleased with us as we "w*alk as children of Light... trying to learn what is pleasing to the Lord.*"

Walk as Children of Light
—EPHESIANS 5:8

---

1. "G1381 - dokimazō - Strong's Greek Lexicon (kjv)." *Blue Letter Bible,* blueletterbible.org/lexicon/g1381/kjv/tr/0-1/.

IN JUST A LITTLE WHILE

SEPTEMBER 11, 2019

"This hope we have as an anchor of the soul, a [hope] both sure and steadfast and one which enters within the veil" Hebrews 6:19

I awoke early this morning with a heavy heart for some dear fellow sojourners on this painful path of child loss. While weeping and interceding for them I was reminded of the significance of today's date and the thousands of others who bear the anguish of death with us as a result of the atrocities of September 11, 2001. It is now eighteen years later, but I am certain many of them are weary today as the sorrow of the absence of their loved ones remains ever-present.

Recently, as my wrestling with my own weariness was compounded by the weight of weariness I see in my precious brothers and sisters in suffering, I found encouragement in the last chapter of Revelation.

Christ concludes His Revelation by saying three times that He is coming quickly.

> And behold, I am coming quickly. Blessed is he who heeds the words of the prophecy of this book. (Rev. 22:7)

> Behold, I am coming quickly, and My reward [is] with Me, to render to every man according to what he has done. (Rev. 22:12)

> He who testifies to these things says, 'Yes, I am coming quickly.' Amen. Come, Lord Jesus. (Rev. 22:20)

Paul echoed the same truth of His imminent return.

> For, "In just a little while, he who is coming will come and will not delay. (Heb. 10:37 NIV)

Habakkuk spoke similarly of the certainty of God doing all that He has promised.

> For the vision is yet for the appointed time; It hastens toward the goal and it will not fail. Though it tarries, wait for it; For it will certainly come, it will not delay. (Hab. 2:3)

In the midst of crippling and consuming sorrow, as we gasp for each breath, the path ahead can appear endlessly long and barrenly bleak. Weariness can quickly and easily give way to hopelessness.

Our omniscient and compassionate Lord and Savior sees and knows our frailty and weakness and speaks to it directly as He reminds us repeatedly that He is coming quickly. Reminders of the hope of His imminent return are ever so graciously given to shore up weak, weary and faltering faith.

Peter implored us to *"fix our hope completely on the grace to be brought to us at the revelation of Jesus Christ,"* and Christ is reminding us repeatedly that the fulfillment of that hope is coming soon, quickly, in just a little while (1 Pet. 1:13).

He is calling us to intentionally and purposefully fix our hope like an anchor on the gracious promises that will be delivered to us, His children, upon His imminent return. Sin, sorrow, and death will be no more, every tear will be wiped away, and we who believe will abide with Him forever... soon, quickly, in just a little while.

As we hold to that anchor of hope, purposefully fixed on His imminent return, we are called and equipped to persevere. The reminders of His imminent return are always accompanied by exhortations to persevere—living expectantly for His promised and certain return.

> ...we who have taken refuge would have strong encouragement to take hold of the hope set before us. This hope we have as an anchor of the soul, a [hope] both sure and steadfast and one which enters within the veil, where Jesus has entered as a forerunner for us... (Heb. 6:18-20)

> FOR YET IN A VERY LITTLE WHILE, HE WHO IS COMING WILL COME, AND WILL NOT DELAY. BUT MY RIGHTEOUS ONE SHALL LIVE BY FAITH; AND IF HE SHRINKS BACK, MY SOUL HAS NO PLEASURE IN HIM. But we are not of those who shrink back to destruction, but of those who have faith to the preserving of the soul. (Heb. 10:37-39)

The reminder that He is coming soon revives us to serve with perseverance and diligence. Through His blood, our precious Savior rescued us who believe from our sin and eternal death, and gloriously made a way for the world, our loved ones, and us to spend eternity with Him and one another. He is coming back soon, quickly, in just a little while, and I want to be found faithful by Him (John 3:16).

The enemy will continue to cruelly and relentlessly taunt, *"saying, 'Where is the promise of His coming? For ever since the fathers fell asleep, all continues just as it was from the beginning of creation"* (2 Pet. 3:4). But we, being *"strengthened with all power according to His glorious might,"* can persevere by holding *"unswervingly to the hope we profess, for he who promised is faithful"* (Col. 1:11; Heb. 10:23).

Hold on, dear weary one, to the anchor of your hope purposefully fixed firmly and securely on the grace to be brought to us at His coming, for He is certainly coming soon, quickly, in just a little while. *"Come, Lord Jesus."*

A STRANGER WITH A FRIEND'S FACE

❦

OCTOBER 2, 2019

The music of Andrew Peterson has powerfully ministered to me over the past two years. His lyrics deeply resonate within my soul while continually challenging me to hope in Christ and cling to the truths of Scripture. One lyric that has been in the forefront of my mind this week is found in the second stanza of his song titled "Rejoice."

> And when the peace turns to danger
> The nights are longer than days
> And every friend has a stranger's face
> Then deep within the dungeon cell
> You have to make a choice[1]

We were at an event recently that brought us together with many long-time acquaintances and friends, most of whom we have known for ten to twenty years or more. As I was standing in the crowd of people, this song, and specifically the lyric *"every friend has a stranger's face,"* was repeatedly playing in my mind.

Sorrow washed over me as I felt so deeply disconnected standing in the midst of all the friends interacting together. I have such fond memories with so many of them and enjoyed seeing them and hearing about their families, but I felt as though there was a chasm between us.

As we made small talk and interacted as though Sarah was still here, as if life is as it was three, ten, or twenty years ago, I felt as though I was acting—painfully playing the part of the person I once was. It was dreadfully hard.

I left the event feeling a fresh weight of sorrow and a profound sense of loneliness that lingered for the next couple of days. All the while this song continued to repeatedly play in my mind as I lamented the isolating impact of loss and grief.

"Every friend has a stranger's face."

In continuing to ponder the shift in those relationships, I gradually realized that it was not they who had changed, it was I. They are still who they were, but I am not.

I have become a stranger with a friend's face.

When they see me they see who I was before Sarah was killed, before this exceedingly painful and transforming journey through the valley of the shadow of death began. Standing at a distance they have no way of knowing the friend they knew in many ways died the day Sarah did.

I realize now that the chasm I felt that brought such sorrow to my heart is not between them and me. The chasm is within me, the expanse between who I was and who I am. It was simply illumined by their presence as my longing to be known by them clashed with the realization that I have been rendered unknown.

I desperately wish I was still that same woman, the mom with four precious daughters all living on earth, unscathed by the talons of death. I wish Sarah was here, that she had not been killed, that I could once again hold her, talk with her, touch her, and see her grow and be used mightily by the Lord here instead of there. But like the prompting of Andrew Peterson's song, I have to make a choice.

I choose to rejoice that even in the moments when I feel completely alone and unknown, Scripture testifies that I am not only intimately known by the God of the universe, but that I am also eternally loved by Him with a perfect and everlasting love.

I choose to rejoice that God is making me anew in the valley of the shadow of death. I rejoice that through agonizing sorrow He has given me an eternal perspective and a fresh urgency for others to know and understand Him and the hope available in Him.

I sentimentally miss the innocent joy of the person I was, sheltered from life's deepest sorrows. But I rejoice in the continually deepening hope and faith that have been and are being forged through the fierce flames of tribulation and sorrow.

The consuming pain of the past two years is inexpressible, but the grace and provision of our faithful God and Father is equally indescribable. I rejoice that He has faithfully comforted me and has filled me with longing to comfort others with that same comfort (2 Cor. 1:3-4).

I rejoice that through the depths of sorrow, He has taught me the value of weeping with those who weep as well as rejoicing with those who rejoice.

I rejoice that I am not who I was.

I also rejoice that I am not yet who I am going to be as He continues His work of sanctifying and transforming me until that glorious day when I finally see Him face to face, and my sweet Sarah with Him (2 Cor. 3:18; Phil. 3:8-11).

Come, Lord Jesus.

---

1. Peterson, Andrew. "Rejoice." Burning Edge of Dawn. Centricity Music, 2015. CD.

SORROW LOOKS BACK

OCTOBER 21, 2019

A quote credited to Ralph Waldo Emerson circulates periodically: "Sorrow looks back, worry looks around, faith looks up." Surprisingly this quote was recently featured on a church sign, a picture of which was widely circulated on social media. I say surprisingly primarily because of the quote itself, but also because of Emerson's denial of the deity of Christ, rejection of Christianity, and role in the rise of transcendentalism.[1]

At first glance, the quote might seem harmless, and could perhaps even sound right or true. However, void of greater context it can be added to a long list of platitudes and sayings beautifully formatted into memes to be well-meaningly yet injuriously forwarded to grieving people.

The quote seems to make the mistake of countless other platitudes. It implies sorrow is antithetical to something else—in this case, faith. It conveys the idea that to choose one is to put away or reject the other. Sorrow puts away faith, or faith puts away sorrow.

I remember an acquaintance who has not lost a child telling me not long after Sarah died that they don't know how God does it, but they are so thankful that somehow He takes all the pain (i.e. sorrow) away. I was not offended by their words, they had no ill intent.

Instead, I found them helpful in understanding some of the misconceptions about sorrow and grief. I think a similar thought process led to the Emerson quote being enthusiastically shared by so many Christians.

The thought of any sorrow lasting a lifetime is uncomfortable, even unbearable. From the outside looking in it's more comfortable to believe there must be a way to make the sorrow go away, so the hollow exhortations commence:

"You just need to have more faith."
"Stop looking back."
"Focus on the future."
"Just move on."
"You've got to let go of the past."
"You just need to live in the present."

Thankfully God's Word makes it clear that sorrow and faith are not antithetical. They are absolutely not in opposition to one another or mutually exclusive. To the contrary, in Scripture and in life we see over and over again that great faith is uniquely evidenced in the midst of deepest sorrow.

> Those who sow in tears shall reap with joyful shouting. He who goes to and fro weeping, carrying [his] bag of seed, Shall indeed come again with a shout of joy, bringing his sheaves [with him.] (Ps. 126:5-6)

The darkness of sorrow is a backdrop upon which the light of faith shines most brilliantly. Sorrow need not be denied or hidden as if its presence compromises faith. Sorrow should be honestly exposed and shared as a platform to display the beautiful reality of the hope of our faith as followers of Jesus Christ.

Additionally, I would argue that for many, perhaps even most, sorrow is not found looking back. Looking back I see my family intact; I see my precious daughter's short but richly full life of seventeen and a half years. I see joy upon joy and blessing upon blessing when I look back. Looking back, I love and cherish the memories of our intact family.

Another popular yet detrimental quote (often wrongly attributed to Emerson) is, "What lies behind us, and what lies before us, are tiny matters compared to what lies within us." When one is shrouded in sorrow following a deep loss, particularly the loss of a child, what lies before us is anything but a tiny matter. The prospect of the remainder of our earthly lives without our precious children is daunting.

The reality is sorrow is found in looking at the present and the future, not in looking back. Sorrow is found in the ever-present void of our child's absence. Sorrow is found each time her chair sits empty, each holiday, each time she is not here to celebrate her sisters' or her birthday, each of her sisters' weddings where she will be glaringly absent, and on and on the list goes.

Sorrow is an uninvited guest physically abiding where my child once was. My child will not return for the remainder of this earthly life, and the sorrow of her absence will not leave. Those who know the pain of child loss have no qualms acknowledging that fact.

The future will invariably continue to hold sorrow, but it is also the future that holds our hope. As followers of Jesus Christ, we are to *"fix our hope completely on the grace to be brought to us at the revelation of Jesus Christ."* What lies before us is no tiny matter, it is the greatest of matters.

> Therefore, prepare your minds for action, keep sober in spirit, fix your hope completely on the grace to be brought to you at the revelation of Jesus Christ. (1 Pet. 1:13)

There is coming a glorious reunion day in the future, *"in just a little while,"* when my beautiful intact family of the past will once again be made whole (Heb. 10:37). In an instant the complete joy of that future day will eclipse into oblivion the darkness of all the sorrow of the in-between days.

Through the promises and hope of Jesus Christ, we can and do join Paul in enduring and persevering, *"sorrowful yet always rejoicing"* (2

Cor. 6:10). The certainty of Sarah's present glorious well-being and the confidence that I will soon see her again liberate me to find joy even in the presence of the persisting sorrow of her absence.

> but in everything commending ourselves as servants of God, in much endurance, in afflictions, in hardships, in distresses, … as sorrowful yet always rejoicing, as poor yet making many rich, as having nothing yet possessing all things. (2 Cor. 6:4, 10)

May we as believers never be guilty of shaming the sorrowful into silence by implying their sorrow reflects a lack of faith. May we instead compassionately encourage the brokenhearted among us to freely and boldly offer up their costly songs of mingled sorrow and praise to Him—*sorrowful yet always rejoicing*. Each a fragrant offering to Him and a glorious display of His miraculous provision, amazing grace, overflowing mercy, and sustaining power; all beautifully magnified against the backdrop of their sorrow. To Him be the glory.

Come, Lord Jesus.

> For here we do not have a lasting city, but we are seeking the city which is to come. Through Him then, let us continually offer up a sacrifice of praise to God, that is, the fruit of lips that give thanks to His name. (Heb. 13:14-15)

---

1. Mohler, Albert. *Ralph Waldo Emerson at 200: Still shaping the American mind.* (2003, December 12). AlbertMohler.com. albertmohler.com/2003/12/12/ralph-waldo-emerson-at-200-still-shaping-the-american-mind

KEEP CRYING OUT AND TESTIFYING

NOVEMBER 30, 2019

"Come and hear, all who fear God, And I will tell of what He has done for my soul." Psalm 66:16

I've not written much lately for a variety of reasons. But one of the primary reasons has been a fear of becoming a clanging cymbal repeatedly saying the same thing over and over. The overarching cry of my heart is, "Come, Lord Jesus!" Anything I might write flows directly from my waiting upon Him with both an urgent longing for His return and a consuming desire to ready myself, and to see His church readied.

I've felt growing apprehension that I was essentially writing the same things over and over again. That concern was reinforced recently when someone brought up the blog to me with disapproval. When I asked what about the blog bothered them, they responded that it seemed to be "dragging on and on."

Despite the obvious sting of those words, I knew I had to weigh them. I had to allow room for them to be true, for me to be wrong, and for me to be corrected by them.

The deep sorrow of Sarah's absence and my anguish over the tragic brokenness of this world remain constant whether I acknowledge them or not. But those words caused me to ponder, is it wrong to continue to acknowledge their reality?

If I continue to write knowing my message from this day forth will at its core be a continual rewriting of the same central truths, am I harming or helping? Am I a clanging cymbal or am I a consistent reminder of hope in the dark brokenness of this world?

How Long?

In the still of the night, as I was once again prayerfully wrestling with burgeoning insecurity from those words, I was reminded of the Psalmists' repeated cries of *"How long?"*

> Be gracious to me, O LORD, for I [am] pining away; Heal me, O LORD, for my bones are dismayed. And my soul is greatly dismayed; But You, O LORD–how long? (Ps. 6:2-3)

> How long, O LORD? Will You forget me forever? How long will You hide Your face from me? How long shall I take counsel in my soul, [Having] sorrow in my heart all the day? How long will my enemy be exalted over me? (Ps. 13:1-2)

> How long, O God, will the adversary revile, [And] the enemy spurn Your name forever? Why do You withdraw Your hand, even Your right hand? From within Your bosom, destroy [them!] (Ps. 74:10-11)

> How long, O LORD? Will You hide Yourself forever? Will Your wrath burn like fire? (Ps. 89:46)

> Do return, O LORD; how long [will it be?] And be sorry for Your servants. (Ps. 90:13)

> Rise up, O Judge of the earth, Render recompense to the proud. How long shall the wicked, O LORD, How long shall the wicked exult? (Ps. 94:2-3)

The Psalmists' cries of *"How long?"* were birthed through pangs of waiting. With each cry for deliverance, the Psalmists acknowledged the dragging on and on of the trials, sorrows, brokenness, and sufferings of this world. Their testimonies of faith were bolstered by sharing their urgency for deliverance along with their proclamation of God Almighty as the one and only worthy Deliverer.

Our Testimony

> Therefore, prepare your minds for action, keep sober [in spirit,] fix your hope completely on the grace to be brought to you at the revelation of Jesus Christ. (1 Pet. 1:13 ESV)

Like the Psalmists', our cries of *"How long?"* testify that we know something gloriously better is coming. Our longing for Christ's imminent return is testimony to our confidence in Him and His promises. The brokenness of this world will drag on and on until His return, as will our cries for Him until that day.

> For we know that the whole creation groans and suffers the pains of childbirth together until now. And not only this, but also we ourselves, having the first fruits of the Spirit, even we ourselves groan within ourselves, waiting eagerly for [our] adoption as sons, the redemption of our body. For in hope we have been saved, but hope that is seen is not hope; for who hopes for what he [already] sees? But if we hope for what we do not see, with perseverance we wait eagerly for it. (Rom. 8:22-25)

Faithful followers of Christ who bear great sorrow are unavoidably and acutely aware of the brokenness of this world. With shattered hearts fixed on Christ, they can't help but be intently focused on the hope of eternity. We are an eagerly waiting people. Like a young child waiting for Christmas, the certainty of our hope compels us to speak repeatedly and enthusiastically about it.

Eternally Focused and Fruitfully Laboring

> For momentary, light affliction is producing for us an eternal weight of glory far beyond all comparison, while we look not at the things which are seen, but at the things which are not seen; for the things which are seen are temporal, but the things which are not seen are eternal. (2 Cor. 4:17-18)

On occasion, some will argue that it is possible to be too focused on eternity, yet Scripture is continually pointing us toward eternity. Our hope is hinged on eternity. Our focus on eternity renders us neither useless nor unfruitful. On the contrary, a biblically proper eternal focus stirs within our souls an urgency for the spread of the gospel and the purification of the church.

> For to me, to live is Christ and to die is gain. But if [I am] to live [on] in the flesh, this [will mean] fruitful labor for me; and I do not know which to choose. But I am hard-pressed from both [directions,] having the desire to depart and be with Christ, for [that] is very much better; yet to remain on in the flesh is more necessary for your sake. Convinced of this, I know that I will remain and continue with you all for your progress and joy in the faith" (Phil. 1:21-25)

For those with precious loved ones who have gone ahead, there is a clear recognition that physical death is imminent, and eternity is uniquely tangible. As a result, with each beat of our hearts we urgently long for the effective spread of the gospel, the salvation of souls, revival, and the discipleship of believers. Like Paul, our longing to be with Christ stirs our commitment to *"number our days aright,"* to be fruitfully used by Him until He comes or calls us home (Psalm 90:12; Phil 1:22).

Not Silenced

> But you are A CHOSEN RACE, A royal PRIESTHOOD, A HOLY NATION, A PEOPLE FOR [God's] OWN POSSESSION, so that you may proclaim the excellencies of Him who has called you out of darkness into His marvelous light (1 Pet. 2:9)

The Psalmists were not silent in their waiting and, unless God is impressing upon us to be silent, we should not be either. Our trials and tribulations may drag on and on, and our testimonies may be echoes of the same truths over and over again, but we should continue to testify nonetheless.

Our testimonies are not for everyone. Those who complain about our testimonies dragging on and on reveal by their response that our testimonies are not for them.

We are commanded to comfort others with the comfort we ourselves have received (2 Cor. 1:3-4). I find deep satisfaction and joy in my testimony of God's faithfulness and provision being of comfort or encouragement to others. But our testimonies are not ultimately for those encouraged by them, either.

The sharing of our personal testimonies is an offering of praise and worship to our God. Our unceasing proclamation of His eternal truths, gracious provision, sanctifying work, sustaining power, and eternal hope is part of the fulfillment of our calling to: *"proclaim the excellencies of Him who has called you out of darkness into His marvelous light."* Our cries of *"How Long?"* are our expressions of believing, trusting, and desiring Him above all else.

> And when they had summoned them, they commanded them not to speak or teach at all in the name of Jesus. But Peter and John answered and said to them, "Whether it is right in the sight of God to give heed to you rather than to God, you be the judge; for we cannot stop speaking about what we have seen and heard. (Acts 4:18-20)

Like Peter and John, we should be unable to stop *"speaking about what we have seen and heard."* May we each faithfully and urgently wait for Him, relentlessly clinging to the promise that, *"In just a little while, He who is coming will come and will not delay"* (Heb. 10:37). May we be found continually praising, testifying, and crying out in unison with the Psalmists who have gone before us, and the saints beneath the altar, *"How long, Sovereign Lord?"* (Rev. 6:10).

Come, Lord Jesus.

And we know that in all things God works for the good of those who love Him

A SWORD PIERCED SOUL

DECEMBER 9, 2019

"And Simeon blessed them and said to Mary His mother, "Behold, this Child is appointed for the fall and rise of many in Israel, and for a sign to be opposed–and a sword will pierce even your own soul–to the end that thoughts from many hearts may be revealed." Luke 2:34-35

Reading through Luke this week, verse 35 of chapter 2 struck me. In the past, I've been so focused on the prophecy regarding Christ that I more or less read past what was spoken to Mary. This time, however, as I read *"a sword shall pierce even your own soul,"* I intimately knew and felt the deep searing pain of a mother bearing the death of her beloved child.

Precious Mary, she who found favor with God and had responded in complete humble surrender to Him, having said of herself, *"Behold, the bondslave of the Lord; may it be done to me according to your word"* (Luke 1:30, 38). Her favor with God, her humble surrender, and her obedience to Him led directly to her soul being pierced by a sword.

The day before my child was killed I sat wrestling in prayer with the choice to place her on that bus the next day. With palms lifted open to the heavens I prayerfully entrusted her to God, praying Psalm 91 over her. In the months since Sarah left, I have struggled with jealously resenting the account of Abraham and Isaac. I, too, placed my child on the altar, but God did not stay the knife. Though I rejoice in the confidence that my child yet lives, I continually bear the soul-piercing sorrow of her physical death on the altar of that bus.

My sword pierced soul finds comfort and courage in the example of precious Mary. I long to have her humble servant's heart to respond to each and every life circumstance in full surrender, *"Behold, the bondslave of the Lord; may it be done to me according to your word."* I long to have a gentle and quiet spirit like that of Mary who *"treasured"* the prophecies and truths of Christ, *"pondering them in her heart"* (Luke 2:19). And I long to walk as righteously and faithfully as Mary in the painful absence of her child. With a sword pierced soul, she was found of one mind with the disciples continually devoting herself to prayer (Acts 1:14).

I praise God for the death of Mary's child, and more so for the resurrection of Mary's child. That which caused the sword piercing pain of Mary's soul is also that which He used to shine His light *"upon those who sit in darkness and the shadow of death, to guide our feet into the way of peace"* (Luke 1:79). Praise God that through the atoning work of Christ Jesus, we no longer sit hopelessly in the shadow of death.

We who believe are tenderly cared for by the Good Shepherd who, through His death, burial, and resurrection, has enabled us to confidently say, *"Even though I walk through the valley of the shadow of death, I fear no evil, for You are with me; Your rod and Your staff, they comfort me"* (Ps. 23:4).

We are pilgrims on a journey—though part of our journey may be through the valley of the shadow of soul-piercing death—we will emerge *"in just a little while"* to the dawning of the Bright Morning Star who will forever cast out death and its shadow (Heb. 10:37; 2 Pet. 1:19; Rev. 22:16).

Until that glorious day, we, too, can faithfully journey like Mary: Praising Him all along the way for He has promised to be with us and to faithfully *"guide our feet into the way of peace"* with His rod and His staff, *"for He Himself is our peace"* (Eph. 2:14). And He will strengthen us to walk in that peace *"with all power, according to His glorious might, for the attaining of all steadfastness and patience"* enabling us to *"joyously give thanks to the Father, who has qualified us to share in the inheritance of the saints in Light"* (Col. 1:11-12).

> Now the God of peace, who brought up from the dead the great Shepherd of the sheep through the blood of the eternal covenant, [even] Jesus our Lord, equip you in every good thing to do His will, working in us that which is pleasing in His sight, through Jesus Christ, to whom [be] the glory forever and ever. Amen. (Heb. 13:20-21)

Come, Lord Jesus.

I heard my Savior say
thy strength indeed is small
Child of weakness
WATCH AND PRAY
find in me thine all in all
~ JESUS PAID IT ALL

NOT A HAPPY BIRTHDAY

DECEMBER 20, 2019

This morning I feel the full weight of sorrow. Through the still of the night last night, I tearfully sat awake in our living room gazing at six carefully hung stockings gently illuminated by the light of the Christmas tree. I was awake remembering December 20, 1999, each December 20th since, and a myriad of memories in between.

Today is Sarah Lauren Harmening's birthday. If she were here she would be twenty years old, but she's not here. For a variety of reasons I don't believe earthly birthdays matter to those in heaven, so I don't envision her celebrating her birthday today. Those feelings and thoughts combined leave me sitting here sort of dreading hearing "happy birthday" spoken of her today.

The reality is today is not a happy birthday. A happy birthday would be me wrapping her birthday gifts and seeing her slightly furrowed brow of disapproval if I failed to wrap her gifts in something other than Christmas wrap. I would be busily fixing some of her favorite foods for a big family dinner tonight. Her chosen menu would likely consist of taco soup and sausage dip, although spaghetti and Texas Toast would certainly be an option. We would have to have Dr. Pepper to drink, but no ice for her. And for dessert, most definitely a homemade fudge cake and Blue Bell ice cream.

We would sing to her and watch her blow out all twenty flaming candles, and we would be filled with anticipation of what her twenty-first year would hold. As I imagine her beaming after blowing out those candles I am suddenly jarred from the pleasantries of my imagining as I realize I am not seeing twenty-year-old Sarah in my mind's eye, I am seeing seventeen-year-old Sarah. I will never see twenty-year-old Sarah, and my mind is incapable of fabricating any other Sarah than the Sarah I intimately know and love.

Sarah is not here for her birthday today, so for me today is a sorrowful birthday. I feel the full weight of sorrow today. Though our culture, particularly religious culture, pressures me to believe feeling sorrowful today is wrong, I'm comforted by my confidence in the knowledge that it is not wrong. It is never biblically wrong to feel the ramifications and weight of sorrow and death in this world. It is completely appropriate to feel sorrowful at the absence of our loved ones and the brokenness of this world.

Deep sorrow is actually a powerful impetus for properly fixed hope. The ever-present painful sting of Sarah's absence is a continual reminder that all my hope must be fixed completely on the promised and certain hope of Christ's return. All other points of hope will eventually disappoint and fail, but hope fixed on the grace to be brought to us at the revelation of Jesus Christ will never disappoint or fail.

> Therefore, prepare your minds for action, keep sober [in spirit,] fix your hope completely on the grace to be brought to you at the revelation of Jesus Christ. (1 Pet. 1:13)

Our adversary is masterfully scheming to lull all humanity into complacency and damnation. To do so he must prevent us from thinking about suffering, sorrow, death, and the brevity of this life. Such things strip away all false and temporal hopes leaving only Jesus Christ and the eternal hope He is freely offering. Sorrow shaming is yet another scheme of our deceitful foe intent on devouring souls.

> Be alert and of sober mind. Your enemy the devil prowls around like a roaring lion looking for someone to devour. (1 Pet. 5:8 NIV)

I am not thankful for the source of my sorrow, Sarah's death. However, I am exceedingly thankful for how God is redemptively using my sorrow daily. My sorrow ultimately keeps me hopeful. Although today is not a happy birthday for me, it is very much a hopeful birthday. Being hopeful is of far greater value and worth than being happy. Happy comes and goes with happenstance, but hope fixed on Jesus Christ creates an unquenchable inner joy that perseveres even through the flames of deepest sorrow.

With an aching in my heart and glistening trails of tears on my cheeks, I don't feel happy this morning. But, praise God, by His grace I am hopeful and joyful. This aching heart is firmly anchored by and to the hope of Him who holds eternity. On this side of eternity, tears will continue to flow today and countless other days yet to come, but, praise God, they are and always will be in the sweet company of His everlasting hope.

> Because God wanted to make the unchanging nature of his purpose very clear to the heirs of what was promised, he confirmed it with an oath. God did this so that, by two unchangeable things in which it is impossible for God to lie, we who have fled to take hold of the hope set before us may be greatly encouraged. We have this hope as an anchor for the soul, firm and secure. It enters the inner sanctuary behind the curtain, where our forerunner, Jesus, has entered on our behalf. He has become a high priest forever, in the order of Melchizedek. (Heb. 6:17-20 NIV)

FLEEING FOR REFUGE

DECEMBER 27, 2019

Christmas Eve, we attended our church's Christmas Eve worship service. We arrived early and had a bird's eye view of the entire evening as we sat perched on the back row of the risers. We watched as family after family filed in together, complete families delightfully celebrating their time together. Those we spoke to greeted us with beaming smiles and heartily shared greetings of "Merry Christmas!" It was a beautiful service full of festive celebration of the birth of Christ.

As the gleeful celebration progressed I knew I was in trouble. I was filled with longing for someone to acknowledge the gaping hole in our family, to not pretend that Sarah had never existed and that we were not painfully missing her. Tears began to well. Recognizing it was unavoidable, I allowed them to flow while taking the Lord's Supper. But as the end of the service drew near I urgently employed my best efforts to stifle them. I successfully regained control just as the service concluded.

Immediately after the conclusion of the service everyone began joyfully mingling again. I barely had control of my tears and immediately realized I was in a terrible predicament. To exit I was going to have to walk through all of them with countless gay happy greetings of "Merry Christmas!" to which a like response is expected. My heart raced as I felt my grip on the sorrow slipping. A warm stream of tears quickly turned to sobbing. In desperate need of an escape, the "no exit" stairwell behind me caught my eye and I quickly fled there.

> …he guaranteed it with an oath, so that… we who have fled for refuge might have strong encouragement to hold fast to the hope set before us. (Heb. 6:17-18 ESV)

As I have been meditating on Hebrews 6 over the past week, the phrase *"we who have fled for refuge"* resonated deeply within my heart. Prior to Sarah's departure, I had experienced loss and heartache but nothing that would have enabled me to truly identify with the raw desperation of one who has literally *"fled for refuge."*

Since Sarah's departure, I find myself in a somewhat continual state of fleeing for refuge. The crushing weight of sorrow has not lifted. The void of Sarah's absence and the resulting painful aching of missing and longing for her presence remain constant.

> …Be merciful to me, O God, be merciful to me, for in you my soul takes refuge; in the shadow of your wings I will take refuge, till the storms of destruction pass by. (Ps. 57:1 ESV)

Over the past two and a half years I have learned valuable skills for navigating daily life amid the sorrow. I have learned to recognize and avoid certain triggers, to quickly take thoughts captive, to fix my focus on eternity and the hope set before me, and to allow myself specific times for the sorrow to overflow.

I was optimistic that this Christmas those acquired skills would render me better able to navigate the many traditions and events that shine like spotlights on the void of her absence. For the most part, I think that was true, I was better able to navigate it. But in hindsight, I realize I had a false expectation of that skillful navigating preventing the moments of crushing sorrow when in reality it only puts them off to another time and place.

> My soul, wait in silence for God only, For my hope is from Him. He only is my rock and my salvation, My stronghold; I shall not be shaken. On God my salvation and my glory [rest;] The rock of my strength, my refuge is in God. Trust in Him at all times, O people; Pour out your heart before Him; God is a refuge for us. Selah. (Ps. 62:5-8)

So once again I find myself reminded that the weight of sorrow and the pain of aching and longing will remain indefinitely, and I am powerless beneath them. God alone can bear them for me, shouldering them and upholding me beneath them with His righteous right hand. There is no satisfaction, reprieve, or relief apart from Him.

> Do not fear, for I am with you; Do not anxiously look about you, for I am your God. I will strengthen you, surely I will help you, Surely I will uphold you with My righteous right hand. (Isa. 41:10)

In the midst of this, I find myself thankful for the realization that my sorrow works in me like the thorn in Paul's flesh. The sorrow does not create my weakness, it simply exposes it. I have always been powerless to save myself and in desperate need of a Savior, but the ease of life prior to Sarah's death buffered my perception of the desperation of my need. Through sorrow's revealing of my weakness, I am actually made strong. As I flee to Him for refuge, His power and strength are manifested in me as He strengthens me *"with all power according to His glorious might"* (Col. 1:11).

> Concerning this I implored the Lord three times that it might leave me. And He has said to me, "My grace is sufficient for you, for power is perfected in weakness." Most gladly, therefore, I will rather boast about my weaknesses, so that the power of Christ may dwell in me. (2 Cor. 12:8-9)

The omnipotent God of the universe knows and reminds us of our weakness and frailty, *"He is mindful that we are but dust"* (Ps. 103:14). He has clearly revealed through His word that we are incapable of bearing up under the unbearable weight of sin, sorrow, suffering, and death. He is actively beckoning us to flee to Him for refuge.

> Behold, I stand at the door and knock; if anyone hears My voice and opens the door, I will come in to him and will dine with him, and he with Me. (Rev. 3:20)

He who is incapable of lying has guaranteed with an oath the certainty of the hope of eternity for those who flee to Him for refuge. He graciously and lovingly reminds us of His unchangeable character and the certainty of His promises in order to provide us with *"strong encouragement to hold fast to the hope set before us."*

Praise God that through Him and Him alone—victory is found in fleeing, strength is found in weakness, and hope is found in the midst of hopelessness.

Come, Lord Jesus.

> So when God desired to show more convincingly to the heirs of the promise the unchangeable character of his purpose, he guaranteed it with an oath, so that by two unchangeable things, in which it is impossible for God to lie, we who have fled for refuge might have strong encouragement to hold fast to the hope set before us. We have this as a sure and steadfast anchor of the soul, a hope that enters into the inner place behind the curtain, where Jesus has gone as a forerunner on our behalf, having become a high priest forever after the order of Melchizedek. (Heb. 6:17-20 ESV)

COMFORTED AND COMFORTING

JANUARY 15, 2020

This morning I sent a text message to my daughters and husband as I frequently do. Each and every time I enter their names I feel the sting of leaving Sarah's off. Today as I felt it I refused to leave her off. I entered her name and began reading our previous messages. Normally, I would not allow myself such an indulgence, knowing it comes at a great cost, but today my open schedule accommodated my desperation for her. Reading each message I slowly scrolled backward in time. Laughter and tears once again joined as I "heard" her quirky sense of humor, and my heart longed all the more for her presence.

Today is just a Wednesday. It's not a holiday or special day or date for my family and me. It's not the first week, month, or year without her here. It is the 951st day, and tomorrow will be 136 weeks of living in her absence. Nonetheless, I find myself unable to push away the ever-beckoning arms of memories and sorrow today.

> Blessed [be] the God and Father of our Lord Jesus Christ, the Father of mercies and God of all comfort, who comforts us in all our affliction so that we will be able to comfort those who are in any affliction with the comfort with which we ourselves are comforted by God. For just

as the sufferings of Christ are ours in abundance, so also our comfort is abundant through Christ. (2 Cor. 1:3-5)

But in the midst of this, I rejoice. I was meditating earlier this week on 2 Corinthians 1 and it immediately came to mind this morning as sorrow gripped me. It is only through the abundance of my sorrow that I have been enabled to experience the abundance of God's comfort. There is an intimacy that comes only in the midst of suffering, the intimacy of comforting and being comforted. I know Him more intimately because of my sorrow, and in that, I greatly rejoice.

> But if we are afflicted, it is for your comfort and salvation; or if we are comforted, it is for your comfort... (2 Cor. 1:6)

More than that, I rejoice in the knowledge that my sorrow is not fruitless. There is a redeeming of our affliction as it combines with His gracious comfort. Through the receiving of His comfort, our affliction has the potential for exceeding fruitfulness. He comforts us in *"all our affliction"* so that we will be able to comfort those who are in *"any affliction"* with the comfort with which we ourselves are comforted by Him. His comfort is desperately needed in this fallen world and, by His design, our personal testimonies of affliction and our received comfort are effective for the comforting of others.

> ...if we are comforted, it is for your comfort, which is effective in the patient enduring of the same sufferings which we also suffer (2 Cor. 1:6)

I also find tremendous encouragement in a specific understanding of His comfort provided in this passage. His comfort is not a promised removal of our affliction, suffering, sorrow, or pain. His comfort is His effective enabling of patient endurance in the midst of suffering. The fact that I am not cured of my sorrow is not a sign of my failing to receive His comfort. On the contrary, His Word makes it clear that *"patient enduring"* in the midst of suffering is the mark of having received His comfort.

So this morning with tears and rejoicing I echo Paul and Timothy saying, *"Blessed be the God and Father of our Lord Jesus Christ, the Father of mercies and God of all comfort. who comforts us in all our affliction."*

Come, Lord Jesus.

> THE MOST Beautiful THINGS IN THE WORLD cannot be seen or touched THEY MUST BE FELT with the Heart
> — HELEN KELLER

PRAY BELIEVING

FEBRUARY 7, 2020

"Truly I say to you, whoever says to this mountain, 'Be taken up and cast into the sea,' and does not doubt in his heart, but believes that what he says is going to happen, it will be [granted] him. 'Therefore I say to you, all things for which you pray and ask, believe that you have received them, and they will be [granted] you'" Mark 11:23-24

I routinely stumble across articles and memes proclaiming God will give us anything we desire and ask of Him *if we believe without doubt that He will*. Name it, claim it, believe it, and you are guaranteed it. I generally dismiss that notion without any struggle, confident that it is not the message of the totality of Scripture.

However, This week I was exposed to it in a different form that was more difficult to slough off. As a result, I found myself wrestling at length with the unwelcome idea that Sarah's life was not physically saved because as I pleaded with God for her safety I had not done so fully believing she would be kept physically safe. In other words, my failure to fully believe my requests for her physical safety would be granted resulted in her not being kept safe.

My mind knew this belief was not theologically correct, but my shattered heart was vulnerable to it, and it pierced with the searing pain of a flaming arrow. Consequently, I've spent the better part of the week wrestling through Scripture to regain confidence in what is and is not biblical truth.

With a disturbed and aching heart, I cried out to God pleading with Him to show me His truths and grant me His peace. He immediately brought to mind Christ in the Garden before the crucifixion. Specifically, He reminded me of Christ's words: *"Father, if You are willing, remove this cup from Me; yet not My will, but Yours be done"* (Luke 22:42).

The day before Sarah left I was deeply unsettled about her trip. I spent hours that day pleading with God to protect her. But beyond that, I simultaneously spent that time crucifying my flesh, entrusting her to Him, and asking Him to use our family however He saw fit for His glory.

When I prayed the day before Sarah died I did not pray believing that God would keep her physically safe. I did not claim her physical safety in the name of Jesus Christ. I did, however, pray confidently knowing that God is all-powerful and perfectly capable of keeping her physically safe. Far more important than that, I prayed knowing beyond any shadow of doubt that God would preserve her soul regardless of what happened to her physically.

I did not pray believing in a specific temporal outcome, but I prayed wholly believing and trusting in the One who determines the outcome. I pled for my will to be done but then surrendered mine to His.

Many who advocate boldly claiming specific things in the name of Jesus view the idea of praying and presenting requests to God with, "if it be Your will," as a cop-out. They deem it a safety net for those who don't truly believe that God will answer or grant their requests. If that is the case, Jesus Christ himself is lumped with us in the cop-out camp: *"Remove this cup from Me; yet not My will, but Yours be done."*

There are requests we can confidently make and claim as guaranteed in prayer. Those are the requests that are found in the revealed promises of His Word. Temporal requests such as those for physical needs, physical healing, and physical safety are not promised to be granted. But the weightier more valuable requests, the ones focused on our spiritual security and eternal hope, are guaranteed.

> For as many as are the promises of God, in Him they are yes; therefore also through Him is our Amen to the glory of God through us. (2 Cor. 1:20)

> These things I have spoken to you, so that in Me you may have peace. In the world you have tribulation, but take courage; I have overcome the world. (John 16:33)

Maclaren clarified this when he wrote, "Wherever a distinct and unmistakable promise of God's goes, it is safe for faith to follow; but to outrun His word is not faith, but self-will…"[1] Wiersbe similarly wrote, "Nor should we interpret Mark 11:24 to mean, 'If you pray hard enough and *really believe*, God is obligated to answer your prayer no matter what you ask.' That kind of faith is not faith in God; rather it is nothing but faith in faith, or faith in feelings."[2]

I have compassion for those who believe the "name it and claim it" false teaching. I can see why they have fallen victim to it. Multiple references used out of context can easily be used to support it, including Mark 11:23-24. Context is vital to the formation of our beliefs, as well as interpreting Scripture with Scripture. We must be diligent in considering important factors such as who each passage was spoken to and if it was addressing spiritual matters or temporal desires. Our beliefs must be shaped by the totality of Scripture and not by individual passages plucked and elevated above others.

May we all with confidence continue to present our requests before Him, not believing in a specific temporal outcome, but wholly believing and trusting in Him, the One who determines the outcome. May we do so confidently knowing His peace that passes understanding will prevail regardless of the outcome or circumstances because *"as many as are the promises of God, in Him they are yes"* (2 Cor. 1:20).

> Be anxious for nothing, but in everything by prayer and supplication with thanksgiving let your requests be made known to God. And the peace of God, which surpasses all comprehension, will guard your hearts and your minds in Christ Jesus. (Phil. 4:6-7)

He who promises to never leave and never forsake, to strengthen, sustain, empower, and uphold, and to grant peace and courage, is faithful and true and cannot lie. And praise be to Him, He is coming again *"in just a little while"* and *"He will wipe every tear from [our] eyes. There will be no more death or mourning or crying or pain"* (Heb 10:37; Rev 21:4).

Come, Lord Jesus.

> Pray, then, in this way: Our Father who is in heaven, Hallowed be Your name. Your kingdom come. Your will be done, On earth as it is in heaven. Give us this day our daily bread. And forgive us our debts, as we also have forgiven our debtors. And do not lead us into temptation, but deliver us from evil. For Yours is the kingdom and the power and the glory forever. Amen. (Matt. 6:9-13)

---

1. Maclaren, Alexander. "The Omnipotence of Faith (Mark 9:23)." *Blue Letter Bible.* blueletterbible.org/comm/maclaren_alexander/expositions-of-holy-scripture/mark/the-omnipotence-of-faith.cfm
2. Guzik, David. "Study Guide for Mark 11." *Blue Letter Bible.* blueletterbible.org/Comm/archives/guzik_david/StudyGuide2017-Mar/Mar-11.cfm

GRIEVING TOO LONG

FEBRUARY 20, 2020

I've been reading through Genesis again recently and noticed a phrase this week that I had missed in previous readings. Israel (Jacob) has just been told by his sons that his beloved son Joseph, whom he had presumed dead, is actually alive and he will soon see him again. God's Word records that in response to this news *"the spirit of their father Jacob revived"* (Gen. 45:27).

> They told him, saying, "Joseph is still alive, and indeed he is ruler over all the land of Egypt." But he was stunned, for he did not believe them. When they told him all the words of Joseph that he had spoken to them, and when he saw the wagons that Joseph had sent to carry him, the spirit of their father Jacob revived. Then Israel said, "It is enough; my son Joseph is still alive. I will go and see him before I die." (Gen. 45:26-28)

I believe Albert Barnes rightly commented on this text, "He is satisfied. His only thought is to go and see Joseph before he dies. A sorrow of twenty-two years' standing has now been wiped away."[1] His love for his beloved Joseph had continued and the reviving of his

GRIEVING TOO LONG

spirit at the news that he would soon see him again testifies that his sorrow at Joseph's absence had continued as well. In his spirit, he had borne the weight of the sorrow of Joseph's absence for twenty-two years.

Even after the reviving of his spirit and his reunion with Joseph, upon meeting Pharaoh he described the days of his life as having been unpleasant or, more literally translated, "evil" (Gen. 47:9). That description was almost undoubtedly heavily shaped by the grief of his twenty-two-year separation from Joseph, as well as the loss of his favored wife, Rachel, in childbirth.

> Pharaoh said to Jacob, "How many years have you lived?'" So Jacob said to Pharaoh, "The years of my sojourning are one hundred and thirty; few and unpleasant have been the years of my life, nor have they attained the years that my fathers lived during the days of their sojourning." (Gen. 47:8-9)

It's not uncommon to hear concerns expressed that someone may be "grieving too long." I've been privy to several such conversations recently. The behavior that aroused concern in those instances was not a failure to function, such as staying in bed or not caring for themselves or their remaining family. The individuals being described were actively living life. The behavior that was cited as concerning was their continuing to speak about their loved one and sharing that the sorrow of their loved one's absence still remains. In each situation, the conversation about grieving too long was concluded with the concerned individual imploring the need for the grieving person to "let it go" or "move on."

Those disappointingly common statements raise many questions: How long is too long? What exactly are they supposed to let go of or move on from? What is the acceptable timeframe to miss one's loved one? Moving on can't simply mean living life, because they are undeniably already doing that, so it must mean something more, but what?

Moving on and letting go both carry the same implication of

leaving behind, so is the expectation that they are to leave their loved one in the past? Could the expectation be that they should stop remembering and loving their loved one?

Regardless of how you define or clarify those statements they invariably remain exceedingly peculiar, unrealistic, and inappropriate expectations, particularly when the concerned individual is a professing follower of Jesus Christ.

For most, if not all believers who have lost someone precious to them, the hope of seeing that loved one again is second only to their hope of seeing their God and Savior. My hope of being reunited with Sarah and spending eternity with our family once again intact is second only to my hope of seeing my Lord and God face to face and spending eternity with Him. With the same degree of certainty, both will happen and I am eagerly anticipating both. Until that day I will continue to long for Sarah's presence and bear a weight of sorrow in her absence.

For we who have loved deeply and lost temporally, the longing for the presence of our loved one and the sorrow of their absence is grief. That longing and sorrow of grief is the weight that Israel had borne for twenty-two years. Upon hearing the news that he would soon see his beloved son again, Israel's twenty-two-year-long grief was suddenly lifted resulting in the reviving of his spirit.

I often think of families with loved ones deployed, and how our hearts ache for theirs as the days of their separation tick by. As days turn to weeks, weeks turn to months, and months turn to a year or perhaps even years, we agonize with them as they increasingly long for their reunion day. The same is true for us who believe and are separated by physical death from our loved ones. We are longing for that impending reunion day and that longing only increases with time—it does not decrease.

Unlike Israel, we have the profound blessing of living on this side of Calvary. We have the tremendous hope of knowing death is defeated and will one day be destroyed (1 Cor. 15:26, 55-58). We know through faith in Christ Jesus and His shed blood and resurrection that we have the hope of eternity with our loved ones who also believe. Our spirits are revived in part now because we know with certainty that glorious reunion day is coming, but they will not be fully revived, or relieved of the weight of sorrow until that day actually dawns.

Praise God that His Word makes it clear that there is no sin or shame in our ongoing sorrow at the painful ramifications of sin and death in our lives and this world (Ecc. 7:2; James 4:9-10). He doesn't require us to muster a stiff upper lip or stifle or dry our own tears. There is no condemnation for our sorrow or our tears. On the contrary, we are encouraged by His Word, *"Those who sow in tears shall reap with joyful shouting. He who goes to and fro weeping, carrying [his] bag of seed, Shall indeed come again with a shout of joy, bringing his sheaves [with him.]"* (Ps. 126:5-6).

What glorious encouragement that His Word does not say we should not grieve, and it does not say there is a time limit for grief. We are only told that our grief should not be like those who have no hope (1 Thess. 4:13-14). We who grieve with hope are called to wait eagerly with perseverance.

> But if we hope for what we do not see, with perseverance we wait eagerly for it. (Rom. 8:25)

With eager expectation, we *fix our hope completely on the grace to be brought to us at the revelation of Jesus Christ* (1 Pet. 1:13). *Strengthened with all power according to His glorious might* we are empowered to persevere in trusting, following, and serving Him, with or without tear-streaked faces, knowing that one day soon, *in just a little while,* with great compassion and lovingkindness He personally will permanently wipe every tear from each of our eyes. (Col. 1:11; Rev. 21:3-5).

> And I heard a loud voice from the throne, saying, "Behold, the tabernacle of God is among men, and He will dwell among them, and they shall be His people, and God Himself will be among them, and He will wipe away every tear from their eyes; and there will no longer be [any] death; there will no longer be [any] mourning, or crying, or pain; the

first things have passed away." And He who sits on the throne said, "Behold, I am making all things new." And He said, "Write, for these words are faithful and true." (Rev. 21:3-5)

> *Crying does not indicate that you are weak. Since birth, it has always been a sign that you're alive.*
> — Charlotte Brontë

---

1. Barnes, Albert. *Genesis 45 Barnes' Notes*. (n.d.). biblehub.com/commentaries/barnes/genesis/45.htm

WORSHIP IN AFFLICTION

MARCH 7, 2020

When I think of the Israelites in the exodus from Egypt I confess the first thought that frequently comes to mind is their seemingly constant fear, doubting, grumbling, and turning away. But as I was reading through Exodus again this week I was struck by a beautiful and compelling example set by them.

The affliction of the Israelites in Egypt had peaked, their condition and God's notice of them is described in Exodus 2:23-25.

> During those many days the king of Egypt died, and the people of Israel groaned because of their slavery and cried out for help. Their cry for rescue from slavery came up to God. And God heard their groaning, and God remembered his covenant with Abraham, with Isaac, and with Jacob. God saw the people of Israel–and God knew. (Ex. 2:23-25 ESV)

In response to the cries of the people, God appointed and sent Moses as a messenger and leader for their deliverance. Moses and Aaron went to the people and told them of God's impending deliverance for them, and demonstrated God's hand upon them by the signs

He had designated for them to perform. The response of the Israelites is recorded in Exodus 4:30-31.

> Aaron spoke all the words that the LORD had spoken to Moses and did the signs in the sight of the people. And the people believed; and when they heard that the LORD had visited the people of Israel and that he had seen their affliction, they bowed their heads and worshiped. (Ex. 4:30-31 ESV)

In the midst of their severe affliction, they bowed their heads and worshiped *"when they heard that the LORD had visited the people of Israel and that he had seen their affliction."* They had not yet been delivered, but they had been given the Word that God saw them and He would deliver them. They didn't wait until after deliverance came to bow down and worship. They worshiped in their affliction.

Their worship amid affliction hinged on a powerful statement, though—*"And the people believed."* They were strengthened to worship in the midst of their affliction because they believed Him and His Word to be true.

Throughout Scripture, God is ultimately pointing to Christ and the coming deliverance, redemption, and life available through belief in Him, His shed blood, and resurrection. The recording of this account is no exception.

> For if you believed Moses, you would believe Me, for he wrote about Me. (John 5:46)

Regardless of the depth and longevity of our affliction, our cry for rescue, like that of the Israelites, goes up to God. God hears our groaning. God remembers His covenant with us, His children, through the blood of Jesus Christ. And just as He *saw* the Israelites and *knew* their affliction, God sees us, and God knows our affliction.

More than that, just as the Israelites had been given a promise of God's impending deliverance through Moses and Aaron, we have been given a promise of God's impending deliverance through Christ Jesus.

He is coming back and He will guide us who believe *to springs of living water.* The day is coming when the *"tabernacle of God will be among men, and He will dwell among us, and we shall be His people, and God Himself will be among us."* And on that day God *"will wipe away every tear from our eyes, and death shall be no more, neither shall there be mourning, nor crying, nor pain anymore"* (Rev 7:17; 21:3-4).

In the meantime, we have a choice to make. The Israelites in Exodus demonstrate both options and their outcomes.

Will we believe Him or not?

Believe. Believe Him. Believe Him for His promised deliverance. He is coming and His deliverance is with Him. Believe His promises of His presence, His faithfulness, His compassion, His lovingkindness, His perfect justice, His patience, His righteousness, His daily provision, His new mercies each morning, His sustaining strengthening power, His abundant amazing grace, His intercession on our behalf, and His ever-present never-failing help.

> For as many as are the promises of God, in Him they are yes; therefore also through Him is our Amen to the glory of God through us. (2 Cor. 1:20)

He and His Word are true. By His grace we can and must daily, hour by hour, and moment by moment choose to believe and rest in each and every promise.

Believe. Believe and be moved to worship today. Worship in the midst of affliction because His Word is true, His promises are certain, and His deliverance is coming... *"For, 'In just a little while, he who is coming will come and will not delay'"* (Heb. 10:37).

GOOD FRIDAY AND SIBLINGS DAY

APRIL 10, 2020

Since Sarah's death, each time National Daughters Day and National Siblings Day roll around, I cringe. For me, they highlight the incompleteness of our family and the fact that we will never have any new memories or photos together to share.

When I realized today, Good Friday, was also National Siblings Day my initial reaction was disappointment. It seemed an unfortunate distraction from the greater significance of today, the crucifixion of Jesus Christ.

Almost as quickly as the disappointment washed over me, though, I was gently reminded that because of Good Friday and Resurrection Sunday, the most precious sibling set in my life will one day be complete again.

I am struck by the heaviness of Good Friday, reminded of the incomprehensible weight of sin and sorrow our Savior bore on Calvary. It resonates with the deep sorrow that always flows just below the surface of my heart.

We will never again have a complete sibling set picture because of sin. Sarah's death is the result of sin. God's perfect creation included no death. Apart from sin, there would be no death. Apart from sin, Sarah would be here.

> Therefore, just as through one man sin entered into the world, and death through sin, and so death spread to all men, because all sinned (Rom. 5:12)

So often people point to God's sovereignty in death, and indeed He is sovereign over it, but I think it is much better to point to His grace instead. In His sovereignty, He chose to pour out His grace through the blood of Jesus Christ on Calvary to remove the sting of death from those who will believe.

Our Savior tasted death, saying of Himself in the process, *"My soul is deeply grieved, to the point of death..."* (Matt. 26:38). Yet even in the midst of His deep grief He persevered in surrendering His life for ours.

> ...I came that they may have life, and have [it] abundantly. I am the good shepherd; the good shepherd lays down His life for the sheep. (John 10:10-11)

Because of His incomprehensible love and grace for us, He came, suffered, bled, and died to pay the penalty for our sins. He came to replace death with life, abundant life. Because He came, died, and rose again we can say of those who believe, "they live even if they die."

> ...I am the resurrection and the life; he who believes in Me will live even if he dies. (John 11:25)

My death holds no sting for me because of the price Christ paid at Calvary. As a result, I profess emphatically with Paul *"the desire to depart and be with Christ, for [that] is very much better"* (Phil. 1:23).

But the death of those we love and our separation from them stings deeply. My separation from and longing for Sarah over the past thirty-four months has been a crushing weight that has repeatedly left me tearfully crying out to God, "My soul is deeply grieved, to the point of death."

But even so, in the midst of the missing and sorrow I can joyfully praise God. Because of the suffering and sacrifice of Good Friday and Sarah's faith in Jesus Christ and His finished work, I have the confidence of knowing that she lives even though she died. Because Jesus Christ is my Lord and Savior as well, I also know I will see her again *"in just a little while"* (Heb. 10:37).

In the meantime, in the midst of the continued longing and sorrow, I have my Savior, my gentle Shepherd, my Great High Priest who lives to intercede for me. The One who sees my sorrow, catches my tears, and carries my burdens knows intimately, in a deeper way than I ever will, what it truly means to feel and say *"My soul is deeply grieved, to the point of death."*

> For we do not have a high priest who cannot sympathize with our weaknesses, but One who has been tempted in all things as [we are, yet] without sin. (Heb. 4:15)

I can't post a new sibling photo of my favorite sibling set today, and that makes me sad. But, praise God, because of Good Friday (and Resurrection Sunday), I have the confident overflowing hope of my family once again being complete on a promised and impending glorious reunion day that will last for all of eternity.

> Therefore when Jesus had received the sour wine, He said, "It is finished!" And He bowed His head and gave up His spirit. (John 19:30)

tetelestai

EAGERLY WAITING

APRIL 25, 2020

"And just as it is appointed for man to die once, and after that comes judgment, so Christ, having been offered once to bear the sins of many, will appear a second time, not to deal with sin but to save those who are eagerly waiting for him." Hebrews 9:27-28 ESV

Easter of 2017 is the last day I have vivid cohesive memories with Sarah prior to the week of her death. All the in-between days were normal days that blur together in my mind's eye, but I can clearly remember what that Easter Sunday felt like.

I remember holding the camera as I took her picture that morning, the one now enlarged and hanging in our living room. I remember her not being satisfied with the way her curls were turning, and her rearranging them as I got her to scoot over so we could get the beautiful lavender Iris in the photo with her. I remember sitting at the table and laughing at lunch, and spending the day together.

The next vivid memories I have are the day before she died and, of course, the day of her death. In my mind, Easter memories are immediately followed by the memories from the week of her death. I assume that is the reason the passing of Easter each year has initiated my feeling as though I have entered a steep slide hurling me involuntarily toward Sarah's death.

I was hopeful that perhaps this year would be different. Sadly, in some ways, it is still much the same as the previous two years, though not quite as raw. Over the past two weeks, shared memories and photos from before Sarah's death have continued to bring the joy of seeing her, but they also bring the sharper sting of the unavoidable reliving of the days leading up to her death. I repeatedly find myself tearfully wincing and instantly thinking how blissfully clueless we were as we had no idea what agony was headed our way.

Some who have not experienced such loss might admonish me to simply not think about it, but those who have experienced similar loss recognize the foolishness of such suggestions. The void of our loved one's absence, particularly the absence of one's child, is so cavernous it is impossible to avoid or forget. I am constantly aware of her absence and forever desperate to see her, to touch her, to hug her and hold her, to tell her how much I love her, to see her smile and hear her laugh. She is intimately known and loved by me, and she forever will be. It is that unending love that drives my endless longing to be with her.

I have been convicted since Sarah left that prior to her leaving I failed to love Jesus in the same way.

Though I had surrendered my life to Him many years before and was certainly desiring and striving to live for and honor Him, I realize now the fervor of my love for Him fell short of my love for my children. I was not desperate to see Him face to face. I had much I still wanted to see and do here. Honestly, if given the option I think I would have opted to delay His return so I could see the earthly future I imagined for my family become reality. In truth, I was not *"eagerly waiting for Him,"* I was hoping He would wait for me to see and experience all the things I wanted to see and experience here.

The day Sarah was killed we prayed Romans 8:28 as a family, believing God would indeed work miraculously to bring good from the great agony of her physical death and resulting absence. Though Sarah's physical death was and is not good, He has brought immeasurable good from it. The greatest "good" to emerge in my life from that inferno is the forging of sure and certain hope in my heart, and my sincere and eager longing for Christ's return.

> And we know that God causes all things to work together for good to those who love God, to those who are called according to [His] purpose. (Rom. 8:28)

In the depths of the darkness of the valley of the shadow of death, He has faithfully poured out His new mercies. In His lovingkindness and compassion, He has ministered to my shattered heart day by day. When I felt time and time again as though I would surely drown in the pit of despair, He faithfully upheld me by His righteous right hand.

He has sustained me day by day, and in the process, He set and fortified His unshakable hope in my heart. Experiencing His intimate and unwavering love and care for my family and me in the midst of suffering radically deepened my love for Him, and my desperation for His coming. Because of His great love for us, I am *"eagerly waiting for Him."*

> We love because He first loved us. (1 John 4:19)

In retrospect, I realize before Sarah left my hope was not fully fixed on His coming. Some of my hope was resting on my perceptions or expectations of my family's future. The things I desired were good: seeing my children grow up, get married, and have their own families. But they should not have been, and can not be, the source or place of my hope. He alone is able to securely hold our hope, all of His promises being sure and certain.

While we may look forward to special times here on earth, our hope must remain completely fixed on Him and His eternal promises. Our fixed focus on our glorious eternal future allows us to see beyond the temporal storms of this life, enabling us to confidently weather them all, even the most severe.

> Therefore, prepare your minds for action, keep sober [in spirit,] fix your hope completely on the grace to be brought to you at the revelation of Jesus Christ. (1 Pet. 1:13)

I am not thankful for Sarah's death. I selfishly wish she was still here. But I am exceedingly thankful for God's continuing redemptive use of the resulting suffering to refine and purify me.

> Not only so, but we also glory in our sufferings, because we know that suffering produces perseverance; perseverance, character; and character, hope. And hope does not put us to shame, because God's love has been poured out into our hearts through the Holy Spirit, who has been given to us. (Rom. 5:3-5 NIV)

If you are suffering, I pray you will be encouraged that the God of the universe intimately loves you and is able, willing, and desiring to redemptively use the suffering in your life for good.

Through the flames of suffering, our hearts can be refined, purified, and sanctified, producing within us perseverance, character, and hope rooted and fixed in eternity. He can use the flames to melt away temporal worldly hopes like dross, leaving only the one true hope that will never disappoint. By which we are forged, strengthened, and equipped to wait with perseverance—sorrowfully yet joyfully crying out in eager anticipation with all the saints before and yet to come, "Come, Lord Jesus!"

> We who have fled to take hold of the hope set before us may be greatly encouraged. We have this hope as an anchor for the soul, firm and secure. (Heb. 6:18-19 NIV)

> For in hope we have been saved, but hope that is seen is not hope; for who hopes for what he [already] sees? But if we hope for what we do not see, with perseverance we wait eagerly for it. (Rom. 8:24-25)

HOPE AGAINST HOPE

MAY 19, 2020

*"...In the world you have tribulation, but take courage;
I have overcome the world."* John 16:33

Life can be so very hard in this broken and fallen world. At times it's indescribably hard. No doubt, this is the reason we are repeatedly implored in Scripture to endure, to persevere, to be steadfast and unwavering, to not grow weary, and to wait eagerly.

- For consider Him who has endured such hostility by sinners against Himself, so that you will not grow weary and lose heart. (Heb. 12:3)
- Let us not lose heart in doing good, for in due time we will reap if we do not grow weary. (Gal. 6:9)
- And not only this, but we also exult in our tribulations, knowing that tribulation brings about perseverance (Rom. 5:3)
- But if we hope for what we do not see, with perseverance we wait eagerly for it. (Rom. 8:25)

I long to wait well, but at the same time, I feel my frailty with every breath. I continually bear in my soul the deeply piercing thorn of Sarah's absence. Indeed, God ever so faithfully strengthens me to persevere despite its constant presence. But it renders me uniquely vulnerable to the sting of every other sorrow, hurt, evil, or wrong. Each one is like a hammer tapping the thorn a bit deeper still.

> For He Himself knows our frame; He is mindful that we are [but] dust. (Ps. 103:14)

Paul's words to the Corinthians resonate loudly within my heart, soul, and mind. I, too, *"groan, longing to be clothed instead with our heavenly dwelling, because when we are clothed, we will not be found naked. For while we are in this tent, we groan and are burdened, because we do not wish to be unclothed but to be clothed instead with our heavenly dwelling, so that what is mortal may be swallowed up by life"* (2 Cor. 5:2-4).

As I, in my brokenness, look hopefully to the future, both temporally and eternally, I've often found myself grappling to believe. In weariness I repeatedly whisper to the Lord, *"I do believe, help my unbelief"* (Mark 9:24).

As I was reading through Romans last week, verses 18-21 of chapter 4 jumped off the page at me. In speaking of Abraham, God's Word says, *"In hope against hope he believed... yet, with respect to the promise of God, he did not waver in unbelief but grew strong in faith, giving glory to God, and being fully assured that what God had promised, He was able also to perform."*

"In hope against hope," when all hope logically seemed lost, *"he believed."* But He didn't believe something arbitrarily or randomly hopeful, wishing in uncertainty for something better. He believed *"the promise of God,"* knowing it to be true and certain. He believed that God was *able to perform all that He had promised*, and as he walked *"unwaveringly"* in belief he grew strong in faith.

I am convicted by the unwavering belief of Abraham.

I urgently long to possess the same testimony—*in hope against hope* —believing, growing strong in faith, and giving glory to God. I am challenged anew to cling to the sure and certain promises of God. The confidence and urgency of my prayers are bolstered, *"being fully assured that what God has promised, He is able also to perform."*

"Lord, *I do believe, help my unbelief."*

> I do believe You are compassionate and long-suffering, that You have not and will not weary of consoling me in my sorrow. *"You have kept count of my tossings; put my tears in Your bottle. Are they not in Your book?"* Help my unbelief (Ps. 56:8).
>
> I do believe the deep sorrow and anguish of my heart is but *"momentary, light affliction producing for [me] an eternal weight of glory far beyond all comparison."* Help my unbelief (2 Cor. 4:17).
>
> I do believe that You will powerfully strengthen me to faithfully endure *"with all power, according to [Your] glorious might, for the attaining of all steadfastness and patience."* Help my unbelief (Col. 1:11).
>
> I do believe that *"[You] who began a good work in [me] will perfect it until the day of Christ Jesus."* Help my unbelief (Phil. 1:6).
>
> I do believe that even when I waver, stumble, or fall, your lovingkindness and willingness to forgive and restore me remain constant. *"As high as the heavens are above the earth, So great is [Your] lovingkindness toward those who fear [You]. As far as the east is from the west, So far have [You] removed our transgressions from us."* Help my unbelief (Ps. 103:11-12).
>
> I do believe the time will come when You will *"bring to light the things hidden in the darkness"* and you will *" judge Your people with*

righteousness And Your afflicted with justice." Help my unbelief (1 Cor. 4:5; *Ps. 72:2).*

I do believe there is coming a day when You *"will wipe away every tear from [our] eyes; and there will no longer be [any] death; there will no longer be [any] mourning, or crying, or pain..."* Help my unbelief (Rev. 21:4).

I do believe that *"in just a little while"* You *"will descend from heaven with a shout, with the voice of [the] archangel and with the trumpet of God, and the dead in Christ will rise first. Then we who are alive and remain will be caught up together with them in the clouds to meet [You] in the air, and so we shall always be with [You]."* Help my unbelief. (Heb. 10:36; 1 Thess. 4:16-17)

Amen. Come, Lord Jesus.

> TO PLANT A GARDEN IS TO BELIEVE IN TOMORROW
> — AUDREY HEPBURN

THREE YEARS AGO TODAY

JUNE 7, 2020

I realized a few days ago that I was approaching a very difficult Psalm in my quiet time, Psalm 91. June 7, 2017, the day before Sarah left for her mission trip, never to return, I spent a prolonged amount of time meditating on and praying Psalm 91 over her. Through it, I begged God in His faithfulness to care for and protect my precious child.

I believe it is providential that my daily Scripture reading through the book of Psalms has me reading this exact Psalm three years later to the day, June 7, 2020. When I first realized it was aligning that way I hesitated and considered altering my reading plan. I had felt betrayed by the words of that Psalm in the days and weeks following Sarah's death. The thought of revisiting those feelings made me shudder.

About a month after Sarah's death I mustered the courage to return to Psalm 91 to read and meditate and found peace in a deeper understanding. In "Why Sarah? Why Us?" I wrote about how God adjusted my perspective at that time.[1] Even so, this Psalm still holds a particularly deep sting for me, and likely always will.

Reading Psalm 91 instantly transports me to my screened porch on June 7, 2017. I can feel the warmth of the air that day and the coolness of the metal table beneath my arms as I place my hands on the delicate pages of my Bible to pray that passage over Sarah. I can see her through the porch window sitting safely in the living room in her usual spot, snuggled securely in a nest of blankets, with books scattered about her. With each reading of it I once again feel the emotions of that day, the consuming unsettledness in my spirit, and the pulsing fervor with which I tearfully pled for her protection.

Nonetheless, I chose to trust Him and press forward in my rereading of Psalm 91 on this day, three years later.

Psalm 91

He who dwells in the shelter of the Most High Will abide in the shadow of the Almighty. I will say to the LORD, "My refuge and my fortress, My God, in whom I trust!" For it is He who delivers you from the snare of the trapper And from the deadly pestilence. He will cover you with His pinions, And under His wings you may seek refuge; His faithfulness is a shield and bulwark. You will not be afraid of the terror by night, Or of the arrow that flies by day; Of the pestilence that stalks in darkness, Or of the destruction that lays waste at noon. A thousand may fall at your side And ten thousand at your right hand, [But] it shall not approach you. You will only look on with your eyes And see the recompense of the wicked. For you have made the LORD, my refuge, [Even] the Most High, your dwelling place. No evil will befall you, Nor will any plague come near your tent. For He will give His angels charge concerning you, To guard you in all your ways. They will bear you up in their hands, That you do not strike your foot against a stone. You will tread upon the lion and cobra, The young lion and the serpent you will trample down. "Because he has loved Me, therefore I will deliver him; I will set him [securely] on high, because he has known My name. He will call upon Me, and I will answer him; I will be with him in trouble; I will rescue him and honor him. With a long life I will satisfy him And let him see My salvation."

As I was praying for Sarah's protection three years ago, I asked the

Lord to speak to me and guide me through His Word in my prayers for her. I believed it was He who led me specifically to Psalm 91 as I interceded for her protection. Though I stopped decidedly short of "claiming" her safety (in a prosperity gospel or word of faith manner), I found encouragement in the words of the Psalm and was hopeful for her physical safety.

When I revisited Psalm 91 the month after her death, I saw the eternal significance and hope of the Psalm rather than the temporal hope I had previously clung to. I was encouraged as I focused on the truths eternally applied to her, most importantly that God has finally and permanently delivered Sarah and set her securely on high with Him.

But as I reread it on this date He instantly and profoundly impressed upon my heart that His leading me to Psalm 91, three years ago today, from the beginning was His tender promise of provision for my soon-to-be shattered heart. The number of Sarah's days had been recorded in His book (Ps. 139:16). On June 7, 2017, as I pled for more days, He already knew it was both the day before her last and the day before the melting of my soul.

> My soul melts away for sorrow; strengthen me according to your word! (Ps. 119:28 ESV)

Revisiting Psalm 91 this morning I was moved to tears. As I read each word, phrase, and sentence I realized this is my story; this is my testimony, not by my strength or might, but by His. He has faithfully strengthened me according to His Word over these three years, and in so doing He has made the words of this Psalm the anthem of my soul.

> He who dwells in the shelter of the Most High Will abide in the shadow of the Almighty. I will say to the LORD, "My refuge and my fortress, My God, in whom I trust!" (Ps. 91:1-2)

Death casts a large shadow. The valley of the shadow of death is cold, dark, and lonely. But as I have run to Him for comfort, dwelling in His shelter, drawing near to Him, He has drawn near to me. His shadow has overtaken the shadow of death. Death still stands and casts its shadow for now, but just as the shadow of a larger building standing behind a smaller building overtakes the shadow of the smaller, the shadow of the Almighty now overshadows the shadow of death. He has been ever faithful these three years and like never before He has become *"my refuge and fortress, My God in whom I trust!"*

> For it is He who delivers you from the snare of the trapper And from the deadly pestilence. He will cover you with His pinions, And under His wings you may seek refuge; His faithfulness is a shield and bulwark. (Ps. 91:3-4)

Our adversary's end goal is not temporal. Though he delights in physical destruction and death, his end goal is much more sinister—spiritual death. In the moments after learning Sarah was gone, God clearly impressed upon my heart that Satan had asked to sift us. Satan in the past three years has brilliantly schemed for the spiritual destruction of our nuclear family and each of us individually. We have seen his snares and the dangers of the deadly pestilence, but God has kept His wing about us. In the darkest of days there were times I questioned His presence, but looking back I clearly see His unwavering faithfulness. He has safely delivered our family and me to this day, and He will safely deliver each of us home.

> You will not be afraid of the terror by night, Or of the arrow that flies by day; Of the pestilence that stalks in darkness, Or of the destruction that lays waste at noon. A thousand may fall at your side And ten thousand at your right hand, [But] it shall not approach you. (Ps. 91:5-7)

By His faithfulness and His lifting of my eyes from the temporal to the eternal, He has taught me to not be afraid. Though the terror of night is real, the arrows flying by are sharp, and pestilence and destruction are on every side, they are all incapable of eternal impact.

Certainly, their impact is painful here at this moment, but just as my sweet Sarah said, "We are like a wisp of smoke. We are only here a moment." My soul is eternally sealed and preserved by Him who holds me fast. Therefore, I am not afraid.

> You will only look on with your eyes And see the recompense of the wicked. For you have made the LORD, my refuge, [Even] the Most High, your dwelling place. No evil will befall you, Nor will any plague come near your tent. For He will give His angels charge concerning you, To guard you in all your ways. They will bear you up in their hands, That you do not strike your foot against a stone. You will tread upon the lion and cobra, The young lion and the serpent you will trample down. (Ps. 91:8-13)

There have been so many deeply painful trials in conjunction with Sarah's death; countless tearful nights crying out to Him to intervene and thwart the schemes of the adversary. Through them all He has guarded our hearts and has faithfully kept us from falling. We stand as a family in faith today because He has powerfully ministered to and preserved us. For the past three years, He has continually and faithfully given victory over that serpent of old, the roving lion seeking to devour our souls.

> "Because he has loved Me, therefore I will deliver him; I will set him [securely] on high, because he has known My name. He will call upon Me, and I will answer him; I will be with him in trouble; I will rescue him and honor him. With a long life I will satisfy him And let him see My salvation." (Ps. 91:14-16)

Oh, how I love Him! How can I not? He is so faithful, patient, loving, gracious, merciful, and kind. Through the blood of Christ He has once and for all delivered me. Though I have and will continue to have trouble in this life, He is with me. His faithfulness is my shield and bulwark. My soul confidently and fervently praises Him, knowing in just a little while He will once and for all rescue me. I will live eternally with Him, seeing Him and beholding Him face to face, and my sweet Sarah with Him.

Thank you, Lord, for redeeming, sustaining, delivering, and preserving my family and me. Thank you, Lord, for making Psalm 91 my story and my testimony for your glory.

Come Lord, Jesus.

But he who dares not grasp the thorn should never crave the rose

—ANNE BRONTË

---

1. see "Why Sarah? Why Us?" pp. 35-39.

JOY INEXPRESSIBLE

JULY 18, 2020

*Y*esterday Scott and I had the tremendous blessing of witnessing our daughter, Kristen, enter into the covenant of marriage. As I was lying awake this morning thinking about yesterday and all the days preceding it, 1 Peter 1:8 came to mind.

> And though you have not seen Him, you love Him, and though you do not see Him now, but believe in Him, you greatly rejoice with joy inexpressible and full of glory. (1 Pet. 1:8)

Lying there in silence, as the orange rays of the rising sun pierced the darkness of our room, I was overwhelmed by the graciousness of God. In the quietness of those moments, He whispered to my heart, *"Joy inexpressible and full of glory."* This is it. I am tasting it now. This is joy inexpressible and full of glory.

As everyone slept I quietly slipped into the living room and watched the video of the wedding ceremony, I watched as three of my four daughters and Scott and I walked a stone path in our backyard leading to a swing arbor built for our four daughters ten years ago. I watched as our precious Kristen stood beneath that arbor and entered into a holy covenant with a little boy we have watched become a strong young man after God's heart over those same ten years.

But what I didn't see was Sarah. There was a gaping hole where our sweet Sarah should have walked and stood. Her absence, though a constant painful void, uniquely pierces our hearts in precious life moments like these.

The sharp bitterness of the sorrow and anguish that we feel and taste from Sarah's absence affects our perception of every other moment and experience. Every moment of every day, good and bad is tinged by the sorrow of her absence. Every other sorrow and difficulty amplifies the constant reverberating groan within our souls, but every joy is magnified against that groaning as well.

For many watching the ceremony yesterday, it was likely just another wedding not unlike any other. But as I watched, I saw a breathtaking display of the mighty hand of our righteous God.

I was taken back to June 8, 2017, as Scott and I sat broken and huddled on a hotel bed with Katelyn, Kristen, and Sophie, telling them that, though our hearts were completely shattered at Sarah's absence, we, as their parents, would continue to be fully present with them in their lives. We promised them in those moments that we would rejoice and fully celebrate every life event with them. Though I spoke those words fully meaning them, it was impossible to fathom how we could carry this crushing sorrow and yet simultaneously fully celebrate them.

As I watched the ceremony I saw God's answer to shield, protect, and guide our family through the schemes and attacks of the adversary, and to draw each of us closer to Himself. I saw the rich fruit of His tenderly and faithfully guiding us and of our obediently following Him.

As I watched I saw God's answer to countless nights of pleading for Him to carry us through the darkness and to knit our family tightly together with cords the enemy could not sever.

As I watched the ceremony I saw God's answer for a godly young man who already steadfastly loves and steadily leads our daughter. A godly young man we have fervently prayed for, deeply love, and are thankful to call ours.

As I watched, I saw the righteous right hand of our mighty God: the God who strengthens and sustains, the God who carries and comforts, the God who weeps with us and sings over us, the God who lavishly redeems and restores, the God who is making all things new, and the God who beckons us to look toward our glorious eternal future with Him.

Against the dark backdrop of the anguish and sorrow of Sarah's absence, the celebration of Kristen's and Austin's wedding was a vibrant display of the overwhelming grace, immeasurable mercy, constant faithfulness, and long-suffering lovingkindness of God.

In those precious moments, I kept my promise to be fully present with Kristen and to celebrate and rejoice fully with her.

What I couldn't fathom as we made that promise on June 8, 2017, was that the ongoing deep sorrow of that terrible day would not only not be an impediment to our joy and rejoicing, but it would actually enhance it.

The deep sorrow of Sarah's absence is a constant sanctifying flame, a testing fire, melting away the worthless and causing us to fix our eyes fully on our God and His eternal purposes. Though we have yet to behold Him face to face, we have seen Him. We saw Him yesterday, and today I am basking in that joy, joy tinged with crushing sorrow. A joy rendered by sorrow so deep and precious that it is *"inexpressible and full of glory."*

Reader, I married him.

—JANE EYRE—

PEACE BE WITH YOU

AUGUST 6, 2020

"So when it was evening on that day, the first [day] of the week, and when the doors were shut where the disciples were, for fear of the Jews, Jesus came and stood in their midst and said to them, 'Peace [be] with you.'"
John 20:19

As I was reading through the book of John recently I was struck by the greeting of Jesus to the disciples after His resurrection, *"Peace be with you"* (John 20:19, 21, 26). A common greeting at the time, some readers disregard His use of it as inconsequential. As I consider it against the backdrop of all that had just transpired, though, it becomes clear it is far more than a dismissible common greeting.

In the days between their last meal with Him and this encounter, He had been crucified, died, atoned for the sins of the world, was raised to life again, and defeated death. In that context, His greeting of *"Peace be with you"* is profound. It's an open-handed offer of peace that powerfully prevails regardless of circumstances; a compassionate proclamation of the immediate availability of hope and restoration He stands freely offering through Himself.

Peace be with you:
When your vision for your life is shattered

Not long before this encounter, the disciples were gathered closely around Jesus, the long-awaited Messiah. They knew well the prophecies of Him ruling from the throne of David forever. Surely the restoration of the kingdom of Israel and His visible reigning over it was at hand. As anticipation built, they likely had very clear and hopeful expectations for their earthly future.

But then, in an instant, everything changed. Jesus was seized in the garden, they were scattered, and their expectations and visions for the future were shattered. Jesus had told them what was about to happen, but they didn't understand. *"They did not grasp what was said."*

> And taking the twelve, he said to them, "See, we are going up to Jerusalem, and everything that is written about the Son of Man by the prophets will be accomplished. For he will be delivered over to the Gentiles and will be mocked and shamefully treated and spit upon. And after flogging him, they will kill him, and on the third day he will rise." But they understood none of these things. This saying was hidden from them, and they did not grasp what was said. (Luke 18:31-34 ESV)

I relate so deeply to this. Prior to Sarah's death, I had been closely communing with Jesus, walking with Him daily. Though I embraced my eternal future, I confess my greatest desire was for the future I saw for my family's little earthly kingdom. I could see and almost touch it: my family intact and thriving as they followed Him, my children marrying godly partners, and grandchildren just over the horizon. But then, in an instant, everything changed. Interlocking dreams and expectations painfully fell, shattering at our feet.

> I have said these things to you, that in me you may have peace. In the world you will have tribulation. But take heart; I have overcome the world. (John 16:33 ESV)

> For momentary, light affliction is producing for us an eternal weight of glory far beyond all comparison, while we look not at the things which are seen, but at the things which are not seen; for the things which are seen are temporal, but the things which are not seen are eternal. (2 Cor. 4:17-18)

In retrospect, I realized He had repeatedly warned me through His Word, just as He had the disciples. And I, like them, just didn't understand. I would sing about this world not being my home, but in reality, it was my home. I had forgotten I was just a sojourner here. I had unintentionally allowed part of my hope to rest on the future and well-being of my little earthly kingdom.

> Therefore, prepare your minds for action, keep sober [in spirit,] fix your hope completely on the grace to be brought to you at the revelation of Jesus Christ. (1 Pet. 1:13)

Followers of Christ have in Him a sure and certain future. Hope fixed completely on Him and the grace He will bring at His revelation is unshakable hope. This rightly fixed hope is the anchor of our souls and the source of our peace. This peace prevails and passes all understanding, even in the midst of deep temporal suffering. It is this peace that Christ stood offering the disciples. And He continues freely offering it to each of us today, *"Peace be with you."*

Peace be with you: When you are afraid

The disciples were meeting behind closed doors when Jesus came to them. John 20:19 specifically records that *"the doors were shut where the disciples were, for fear of the Jews."* As their hopes and expectations fell, their fears rose. They were uncertain and afraid. Their fears were justified. Their Lord had just been tortured and crucified, and they were likely to be next.

And yet, as they gathered together in fear and uncertainty, Jesus came to them and greeted them with *"Peace be with you."* He stood before them, having just paid their sin debt and ours, risen from the dead, and having defeated death. He stood before them having secured their eternal future, and the future of all who have and will believe in Him (Acts 16:31).

Though the trials and sorrows of this life are real and painful, they, like this life itself, are but a vapor (Jas. 4:14). We in Christ need not fear, our destination is secure. He is continually with us in the journey, abiding and sustaining, and He will safely lead us home. Look to Him and freely be liberated from fear today. His compassionate offer remains, *"Peace be with you."*

> And do not fear those who kill the body but cannot kill the soul. Rather fear him who can destroy both soul and body in hell. Are not two sparrows sold for a penny? And not one of them will fall to the ground apart from your Father. But even the hairs of your head are all numbered. Fear not, therefore; you are of more value than many sparrows. (Matt. 10:28-31 ESV)

> Peace I leave with you; my peace I give to you. Not as the world gives do I give to you. Let not your hearts be troubled, neither let them be afraid. (John 14:27 ESV)

Peace be with you: When you have failed

As the disciples met behind closed doors that night, shame and disappointment likely loomed alongside the disillusionment and fear they felt. Jesus had predicted they would all fall away and leave Him alone the night He was seized, and it had happened just as He said (Matt. 26:31-35).

Peter bore the tremendous weight of not only falling away but also overtly denying Him. Peter in his fiery love for Jesus had boldly proclaimed he would die with Him before he would deny Him. And yet in the frailty of his flesh, he denied Him, not once but three times, and Jesus knew. After Peter had denied Jesus the third time *"the Lord turned and looked at Peter. And Peter remembered the saying of the Lord, how he had said to him, 'Before the rooster crows today, you will deny me three times.' And he went out and wept bitterly"* (Luke 22:61-62).

I'm optimistic after denying Him and weeping bitterly Peter recalled Jesus' words to him from their last supper together. Jesus had warned Peter that very night that Satan was going to *"sift him."* But that warning was followed with a tremendously hopeful word, Jesus Himself had prayed for Peter, that his faith would not fail. He went on to encourage Peter that when he had *"turned again"* (repented), he should strengthen his brothers.

> "Simon, Simon, behold, Satan has demanded [permission] to sift you like wheat; but I have prayed for you, that your faith may not fail; and you, when once you have turned again, strengthen your brothers." But he said to Him, "Lord, with You I am ready to go both to prison and to death!" And He said, "I say to you, Peter, the rooster will not crow today until you have denied three times that you know Me." (Luke 22:31-34)

Peter's sinful betrayal of Christ took him to the end of himself. He thought he could serve, follow, and stand with Christ in his own strength. Satan's sifting revealed the insufficiency of Peter's sinful self-sufficiency. As His beloved Lord looked upon him in his denial, Peter's eyes were painfully opened to his frailty and depravity. Satan meant it for harm, but God used it for good. Satan's sifting, used by God as a refining flame, sanctified and fortified the faith of Peter.

It is against this backdrop of failure, shame, and sorrow that our compassionate Lord Jesus Christ entered the room with His downcast and fearful disciples. His steadfast love was tenderly displayed as He came to them not with rebukes and chastening in that moment, but freely offering the balm of His prevailing peace.

> For as high as the heavens are above the earth, so great is his steadfast love toward those who fear him; as far as the east is from the west, so

far does he remove our transgressions from us. As a father shows compassion to his children, so the LORD shows compassion to those who fear him. For he knows our frame; he remembers that we are dust. (Ps. 103:11-14 ESV)

He freely offers us this same prevailing peace in the midst of our sins, failures, and brokenness as we turn in repentance toward Him. Just as He prayed for Peter, He is actively praying for those of us who are surrendered to Him. Receive His peace today. He is calling, *"Come to me, all who labor and are heavy laden, and I will give you rest. Take my yoke upon you, and learn from me, for I am gentle and lowly in heart, and you will find rest for your souls. For my yoke is easy, and my burden is light"* (Matt. 11:28-30).

Consequently, he is able to save to the uttermost those who draw near to God through him, since he always lives to make intercession for them. (Heb. 7:25 ESV)

For we do not have a high priest who is unable to sympathize with our weaknesses, but one who in every respect has been tempted as we are, yet without sin. Let us then with confidence draw near to the throne of grace, that we may receive mercy and find grace to help in time of need. (Heb. 4:15-16 ESV)

Peace be with you.

Peace be with you when your vision for your life is shattered.
Peace be with you when you are afraid.
Peace be with you when you have failed.
Peace be with you.

Our peace is not dependent upon our temporal well-being, good or bad circumstances, our courageousness or fearfulness, or our successes or failures. Our peace rests fully on the hope of Jesus Christ. *"For our citizenship is in heaven, from which also we eagerly wait for a*

Savior, the Lord Jesus Christ" (Phil. 3:20). He alone is the source of our unshakable hope and prevailing peace.

> Therefore we do not lose heart, but though our outer man is decaying, yet our inner man is being renewed day by day. For momentary, light affliction is producing for us an eternal weight of glory far beyond all comparison (2 Cor. 4:16-17)

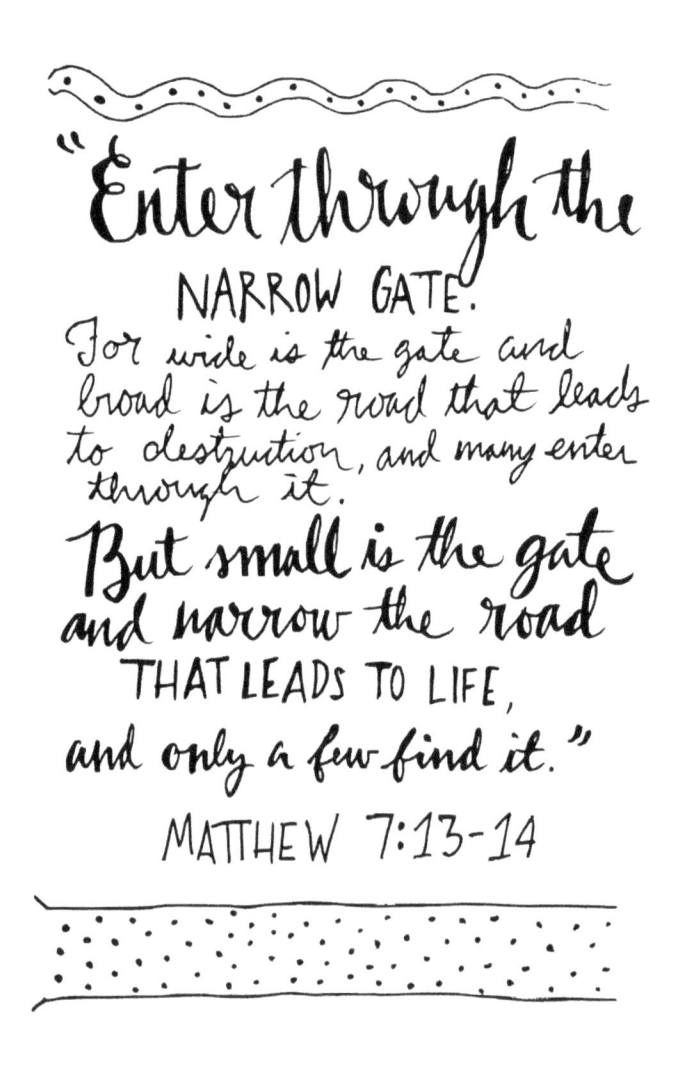

"Enter through the NARROW GATE. For wide is the gate and broad is the road that leads to destruction, and many enter through it. But small is the gate and narrow the road THAT LEADS TO LIFE, and only a few find it."

MATTHEW 7:13-14

FACING DEATH

SEPTEMBER 16, 2020

There's a cemetery just across the street from our house. Until just recently, there was a house across the street in front of the cemetery blocking our view of it. But the house has been removed, so now as I leave my home every day I face the cemetery. It's not just any cemetery, though. It's the cemetery where my seventeen-year-old daughter's body is buried. Now, since the removal of the house, the start of every day for me includes facing her body's grave.

For some, the cemetery is comforting, a place they like to go and remember. That's wonderful, but that's not true of me. I dislike the cemetery. My dislike is not rooted in failure to accept her death or avoidance of death in general. Every moment of every day I am aware of the reality of death. My heart continually bears the painful temporal remains of death's sting, our separation from Sarah.

I dislike the cemetery because seeing her grave invariably transports me back to one of the most excruciating days of my life. So, I rarely go. When I do go, it is raw and painful. The first time I drove down the driveway after they took the house away, my heart was pierced by the painful realization that I would now be forced to face the cemetery at the start of the day, every day, indefinitely.

One morning last week, shortly after my now unavoidable daily routine of facing my child's grave, I heard a song on Christian radio proclaiming, like so many others, God's faithfulness to miraculously deliver us. It linked hope and an absence of fear to His capacity to perform earthly miracles. The song referenced the parting of the sea, walking through fire, and shutting the mouths of lions. Hearing those truths exuberantly sung as a proclamation of hope in miraculous deliverance immediately brought to mind Hebrews 11:37-40.

> They were stoned, they were sawn in two, they were tempted, they were put to death with the sword; they went about in sheepskins, in goatskins, being destitute, afflicted, ill-treated ([men] of whom the world was not worthy), wandering in deserts and mountains and caves and holes in the ground. And all these, having gained approval through their faith, did not receive what was promised, because God had provided something better for us, so that apart from us they would not be made perfect. (Heb. 11:37-40)

Hebrews 11 (vv. 29-34) records each of the miraculous examples of deliverance cited in those song lyrics: the parting of the sea, walking through fire, and shutting the mouths of lions. But they are divinely yoked in Scripture with the equally significant examples of those persecuted and martyred for their faith, listed in the very next verses (vv. 35-38).

I am not thankful for Sarah's death, but I am thankful for the perspective her death has provided. As I face death daily through both the constant void of her absence and facing her grave each morning, I am continually reminded of the temporality of this life and the tremendous hope of the eternal life found in Christ Jesus.

The temporal deliverance He provided and provides in earthly miracles is certainly worthy of our praising Him. But those momentary miracles of deliverance instantly pale in comparison to the miraculous eternal deliverance already secured through the sacrificial death and resurrection of Jesus Christ; the eternal deliverance made freely available to whosoever will believe upon Him.

My certain hope and absence of fear are not found in the idea or hope of miraculously avoiding physical suffering or death here on earth. My certain hope and absence of fear are found in facing the reality and imminence of my physical death—confidently knowing that *"to die is gain"* and to depart and be with Christ is *"very much better"* (Phil. 1:21-23). Through fully facing death I am able to lift my eyes to look just an instant beyond it to the glorious eternity before me in Christ Jesus.

The miracles of temporal deliverance, the parting of the sea, walking through fire, and shutting the mouths of lions, are incredible displays of God's power. But for me, the more inspiring and encouraging displays of God's power are in the verses that follow: the stories of His miraculously sustaining His children to persevere in the absence of deliverance.

In our Christian culture laden with prosperity theology, we must continually be sober and alert to push back against a false gospel that wrongly proclaims promises of guaranteed temporal deliverance from suffering, sickness, and death. It's a lie from the father of lies, a brilliant scheme designed to thwart the salvation of many.

> Yet you do not know what your life will be like tomorrow. You are [just] a vapor that appears for a little while and then vanishes away. (James 4:14)

The prosperity gospel is myopic. It causes its victims to wrongly focus on this life and lose perspective that this life is but a vapor. Those rooted by the seed of a prosperity theology gospel are in grievous peril of becoming *"the ones on whom seed was sown on the rocky places, who, when they hear the word, immediately receive it with joy; and they have no firm root in themselves, but are only temporary; then, when affliction or persecution arises because of the word, immediately they fall away"* (Mark 4:16-17).

Significantly, Scripture says, *"when affliction or persecution arises"* not "if affliction or persecution arises." At some point, most of us, if not all of us, will face flames that will not be extinguished, waters that will not be parted, or lions whose mouths will not be shut. And when that happens, God is faithful still.

> Be of sober [spirit,] be on the alert. Your adversary, the devil, prowls around like a roaring lion, seeking someone to devour. But resist him, firm in [your] faith, knowing that the same experiences of suffering are being accomplished by your brethren who are in the world. After you have suffered for a little while, the God of all grace, who called you to His eternal glory in Christ, will Himself perfect, confirm, strengthen [and] establish you. (1 Pet. 5:8-10)

The miracles He offers in the midst of suffering are just as powerful, if not more so, than the miracles of temporal deliverance. He offers to miraculously strengthen us *"with all power according to His glorious might for the attaining of all steadfastness"* (Col. 1:11). As we fix our eyes and our hope on Him, He will miraculously equip and enable us to persevere in our suffering. He is uniquely *"near to the brokenhearted"* (Ps. 34:18). His intimately ministering to us in the depths of suffering allows us to know and experience Him as never before. As we look to Him, trusting the truths of His promises, He also grants us the incomprehensible miracle of His redemptive power that brings forth beauty after beauty from the ashes of our suffering.

> And we know that God causes all things to work together for good to those who love God, to those who are called according to [His] purpose. (Rom. 8:28)

No doubt temporal deliverance from suffering is a gracious miracle granted by the omnipotent hand of God. But I believe God in Scripture sovereignly linked the accounts of miraculous temporal deliverance with the testimonies of the suffering saints who were miraculously sustained—but not temporally delivered—to remind us His miraculous power as well as His glory are equally displayed in both.

> Beloved, do not be surprised at the fiery ordeal among you, which comes upon you for your testing, as though some strange thing were happening to you; but to the degree that you share the sufferings of Christ, keep on rejoicing, so that also at the revelation of His glory you may rejoice with exultation. (1 Pet. 4:12-13)

It is good and right to remember God is capable of miraculously delivering us from temporal suffering, and it is appropriate to pray for that. But when He does not grant temporal deliverance, we must not be surprised. We must never forget or deny that He, through His Word, has repeatedly forewarned us that we will suffer in this life.

> Indeed, all who desire to live godly in Christ Jesus will be persecuted. (2 Tim. 3:12)

We are absolutely not guaranteed to be delivered from suffering in this earthly life. But with certainty there is coming a day in just a *"very little while"* when we who are found in Him will be finally and gloriously delivered, never to suffer again. So fixing our hope fully on the grace to be brought to us at the revelation of Jesus Christ, we can and should boldly face suffering and death, not as those who shrink back and are fearful, but as those with confident assurance in the glorious hope that awaits us on the other side.

> Therefore, do not throw away your confidence, which has a great reward. For you have need of endurance, so that when you have done the will of God, you may receive what was promised. FOR YET IN A VERY LITTLE WHILE, HE WHO IS COMING WILL COME, AND WILL NOT DELAY. BUT MY RIGHTEOUS ONE SHALL LIVE BY FAITH; AND IF HE SHRINKS BACK, MY SOUL HAS NO PLEASURE IN HIM. But we are not of those who shrink back to destruction, but of those who have faith to the preserving of the soul. (Heb. 10:35-39)

BLESSED MOURNER

OCTOBER 19, 2020

> *"Blessed are those who mourn, for they shall be comforted."*
> Matthew 5:4

Recently I was awake in the middle of the night, unable to sleep, missing Sarah, and thinking about the past forty months. As I was lying there, Matthew 5:4 came to mind and I pondered it at length. Since then it has continued to roll around in my heart and mind.

I vividly remember years ago being taught that the mourning referenced here is specifically and only mourning over our personal sin, not mourning suffering and loss. The argument presented for that view was convincing and I believed it, so much so that I have probably even repeated or taught it at some point.

But as I was lying awake in the still of the night mourning Sarah's absence and our family's loss and suffering, I remembered that teaching and began questioning the validity of its exclusiveness.

Indeed there is a blessedness to mourning over sin, but how disappointingly shortsighted to narrow the application of this precious truth to that alone. In so doing those who mourn over loss and suffering are robbed of the rich hope of the full meaning of this simple yet profound promise.

"Blessed are those who mourn, for they shall be comforted."

Sarah's physical death and the many smaller tragedies surrounding it intimately acquainted me with the gravity of the devastating brokenness and fallenness of this world. Through the agony of mourning, my desire for this world and anything it has to offer has been stripped away. A response repeatedly reinforced by every other tragedy and injustice I see.

Solomon recorded a similar realization in Ecclesiastes 4. *"Then I looked again at all the acts of oppression which were being done under the sun. And behold [I saw] the tears of the oppressed and [that] they had no one to comfort [them;] and on the side of their oppressors was power, but they had no one to comfort [them.] So I congratulated the dead who are already dead more than the living who are still living"* (vv. 1-2).

Unlike Solomon's account, though, I clearly see and know a comforter—the Comforter who longs to comfort. Through my mourning, He has made Himself known, and I am blessed to clearly see and intimately know Him and His comfort.

> Blessed [be] the God and Father of our Lord Jesus Christ, the Father of mercies and God of all comfort, who comforts us in all our affliction so that we will be able to comfort those who are in any affliction with the comfort with which we ourselves are comforted by God. (2 Cor. 1:3-4)

I knew Him and I knew He was a comforter prior to experiencing the depths of sorrow. But I did not truly know and understand the immeasurable magnitude of His comfort until I knew the agony of the deepest depths of sorrow and mourning that require it.

As I plunged deeper and deeper into the depths of sorrow, He proportionately poured out His comfort in a way that profoundly grew my knowledge, understanding, and experience of it and Him.

Through mourning, I know Him in a way I did not, would not, and likely could not know Him apart from mourning. A precious blessedness of intimacy with Him, and trust in Him, is created in the divine colliding of His comfort with our mourning.

"Blessed are those who mourn, for they shall be comforted."

The mourning of my soul in response to Sarah's absence lingers like Paul's thorn. A mother never stops loving and longing for her child. I will always love and long for Sarah and as a result I will mourn her absence until my final breath. But in every moment that I have mourned Sarah's absence, His comfort has faithfully met me there.

Through His proven faithfulness to comfort me in my mourning I am blessed with confidence in the certainty of His faithfulness to continue to comfort me. I will continue to mourn, but He will also continue to comfort me. Though the world will undoubtedly grow weary of comforting me in my mourning, He never will.

"Blessed are those who mourn, for they shall be comforted."

Through mourning my gaze has been lifted and fixed heavenward. My sorrow is a continual reminder that I am just a sojourner here, a stranger in a world not my home. His comfort draws me to Him, to long for Him above all others and all else. My mourning and His comfort cause me to live expectantly, eagerly waiting and longing for Him and His return.

Encouraged by the comfort He has already given, we can be confident in the ultimate comfort yet to come. As He faithfully comforts us in our mourning, by His mercy, grace, and power we are strengthened to fruitfully persevere—comforting others with the comfort He has given. And so our mourning and His comfort work together in us to enable us to boldly and joyfully proclaim the hope and comfort of this great truth: *"Blessed are those who mourn, for they shall be comforted."*

HOPE GRIEVES

DECEMBER 18, 2020

"But we do not want you to be uninformed, brethren, about those who are asleep, so that you will not grieve as do the rest who have no hope. For if we believe that Jesus died and rose again, even so God will bring with Him those who have fallen asleep in Jesus." 1 Thessalonians 4:13-14

The past week my heart has been heavy for multiple reasons, but in large part, it has been the void of Sarah's absence. December 20th would have been her twenty-first birthday. Twenty-one years old, a cultural milestone birthday that has resulted in social media posts of more than a few of her peers celebrating. While I celebrate with each of them, my heart aches from my inability to celebrate with her. In the midst of that aching, I was told there is concern Scott and I are grieving too long.

Daily we are actively living, serving, and celebrating life events with family and friends, so I'm not certain what caused their perception. But if by "grieving" we simply mean that I am continuing to miss Sarah and long for her presence, then I acknowledge that I am still grieving.

The misconception that parents whose children have died should stop grieving their child's absence, and stop within a specified amount of time, is a common one. I was not surprised to hear the words, nor was I offended. But I confess my initial thought was one of self-preservation, to steer clear of all future vulnerability and take a vow of silence regarding the reality of grief. Just as quickly as that thought formed, though, my mind was flooded with the faces of so many journeying this painful path of child loss behind us. So this is for them and all who will follow them.

Missing our children and longing for our reunion with them is not a sin. Missing our children is not an indication we are failing to take hold of the hope of Christ. Hope does not exclude grief. Those who have hope grieve. We who hope in Christ grieve. We, who have all of our hope in its entirety completely and firmly fixed on the grace to be brought to us at the revelation of Jesus Christ, still grieve.

> Therefore, prepare your minds for action, keep sober [in spirit,] fix your hope completely on the grace to be brought to you at the revelation of Jesus Christ. (1 Pet. 1:13)

The hope of Christ has never been more real to me than it is at this very moment. I have never been more certain than I am now of my eternal future and the inconceivable magnitude of what will be delivered to me in that grace. The unrelenting grief of Sarah's death and her ongoing absence has profoundly bolstered my understanding of the reality and certainty of my hope in Jesus Christ.

> For momentary, light affliction is producing for us an eternal weight of glory far beyond all comparison, while we look not at the things which are seen, but at the things which are not seen; for the things which are seen are temporal, but the things which are not seen are eternal. (2 Cor. 4:17-18)

Grief does not diminish my hope, it fortifies it. Grief, if we allow it, is a refining flame. It melts away the dross, enabling us to *"extract the precious from the worthless"* (Jer. 15:19). Grief has rightly shifted my focus from the temporal fully to the eternal. Through my grief, I intimately know and confidently cling to the hope of Jesus Christ like never before. I rejoice in that hope with great joy even as I continue to grieve Sarah's absence.

Conversely, the certainty of that very hope perpetuates my grief. The reality of my hope and my fixed focus on eternity causes my soul to groan with longing, urgent for its culmination and fulfillment. I am so confident He is coming back, and that I will see Sarah again, that I groan with expectant longing for it.

> For we know that the whole creation groans and suffers the pains of childbirth together until now. And not only this, but also we ourselves, having the first fruits of the Spirit, even we ourselves groan within ourselves, waiting eagerly for [our] adoption as sons, the redemption of our body. (Rom. 8:22-23)

Our groaning is an expression of grief, and creation joins us in it. Because of sin, this world bears the pain and scars of suffering, as do we. As a result, we who understand and possess the hope of Christ through His indwelling Spirit, groan with longing within ourselves.

> For indeed in this [house] we groan, longing to be clothed with our dwelling from heaven, inasmuch as we, having put it on, will not be found naked. For indeed while we are in this tent, we groan, being burdened, because we do not want to be unclothed but to be clothed, so that what is mortal will be swallowed up by life. (2 Cor. 5:2-4)

We groan with longing for the end of sin and suffering. We groan with longing for the coming day when all things will be made right. And in the groaning of our souls, we join the chorus of saints throughout Scripture, from beginning to end, crying out to Him, "*How Long, O Lord?*"

> Return, O LORD! How long? Have pity on your servants! (Ps. 90:13 ESV)

There is no sin in my missing and longing for Sarah's presence. There is no sin in your missing and longing for your child's presence. We who are in Christ are groaning with longing because we have hope. We are groaning with longing because we are certain there is coming a day *"in just a little while"* when we will see Jesus face to face, and our precious children with Him (Heb. 10:37).

> For in hope we have been saved, but hope that is seen is not hope; for who hopes for what he [already] sees? But if we hope for what we do not see, with perseverance we wait eagerly for it. (Rom. 8:24-25)

In the meantime, as we wait, we rejoice in the hope that allows us to grieve and enables us to expectantly persevere. We echo Paul in saying, *"I am hard-pressed from both directions, having the desire to depart and be with Christ, for that is very much better... But if I am to live on in the flesh, this will mean fruitful labor for me"* (Phil. 1:22-23).

And *"strengthened with all power, according to His glorious might, for the attaining of all steadfastness and patience"* we persevere, urgently and expectantly following Him (Col. 1:11). Walking in His wisdom and His power, making the most of every opportunity to make Him and His hope known to a hopeless world.

We rejoice in the hope of Christ that allows us to grieve and enables us to persevere. And we eagerly wait, persevering in the midst of our grief, comforted by the knowledge that *"those who sow in tears will soon reap with songs of joy!"* (Ps. 126:5-6).

> In just a little while, he who is coming will come and will not delay. (Heb. 10:37 NIV)

> He who testifies to these things says, "Yes, I am coming quickly." Amen. Come, Lord Jesus. (Rev. 22:20)

Come, Lord Jesus.

GRACE UPON GRACE

MAY 31, 2021

"For from his fullness we have all received, grace upon grace."
John 1:16 ESV

The many painful memories of June 8, 2017, are a daily presence. Among them is a heart-rending image forever etched in my mind of Sarah's sisters shattered and huddled together after their dad told us she was gone. I vividly remember the weight and urgency I felt at that moment to comfort them and assure them we "would be okay." In my spirit, I knew Scott and I would do everything within our power to make into reality what at that moment seemed like a hollow promise. But in that moment, I was also acutely and excruciatingly aware of how very little power we actually have.

But God through His infinite grace has been ever so faithful. In the midst of darkest days and deepest sorrow, He has faithfully heaped grace upon grace on us. Yesterday was another demonstration of His lavish grace.

Our oldest daughter, Katelyn, married yesterday. The weather was perfect for her dream outdoor ceremony. It was a beautiful wedding and reception that I hope held many precious memories for her.

As the bridesmaids stood before me prepared for her to make her entrance, I sat relentlessly taking captive thoughts of Sarah's absence among them. As Katelyn and her dad made their way down the aisle to the front, my eyes were on her groom, Phillip. I saw God's overflowing grace there. Phillip loves Katelyn so well. As she moved toward him he was captivated by her, and I was captivated by his love for her.

God has been so indescribably faithful and gracious to our family. He has taken that shattered huddle of my remaining children and carried them, Scott, and me on Eagle's wings. He has tenderly loved us, compassionately sustained us, and faithfully led us.

Scott and I gained another son last night. A son we deeply love and appreciate because we see how well he loves our daughter.

We gained our first son less than a year ago when Kristen and Austin wed. As I watched our girls with each of their guys last night I couldn't help but be reminded of God's blessings for Job. God has allowed us to walk the indescribably painful path of Sarah's earthly death and absence. He has not filled, and will not fill, the void of Sarah's absence on this side of heaven. But He has undeniably blessed us with the priceless gift of an expanding family through sons who love our daughters well.

Through the years I've said many times that I wished we had six children instead of just four. Last night we gained our sixth. This side of heaven our family will always remain incomplete, the sting of Sarah's absence ever-present. Even so, by and through God's outpouring of grace upon grace, our shattered hearts rejoice in His abundant goodness and faithfulness.

> This I recall to my mind, Therefore I have hope. The LORD'S lovingkindnesses indeed never cease, For His compassions never fail. [They] are new every morning; Great is Your faithfulness. (Lam. 3:21-23)

NESTLESS

NOVEMBER 4, 2021

The phrase "empty nester" has been used repeatedly in recent days to describe me. Each time I hear it my stomach turns and I feel a twinge of pain in my heart.

I have treasured the days of having my children at home. For years I have, in a sense, dreaded their leaving. But as with every passing season of raising our children, I find launching them into adulthood and independence has held blessings, beauty, and privilege that overshadow the sadness of the passing of the previous savored seasons. My heart delights in seeing two of my adult daughters thriving away from home, and one adult daughter soon to complete school and ready to do the same.

I struggle with the term "empty nester," though. Not because my children have matured and left our home, but because one of them never will. Each time I hear that phrase my mind and heart are pierced by the involuntary thought of our enemy intent on stealing, killing, and destroying—physically snatching her from "our nest."

This week I finally looked up the phrase "empty nester." Merriam-Webster defines it as *"a parent whose children have grown and moved away from home."*[1] Validation, I am not an empty nester. The unsettling I felt with that term is appropriate because it does not fit me. That term will never truly fit me because one of my children will never grow up and move away from home.

I have read and been told that parents who have experienced the death of a child are not, and should not be, defined by the loss of their child. While I agree we are not wholly defined by the loss of our children, I disagree that we should not be partially defined by it.

Brittanica lists the meaning of *define* as *"to show or describe (someone or something) clearly and completely."*[2] It is impossible to clearly and completely describe me without including the fact that I bear in my soul the trauma of the physical death of my child and the sorrow of my ongoing separation from her.

If the loss of my child alone wholly defined me it would be a tragic and hopeless definition. But I am more than that, much more. If I could choose only one descriptor to define me, it would be a follower of Jesus Christ. That is the most important determinant of who and what I am, and how I am shaped by every circumstance. The shaping force of every other aspect or descriptor of me is filtered through my relationship with Jesus Christ, including that of child loss.

> I have been crucified with Christ; and it is no longer I who live, but Christ lives in me; and the [life] which I now live in the flesh I live by faith in the Son of God, who loved me and gave Himself up for me. (Gal. 2:20)

I am being wholly transformed through my relationship with Jesus Christ. That transforming work, however, does not remove the painfully defining impact of Sarah's death on my life. He allows that painful mark to remain, and He radically uses it in His overarching work of transforming me. I have been and continue to be profoundly shaped by His redemptively using the defining mark of Sarah's death on my life.

To deny the ongoing defining impact of Sarah's death on my life would wrongly silence my testimony of His ongoing work and provision through it.

> And we know that God causes all things to work together for good to those who love God, to those who are called according to [His] purpose. (Rom. 8:28)

I have been refined in innumerable ways through Sarah's physical death and ongoing absence. The most prominent is undoubtedly in shifting my attention away from the pleasures and comforts of this world to a much more biblical perspective focused squarely on the eternal.

> Therefore we do not lose heart, but though our outer man is decaying, yet our inner man is being renewed day by day. For momentary, light affliction is producing for us an eternal weight of glory far beyond all comparison, while we look not at the things which are seen, but at the things which are not seen; for the things which are seen are temporal, but the things which are not seen are eternal. (2 Cor. 4:16-18)

Through Sarah's physical death, I have been made undeniably and continually aware of the reality that this world is not my home. Her absence sharply guards me from a temporal focus and daily reminds me I am just a sojourner here.

> We are of good courage, I say, and prefer rather to be absent from the body and to be at home with the Lord. (2 Cor. 5:8)

The sorrow of Sarah's absence undeniably remains and plays a pivotal role in defining me. I feel its sting daily. But in the weakness of that persisting sorrow, I am given the indescribable gift of daily experiencing Him powerfully strengthening and sustaining me through His overflowing grace and abundant mercy.

> And He has said to me, 'My grace is sufficient for you, for power is perfected in weakness.' Most gladly, therefore, I will rather boast about my weaknesses, so that the power of Christ may dwell in me. Therefore I am well content with weaknesses, with insults, with

distresses, with persecutions, with difficulties, for Christ's sake; for when I am weak, then I am strong. (2 Cor. 12:9-10)

The sorrow and His sustaining redemptively merge, powerfully fanning the flames of my desire for Him and my ultimate homegoing to Him (and Sarah). In the meantime, that fervent desire to be at home with the Lord and the eternal focus that longing provides, enable and compel me to live hopefully, eagerly, urgently, and fruitfully.

For to me, to live is Christ and to die is gain. But if [I am] to live [on] in the flesh, this [will mean] fruitful labor for me; and I do not know which to choose. (Phil. 1:21-22)

I recently read that many migrating birds migrate alongside rivers and streams and sit or stand on rocks alongside the flowing water to rest and replenish as they migrate. I love that image. "Empty nester" does not appropriately define me, but perhaps "nestless" does. A nestless one migrating home, soaring on wings like an eagle, standing on the Rock, and daily being refreshed by streams of living water.

Do you not know? Have you not heard? The LORD is the everlasting God, the Creator of the ends of the earth. He will not grow tired or weary, and his understanding no one can fathom. He gives strength to the weary and increases the power of the weak. Even youths grow tired and weary, and young men stumble and fall; but those who hope in the LORD will renew their strength. They will soar on wings like eagles; they will run and not grow weary, they will walk and not be faint. (Isa. 40:28-31 NIV)

Come, Lord Jesus.

---

1. "Empty nester, N." *Merriam-Webster Dictionary*, merriam-webster.com/dictionary/empty%20nester. Accessed 4 Nov. 2020.
2. "Define. V. (2)." *The Brittanica Dictionary*, britannica.com/dictionary/define. Accessed 4 Nov. 2020.

A NEW SONG

NOVEMBER 12, 2021

Last night I was awake through the night deeply burdened and fervently praying for someone journeying through an oppressively dark valley. My heart ached with and for theirs. I cried out for God to be near to them, to lift them from the pit, and to allow them to see and experience His powerfully sustaining mercy and grace.

As I prayed for that person, others who are also struggling and suffering came to mind. One by one, I prayed for each of them. My heart ached for theirs as I recalled the anguish of waiting in the pit.[1] As I lingered in prayer, Psalm 40 came to mind and my heart was immediately flooded with gratitude for the new song He has given me.

> …I waited patiently for the LORD; And He inclined to me and heard my cry. He brought me up out of the pit of destruction, out of the miry clay, And He set my feet upon a rock making my footsteps firm. He put a new song in my mouth, a song of praise to our God; Many will see and fear And will trust in the LORD. (Ps. 40:1-3)

I don't remember exactly when it happened, probably sometime around the end of the first year of Sarah's absence, but I vividly remember the sting of realizing some expected that it was time for me to no longer feel the pain of missing Sarah. They were certain I would and should be healed, and the time had come for that to happen.

Our current Christian culture is one in which there is an expectation of total healing and deliverance: right here and now. Suffering is tolerated for a season, but the affliction and resulting sorrow must not last beyond some randomly prescribed time. The expectation is clear and loud—you must be healed.

Our healing is gloriously certain in Christ Jesus, but the timing of it is not. Some wounds are not fully healed here but are instead "bound up" for the remainder of the journey.

> He heals the brokenhearted And binds up their wounds. (Ps. 147:3)

Paul pleaded for healing from the "thorn" that tormented him, but the temporal deliverance he desired was not granted. Likewise, I am not healed from the sorrow of Sarah's death. My heart was shattered the day she died, and it remains shattered. But my God who promises to be near to the brokenhearted has compassionately gathered and bound the shards together.

> Concerning this I implored the Lord three times that it might leave me. And He has said to me, "My grace is sufficient for you, for power is perfected in weakness." Most gladly, therefore, I will rather boast about my weaknesses, so that the power of Christ may dwell in me. Therefore I am well content with weaknesses, with insults, with distresses, with persecutions, with difficulties, for Christ's sake; for when I am weak, then I am strong. (2 Cor. 12:8-10)

He has patiently and gently cared for me in the depths of my brokenness. Like the Psalmist, He has tenderly and graciously bound my heart, lifted me from the pit, and set my feet upon the Rock. With each passing day, He increasingly strengthens me to bear the pain of my sorrow, though it will not be removed this side of heaven.

Before Sarah died I sang a beautiful song of deliverance. The song of my God who delivered me from the weight and bondage of sin through the precious blood of Jesus. I still boldly and gratefully sing that song.

But He's added to that a costly and treasured new song, the song of the sustained. The song of those who have been shattered and one day will be fully healed, but in the meantime have been tenderly "bound up."

I am not ashamed to admit that I am still broken, that I am not healed. Like Paul, *"I will rather boast about my weaknesses, so that the power of Christ may dwell in me."* It is through my brokenness that I experience and know God's sustaining power. It is of that power that I now sing.

Some don't understand the song I sing, but I must sing nonetheless. To the broken and suffering, each note resonates as the sound of hope. Hope that the God of the universe still sees, hears, binds up, and sustains. And hope that He will see, hear, bind up, and sustain them.

Whatever suffering or sorrow you bear, God can and will sustain you, but you must first cry out to Him. As you wait for Him, He will bind your wounds just as He has bound mine. He is faithful and His Word is true. He will strengthen and sustain you *"with all power according to His glorious might,"* and in so doing He will give you a new song to sing as well.

I will never be thankful for Sarah's death or the sorrow of her absence, but I am indescribably grateful for the new song God has given me through it—the song of the sustained.

Come, Lord Jesus.

---

1. see "Waiting in the Pit," pp. 46-47.

HER FIFTH BIRTHDAY

DECEMBER 20, 2021

This morning I was listening to the final episode of the podcast "The Rise and Fall of Mars Hill." A quote at the end deeply resonated with me: "The longer that you live with a mask, the greater the void grows between the mask and the internal reality of who you are. And that void becomes vacuous and empty and hollow, and ultimately you end up being loved for something you're not, rather than who you actually are."[1]

I immediately thought of grieving people when I heard the quote. We live in a culture that seeks to put parameters and time limits on grief. Many grieving quickly learn there can be negative ramifications of transparently sharing their grief, particularly as time goes on. For some who wish to avoid those ramifications, mask-wearing becomes a necessary skill. In 2018 I wrote about my experience with this in "Faking Fine in The Midst of Grief?" and "The Hypocrisy of Grief."[2,3]

In the early days of Sarah's absence, I felt the angst of the void between the mask and reality. But I am so very grateful that God has since encircled us with a precious band of sojourners. There is no mask worn with them, they see and know us as we are. Most of them understand because they also bear the pain of deep grief, many of child loss specifically. But others not yet scathed by deep grief allow us to be maskless because their sincere love for us renders them willing to accept the reality of our sorrow as well as our hope.

If Sarah were here today, we would be excitedly preparing for our traditional family birthday party, her twenty-second. I would be busy in the kitchen cooking and preparing the dinner and homemade cake she had chosen. And her sisters, grandparents, aunt, uncle, and cousins would be preparing to come celebrate her.

Instead of that, though, we find ourselves marking the fifth passing of her birthday in her absence. With each passing birthday we have learned better how to navigate them as a family, we no longer fearfully dread their coming. But the tension between deep sorrow and gratitude remains.

I am exceedingly grateful for the seventeen and a half years I was given with Sarah. And yet the passing of her birthday without her is a profoundly sorrowful experience. My heart longs for her presence, to know what she would be thinking and doing if she were here and turning twenty-two years old. So I find myself once again with a tear-streaked face, simultaneously deeply grateful and sorrowful.

This morning I am sharing this for those who also know the sorrow of deep grief, compelled largely by the quote I previously mentioned. Those who know grief know the tension of which I speak. They know the reality that five years later you long for their presence just as much, or perhaps even more than you did the first birthday without them.

If you find yourself grieving today but painfully hidden behind a mask, be encouraged that there are people who will see, know, and love you without the mask. Don't allow the adversary to isolate you through his shame-filled lies about the realities of grief. Scripture says we do *"not grieve as others do who have no hope,"* but it does not say "we do not grieve" (1 Thess. 4:13).

We grieve the absence of those we love—but with hope. That hope, the hope of Jesus Christ specifically, enables us to persevere living fruitfully, gratefully, and joyfully, in the midst of ongoing sorrow. But that hope also allows us sorrow without shame. He compassionately promises us one day He will wipe away every tear, but that day has not yet come. Condemnation for tears is not from Him.

> He will wipe away every tear from their eyes, and death shall be no more, neither shall there be mourning, nor crying, nor pain anymore, for the former things have passed away. (Rev.21:4 ESV)

There are tears today as we mark Sarah's fifth birthday in heaven. But there is also gratitude, hope, and joy. Sarah had a bucket list, so we checked off one of her bucket list items by going to Graceland in honor of her and her birthday this weekend. Tonight we will gather with her sisters and their guys again for some of Sarah's favorite traditions: family dinner, decorating cookies, and watching a Christmas movie together.

At the close of the night, Scott and I will celebrate, probably tearfully, the incredible gift we were given in Sarah twenty-two years ago today, and the glorious fact that we are five birthdays closer to seeing her again.

> But we do not want you to be uninformed, brethren, about those who are asleep, so that you will not grieve as do the rest who have no hope. For if we believe that Jesus died and rose again, even so God will bring with Him those who have fallen asleep in Jesus. (1 Thess. 4:13-14)

Come, Lord Jesus.

---

1. Cooper, Mike. "Aftermath." *The Rise and Fall of Mars Hill*, Episode 12, Christianity Today, 4 Dec. 2021, christianitytoday.com/ct/podcasts/rise and fall of mars hill/mars-hill-podcast-driscoll-finale-aftermath.html.
2. see "Faking Fine in The Midst of Grief?" pp. 141-144.
3. see "The Hypocrisy of Grief," pp. 205-209.

FIVE YEARS: BEAUTY FOR ASHES

JUNE 8, 2022

A few weeks ago we visited the Big Island of Hawai'i. As we traveled across the island I was captivated by the sight of plants springing up in the charred fields of lava. How impossible it seemed that beauty and life could spring up in the midst of such utter destruction. Each time I saw the brilliant green sprigs of new life piercing through the seemingly endless flows of black-crusted lava I was reminded of the promise of *"beauty for ashes"* in Isaiah 61.

> The Spirit of the Lord GOD [is] upon me; because the LORD hath anointed me to preach good tidings unto the meek; he hath sent me to bind up the brokenhearted, to proclaim liberty to the captives, and the opening of the prison to [them that are] bound; To proclaim the acceptable year of the LORD, and the day of vengeance of our God; to comfort all that mourn; To appoint unto them that mourn in Zion, to give unto them beauty for ashes, the oil of joy for mourning, the garment of praise for the spirit of heaviness; that they might be called trees of righteousness, the planting of the LORD, that he might be glorified. (vv. 1-3 KJV)

The sight of each vibrant green plant, no matter how small, captivated my attention and strummed the chords of hope deep in my soul. Of the countless beautiful sights on the island, I found myself repeatedly drawn to this one. I'm doubtful many would describe it as beautiful, but for me—it was profoundly beautiful.

Evidence of the violent devastation wrought by the volcanoes will always be present on the island. It has been forever transformed and reshaped by their catastrophic eruptions.

Likewise, I am forever marked by the devastating sorrow of Sarah's death and absence. I have been permanently transformed and reshaped through it.

Today marks five years since we were abruptly and violently separated from our sweet Sarah. Five years, that's sixty months apart. Five and sixty, both seemingly small numbers to reflect an incomprehensible 260 weeks of separation. More strikingly, that's 1,825 days since I last saw my child alive, 43,800 hours since I last felt her embrace, and 2,628,000 minutes since I last heard the sound of her precious voice speaking to me.

Five years without my child. Pondering that reality takes my breath away. I am continually, unavoidably, and acutely aware of her now five-year absence, and yet my heart convulses each time I acknowledge its reality.

As the Big Island bears the black crusted mounds and gorges created by the destructive rivers of lava, my heart and soul bear the transforming scars of soul-piercing sorrow.

But just as God is bringing new life and beauty up out of the ashes of the lava fields, He continues to faithfully bring beauty up out of the ashes of my sorrow.

In Luke 4:17-21 Jesus read Isaiah 61:1-2 aloud in the temple, and followed by saying *"Today this Scripture has been fulfilled in your hearing."*

> And the scroll of the prophet Isaiah was given to him. He unrolled the scroll and found the place where it was written, "The Spirit of the Lord is upon me, because he has anointed me to proclaim good news to the poor. He has sent me to proclaim liberty to the captives and

recovering of sight to the blind, to set at liberty those who are oppressed, to proclaim the year of the Lord's favor." And he rolled up the scroll and gave it back to the attendant and sat down. And the eyes of all in the synagogue were fixed on him. And he began to say to them, "Today this Scripture has been fulfilled in your hearing." (Luke 4:17-21 ESV)

Many believe it is significant that He stopped reading prior to saying, *"and the day of vengeance of our God,"* partway through Isaiah 61:2, because that day will be associated with His second coming rather than His first.

Jesus Christ is coming again. And after His second coming, *"and the day of vengeance of our God,"* every tear and sorrow will be wiped away.

> He will wipe away every tear from their eyes, and death shall be no more, neither shall there be mourning, nor crying, nor pain anymore, for the former things have passed away. (Rev. 21:4 ESV)

In that glorious day when tears and sorrows are wiped away, my *ashes* (sorrow), *mourning, and spirit of heaviness* will be completely removed and fully replaced with *beauty, joy, and praise* (Isa. 61:3).

That day has not yet come, but the promise of its coming allows us to experience its fulfillment in a very significant way even now. The hope we have been given through the first coming of Jesus Christ, and His promised second coming, is our source of *beauty, joy,* and *praise* even in the midst of our *ashes, mourning,* and *spirit of heaviness*.

Our *ashes, mourning, and spirit of heaviness* enable us to uniquely see and experience the *beauty, joy, and praise* found through the hope we have in Him.

Like rivers of lava, sorrow and suffering roll through our lives as sanctifying flames, stripping away temporal comforts and distractions and enabling us to clearly see and cling to our only true hope: Jesus Christ, and the glorious future found only in Him.

> Therefore, prepare your minds for action, keep sober [in spirit,] fix your hope completely on the grace to be brought to you at the revelation of Jesus Christ. (1 Pet. 1:13)

Because He came and is coming again, and Sarah's faith was and mine is in Him, I have the promised hope of eternity with Him and her. Through Him, my five long years apart from Sarah sets me five full years closer to seeing her again, this time never to be separated again.

> These things I have written to you who believe in the name of the Son of God, so that you may know that you have eternal life. (1 John 5:13)

> But we do not want you to be uninformed, brethren, about those who are asleep, so that you will not grieve as do the rest who have no hope. For if we believe that Jesus died and rose again, even so God will bring with Him those who have fallen asleep in Jesus. (1 Thess. 4:13-14)

What glorious promises!

And so, as we who grieve choose to continually fix our eyes, hearts, and hope on the *beauty* of this and His many other precious promises, He restores to us the true *joy* of His Salvation. And as we are reminded of and filled with the true joy of His salvation, our souls can't help but erupt in *praise* to Him—rendering us, like Paul, *"sorrowful yet always rejoicing"* (2 Cor. 6:10).[1]

> Purify me with hyssop, and I shall be clean; Wash me, and I shall be whiter than snow. Make me to hear joy and gladness, Let the bones which You have broken rejoice. Hide Your face from my sins And blot out all my iniquities. Create in me a clean heart, O God, And renew a steadfast spirit within me. Do not cast me away from Your presence And do not take Your Holy Spirit from me. Restore to me the joy of

Your salvation And sustain me with a willing spirit. [Then] I will teach transgressors Your ways, And sinners will be converted to You. (Ps. 51:7-13)

To appoint unto them that mourn in Zion, to give unto them beauty for ashes, the oil of joy for mourning, the garment of praise for the spirit of heaviness; that they might be called trees of righteousness, the planting of the LORD, that he might be glorified. (Isa. 61:3 KJV)

He who testifies to these things says, "Yes, I am coming quickly." Amen. Come, Lord Jesus. (Rev. 22:20)

Earth hath no sorrow that heaven can't heal.

— Beth's hymn

---

1. see "Restore to Me," pp. 26-28.

SUICIDE PREVENTION OR AWARENESS?

SEPTEMBER 1, 2022

September is Suicide Prevention Month, this year National Suicide Prevention Week begins September 4th, and September 10th is World Suicide Prevention Day. In the midst of all of the talk of prevention, I find myself grieving with and for my precious friend as the September 5th anniversary of her beloved son's death by suicide rapidly approaches.

Guilt is one of the most formidable foes of grief. Of the many bereaved parents we have spent time with, most have expressed experiencing the crushing weight of guilt at one time or another, and repeatedly for many. I am among the many in that regard. My battle with guilt has been consuming and devastating at times. But I have found great comfort in learning to recognize that guilt for what it is—a powerfully effective, yet not undefeatable scheme of our adversary.

> In order that Satan might not outwit us. For we are not unaware of his schemes. (2 Cor. 2:11 NIV)

Scripture tells us Satan is a liar and the father of all lies. He is the *"accuser of the brethren,"* a thief who has come *"to steal, kill and destroy"* *"like a roaring lion seeking someone to devour"* (Rev. 12:10; John 10:10; 1

Pet. 5:8). Guilt is one of his favored and most insidiously effective schemes, particularly amongst the broken and grieving.

> ...He was a murderer from the beginning, and does not stand in the truth because there is no truth in him. Whenever he speaks a lie, he speaks from his own [nature,] for he is a liar and the father of lies. (John 8:44)

For those left in the devastating wake of suicide, the guilt-laden "what-ifs" and "if onlys" are like the piercing and shredding teeth of the devouring lion's jaws. "You could have prevented this." "You should have prevented this." "This is your fault!" An endless barrage of excruciating accusations and lies. This is his scheme—crippling, life-stealing lies of guilt and shame.

Suicide awareness and mental health awareness are vitally important. Very thoughtfully choosing our words in raising that awareness is equally important. Many who have died by suicide have left family and friends who spent years deeply loving them, faithfully caring for them, and diligently and purposefully working to prevent their suicides. The implication that they could have prevented their loved one's suicide is yet another devastating blow for them. Another brilliant scheme in the hands of a cruel adversary.

If you find yourself battered and broken, pierced by the accusation that "you could have prevented this," I hope you will recognize it today for what it is. I am praying today that you can begin to find victory over those accusations by recognizing their source and purpose. They are the scheme of a ruthless adversary intent on stealing, killing, and destroying *you*. But we are not unaware of his schemes, and there is victory and peace freely available in Jesus Christ.

> Come to me, all you who are weary and burdened, and I will give you rest. Take my yoke upon you and learn from me, for I am gentle and humble in heart, and you will find rest for your souls. For my yoke is easy and my burden is light. (Matt. 11:28-30 NIV)

Through His strength we can resist the accusations and lies by learning to *"take every thought captive to the obedience of Christ"* (2 Cor. 10:5). Throwing off each lie and thinking instead on *"whatever is true, whatever is noble, whatever is right, whatever is pure, whatever is lovely, whatever is admirable"* (Phil. 4:8). *"And the peace of God, which transcends all understanding, will guard your hearts and your minds in Christ Jesus"* (Phil. 4:7).

Jacob Cole Laney
December 23, 1998 - September 5, 2018

Jacob, your mom and I are eagerly waiting together for that glorious reunion day *"in just a little while…"* (Heb. 10:37)

He who testifies to these things says, "Yes, I am coming quickly." Amen. Come, Lord Jesus. (Rev 22:20)

LONG AND NEW SORROW

※

DECEMBER 19, 2022

Tomorrow is the sixth time our family is forced to decide what to do on Sarah's birthday without her, in the middle of our sixth Christmas season without her.

Thankfully, her birthday and this Christmas season are not the cutting of new wounds in our hearts, but more like the pressing of a still tender scar. The passage of time has allowed the experience of these days to shift from the excruciating pain of new sorrow to a throbbing of the deep ache of long sorrow.

The fresh wounds of new sorrow now come less frequently, but more unexpectedly, not as much on specific dates, in predictable moments, or moments of willingly allowing ourselves to think about and mourn all we miss with her.

These days the sharp edge of new sorrow most often slices unexpectedly, camouflaged within everyday life.

I rarely allow myself to willfully ponder what Sarah would be doing were she here. But as her peers reach and share new milestones, the sharp pains of missed experiences are unavoidable. I rejoice with them in each new accomplishment and announcement, but simultaneously my heart is pierced by the new sorrow of her absence in those specific moments.

Sarah was seventeen years old when she died. She didn't turn eighteen. She will never be physically present in our earthly lives again. She won't sit, eat, and laugh at the table with us, celebrate holidays with us, graduate high school, attend college, graduate from college, be in her sisters' weddings, date, get engaged, get married, celebrate the arrival of nieces and nephews and be known by them, or have children of her own. Since she died I have been unavoidably, acutely aware of each of these fully incomprehensible and unforgettable losses, as well as many others.

As a result, one of the largest surprises of grief for me has been experiencing the sharpness of the new sorrow that these long-recognized losses still possess. Each time I am confronted by the reality that if Sarah was here she would likely be experiencing at this moment some specific new milestone, I am shocked by the weight and painful newness of the sorrow that the realization delivers.

It seems impossible that a well-known loss can arrive years later as fresh hurt and new sorrow, and yet it does. As her friends graduated from high school in 2018, almost a year after she died, we grieved her absence as new sorrow. In 2019, 2020, and 2021 as her sisters got engaged and married, in the midst of the rejoicing there was the sharp pain of new sorrow.

This year Sarah's friends graduated from college and are getting engaged and married, and her precious first nephew was born. All moments of great rejoicing accompanied by painful gashes of new sorrow.

I'm thankful Sarah's birthday and Christmas are no longer new sorrows, but instead part of our long sorrow. I intimately know the sorrow these days hold, so they no longer hold the sharp pain of new experiences and daunting unknowns. Instead, they are a throbbing of the now well-known deep aching of long sorrow.

The bitterness of the pain of missing her sweet presence in our family on these days is ever present, but also familiar and known enough to allow room to more fully experience the sweetness of memories with her, and the hopefulness of our future together.

God has been ever-faithful as He has so graciously carried,

sustained, and strengthened us over the past five and half years without our child. We are deeply grateful that, though the long sorrow remains, each year seems to possess fewer sharp edges of new sorrow. We are also thankful that through God's proven faithfulness, we have confidence that each sharp new sorrow yet to emerge will invariably be met with His never-failing new mercies, tender compassion, and empowering grace, that have faithfully met every new sorrow already experienced.

If you are journeying behind us on the painful path of child loss, I pray it will encourage your heart to know the long sorrow is a gentler aching than the piercing pain of new sorrow. And if you, like me, have been surprised by the sharpness of the new sorrow that continues to emerge with long-anticipated occasions, I hope you will find encouragement in knowing you are not alone.

And together we can find encouragement in knowing that even though new sorrows will continue to emerge until we are reunited with our children, they, too, will gradually merge into our long sorrow and no longer bear the sharp sting of newness they once held.

But may we always find our greatest encouragement and hope through faith in Jesus Christ. Reminding ourselves that *"in just a little while, He who is coming will come and will not delay"* (Heb. 10:37). *"For the Lord Himself will descend from heaven with a shout, with the voice of the archangel and with the trumpet of God, and the dead in Christ will rise first. Then we who are alive and remain will be caught up together with them in the clouds to meet the Lord in the air, and so we shall always be with the Lord"* (1 Thess. 4:16-17). *"And He will wipe every tear from our eyes. There will be no more death or mourning or crying or pain, for the old order of things will have passed away"* (Rev. 21:4)... *"Therefore comfort one another with these words"* (1 Thess. 4:18).

He who testifies to these things says, "Yes, I am coming quickly."
Amen. Come, Lord Jesus.
Revelation 22:20

THE CUP OF SALVATION

APRIL 7, 2023

"What shall I render to the LORD For all His benefits toward me? I shall lift up the cup of salvation And call upon the name of the LORD."
Psalm 116:12-13

Easter is bittersweet for me. Sarah didn't die at Easter, but Easter of 2017 holds the last vivid memories I have up until the day before she left. It's the last day of cohesive memories I can in part relive with her through my mind's eye. All the moments of days between then and the day before she left are just snippets of time I'm unable to string together in a satisfying way.

I'm so very thankful for Easter. If there were no Easter—no resurrection of Christ to celebrate—Christianity would be utterly meaningless. If Christ was not raised then there is no future resurrection and, as Paul said, Christians *"are of all men most to be pitied."*

> if Christ has not been raised, your faith is worthless; you are still in your sins. Then those also who have fallen asleep in Christ have perished. If we have hoped in Christ in this life only, we are of all men most to be pitied. (1 Cor. 15:17-19)

Praise God, Jesus was indeed raised! Jesus Christ, God incarnate, came in human flesh, lived a perfect sinless life, died willingly and purposefully for the atonement of our sins, and rose again gloriously defeating death. God in Him reconciling the world to Himself and providing the precious certain hope of eternal life for all who will believe (2 Cor. 5:19).

I believe. I have confident eager hope. I am longing for a future I am certain of because I believe He who promised is faithful. And yet my heart aches and my eyes well with tears as I type. Lamenting cries of Pslamists and saints from centuries ago echo in my ears and reverberate in my heart, *"How Long, O Lord?"* and *"Come, Lord Jesus!"*

So as confident hope and the deep ache of long sorrow once again meld within me this morning, I lift up the inspired words of one of those Psalmists from long ago as my offering to Him.[1]

Psalm 116

I love the LORD, because He hears My voice [and] my supplications. Because He has inclined His ear to me, Therefore I shall call [upon Him] as long as I live. The cords of death encompassed me And the terrors of Sheol came upon me; I found distress and sorrow.

Then I called upon the name of the LORD: "O LORD, I beseech You, save my life!" Gracious is the LORD, and righteous; Yes, our God is compassionate. The LORD preserves the simple; I was brought low, and He saved me. Return to your rest, O my soul, For the LORD has dealt bountifully with you. For You have rescued my soul from death, My eyes from tears, My feet from stumbling. I shall walk before the LORD In the land of the living. I believed when I said, "I am greatly afflicted." I said in my alarm, "All men are liars."

What shall I render to the LORD For all His benefits toward me? I shall lift up the cup of salvation And call upon the name of the LORD. I shall pay my vows to the LORD, Oh [may it be] in the presence of all His people. Precious in the sight of the LORD Is the death of His godly ones. O LORD, surely I am Your servant, I am Your servant, the son of Your handmaid, You have loosed my bonds. To You I shall offer a sacrifice of thanksgiving, And call upon the name of the LORD. I shall pay my vows to the LORD, Oh [may it be] in the presence of all His people, In the courts of the LORD'S house, In the midst of you, O Jerusalem. Praise the LORD!

Any fear I may once have had of my personal physical death evaporated the moment my child was stripped from me. In that instant I was instead entangled, encompassed by the *cords of death*—her death— and the *terror, distress, and sorrow* it brought. Then, like the Psalmist, I, too, *called upon the name of the Lord.*

Because of Easter, I have the hope and joy of saying with the Psalmist, *"You have rescued my soul from death, My eyes from tears, My feet from stumbling. I shall walk before the LORD In the land of the living."*

That first "Easter" He defeated death, and death's destruction day is coming *in just a little while.* He has secured my eternal future with Him, Sarah, and all who will call upon His name. Praise God, there is a certain day coming soon when this sword pierced soul of mine will no longer ache and my eyes will no longer well with tears (Heb. 10:37; Rev. 21:4).

> What shall I render to the LORD For all His benefits toward me? I shall lift up the cup of salvation And call upon the name of the LORD. I shall pay my vows to the LORD, Oh [may it be] in the presence of all His people (vv. 12-14)

His benefits and faithfulness toward me these past 2,129 days without Sarah are innumerable. In response, with tearful yet grateful worship I lift my cup of salvation high to Him, proclaiming His faithfulness in the presence of His people.

In gentleness and compassion, He reminds me, *"Precious in the sight of the LORD Is the death of His godly ones."* Sarah's death is *precious* to Him. It is not forgotten or unnoticed by Him, nor are my tears in her absence.

THE CUP OF SALVATION

He sets no earthly time limit on the ache of my heart or yours. He tenderly collects each of our tears in His bottle. He will faithfully do so until a soon coming day, *in just a little while,* at long last, when He Himself has promised to wipe the final tears from each of our eyes.

Until that day, may we each lift the cup of salvation high to Him, and our hearts with it, boldly and faithfully singing with the Psalmist, *"O LORD, surely I am Your servant, I am Your servant, the son of Your handmaid, You have loosed my bonds. To You I shall offer a sacrifice of thanksgiving, And call upon the name of the LORD. I shall pay my vows to the LORD, Oh [may it be] in the presence of all His people, In the courts of the LORD'S house, In the midst of you, O Jerusalem. Praise the LORD!"*

> BE Joyful in HOPE
> Patient IN AFFLICTION,
> Faithful IN PRAYER
> —Romans 12:12

---

1. see "Long and New Sorrow," pp. 387-389.

MISSING YOU TODAY ESPECIALLY

JULY 25, 2023

My sweet Sarah,

Monday at 2:09 p.m. Katelyn gave birth to your first niece, Lauren Hope. She is so precious, and she reminds me so very much of you. Adorable full cheeks, inquisitive furrowed brow, and a head full of dark hair.

Katelyn and Phillip named her Lauren after you. We all know how much you loved your middle name, so it brings us joy to remember you each time we speak it. Through your absence we have learned the most precious commodity we each possess in this life is hope, so how fitting that they chose to combine your name with it in naming her.

Your dad and I are so completely overjoyed for Katelyn and Phillip as they enter this new season of life. And we already deeply love precious Lauren Hope. But at the same time, it brings me once again to the edge of the abyss of the sorrow of your absence.

It's another new sorrow. As I saw Kristen and Sophie meeting Lauren for the first time, there was the unavoidable awareness that we were incomplete, you were so indescribably missed in that moment. As I watched Kristen and Sophie climb into the hospital bed with Katelyn, Lauren, and Samuel, my heart ached and longed for you to be there, too.

I know your tender heart would be so sad if we were not fully celebrating the arrival of sweet Lauren Hope with Katelyn and Phillip. So I'm thankful to be able to tell you that our rejoicing with them has not been diminished, even by this new sorrow of your ongoing absence. There is a bittersweet mingling of the joy and the sorrow. The stark bitterness of the sorrow of your absence, having taught us to number our days aright, has surprisingly made the sweetness of the present joy sweeter.

The joy and sorrow are always together. I experience the joy fully, but in the midst of it the sorrow wells again as I miss you. I've heard warnings that if bereaved parents express missing their deceased child "too much" they will cause their surviving children to feel less loved. And sort of the opposite of that, I've heard bereaved parents express fear that experiencing joy and celebrating life "too much" after their child's death means they somehow love their deceased child less.

With those thoughts in mind, I'm grateful that I have peace that you and your sisters all know that my love for each of you is forever continually the same, none greater than the other, and none ever diminishing the other. My loving and missing you in no way takes away from my love for them, and my loving, rejoicing with, and celebrating them in no way diminishes my love for you. I will continue to love you the same until I see you again, and then I will love all four of you perfectly for the rest of eternity.

The hope of eternity brings me the greatest joy. I am exceedingly thankful for the inexpressible joy of knowing that because of your faith and hope in Jesus Christ, and ours, you are not behind us in our past, but very much before us in our future. With each passing day, I am reminded I am one day closer to being with you again, and my heart leaps daily at that glorious thought.

But until then I want you to know I'm committed to living life fully with your dad, sisters, brothers, Samuel, and now Lauren Hope. I've got all your favorite books ready to read to Samuel and Lauren. We'll be talking a lot about heaven and you, and how one day, in just a little while, we will all be together with you there.

So I'm writing this letter to you for myself more than anyone else.

Just to remind myself of these things I know to be true and to say once again, "I love you and miss you."

I miss you every single day. But I'm missing you today, especially.

It seems as if I should be homesick for you even from heaven.

—Beth March

HER PRESENT ABSENCE

NOVEMBER 11, 2023

As I sat by the window in the still of the morning, a gust of wind brought a vibrant cascade of orange, red, and brown gracefully flowing from the trees beside me. The beauty of the colors and the melodic rustling of the leaves was pleasant to my soul.

The beauty and pleasure of the moment brought with them a flurry of memories. The memories bore witness to the painful sorrow of Sarah's present absence, and instantly a wave of sorrow crashed over me.

As the unsolicited reel of memories continued to play in my mind's eye I was reminded of the empty yet often-spoken exhortation to "look forward, not back." Empty advice that fails to understand the source of sorrow.

The sweet memories of the past are not the source of our sorrow. The gaping hole of our loved one's absence in each present moment is the source of our sorrow.

It is not looking back that staggers me, it is seeing her absence in this present moment that staggers me. Her present absence triggers the present sorrow. Her felt absence in this moment hurts in this moment.

Six years later her absence remains present, and the sorrow of her absence with it. There is no wrong or shame in acknowledging that reality. On the contrary, that reality is used for great good by our omnipotent Redeemer who promises to use everything for our good, even the worst of things.

> And we know that God causes all things to work together for good to those who love God, to those who are called according to [His] purpose. (Rom. 8:28)

The painful presence of her absence most powerfully spurs me on to live the remainder of my life fruitfully.

> For to me, to live is Christ and to die is gain. But if [I am] to live [on] in the flesh, this [will mean] fruitful labor for me…(Phil. 1:21-22)

Her absence is a constant reminder that this life is but a vapor. The sorrow stirs my awareness that this is not our home, that we are just sojourners here for a moment. Her present absence continually testifies to the transitory nature of what remains, causing me to press into Christ who faithfully strengthens me to persevere, and filling me with urgency and longing to finish the race well.

> Therefore, since we have so great a cloud of witnesses surrounding us, let us also lay aside every encumbrance and the sin which so easily entangles us, and let us run with endurance the race that is set before us, fixing our eyes on Jesus, the author and perfecter of faith, who for the joy set before Him endured the cross, despising the shame, and has sat down at the right hand of the throne of God. (Heb. 12:1-2)

There is an indescribable joy set before us who love the Lord Jesus Christ, and it's just over the horizon. I will soon see my Savior face to face, and my sweet Sarah with Him. *"In just a little while"* He will wipe every tear from our eyes, and there will be no more sorrow. What a glorious day that will soon be!

You need to persevere so that when you have done the will of God, you will receive what he has promised. For, "In just a little while, he who is coming will come and will not delay." (Heb. 10:36-37 NIV)

But in the meantime, the sorrow of her present absence remains. There is no sin in the sorrow we feel in our loved one's present absence, and there is no wrongdoing or shame in acknowledging its reality. It's simply a testimony of our enduring love for them, and our certainty that we will soon see them again.

But we do not want you to be uninformed, brethren, about those who are asleep, so that you will not grieve as do the rest who have no hope. For if we believe that Jesus died and rose again, even so God will bring with Him those who have fallen asleep in Jesus. (1 Thess. 4:13-14)

So let's purposefully pick up our seed for sowing and persevere in living fruitfully, even as our faces remain streaked with the tears of their present absence. There's a glorious day just over the horizon before us. May we each continue laboring so fruitfully that a harvest of righteousness follows us there.

Those who sow in tears shall reap with joyful shouting. He who goes to and fro weeping, carrying [his] bag of seed, Shall indeed come again with a shout of joy, bringing his sheaves [with him.] (Ps. 126:5-6)

Come, Lord Jesus.

STILL TALKING ABOUT IT

DECEMBER 14, 2023

"When will they stop talking about it?" A question that is perhaps thought more often than spoken regarding grieving parents who continue to talk about their children and their sorrow. I've only heard it asked a couple of times, but have thought of it countless times since, and this month in particular.

Sarah's birthday is next week and I am painfully missing her. We're in our seventh holiday and birthday season without her. I'm grateful that the familiarity of the long, ever-present sorrow of her absence has rendered it far less sharp than the newness of the first seasons without her. Over the past six years, we've learned effective ways to best navigate many of the challenges of the season, to minimize the incidences and degrees of awkward situations and unnecessary compounding of sorrow.

To those journeying this path behind us, be encouraged that it has "gotten better."

For many the assumption is that "getting better" means the sorrow and pain of her absence is decreasing. But I am convinced that is a misconception. I don't believe the sorrow of her absence has lessened.

When I allow myself to truly ponder the reality of her absence it still takes my breath away. Each time I allow my eyes and thoughts to drift to and focus on the many ways she would have filled the now empty spaces in our home and lives, that lamentably familiar wave of staggering sorrow and disbelief comes crashing in with crushing force once again.

But it truly has gotten better.

The misconception is that the sorrow gets better. The sorrow has not gotten better, but our strength to bear up under the sorrow has.

The complete shattering of Sarah's death and absence has rendered me undeniably aware of my weakness, of my inability, and of my profound needfulness. The purging of my illusions of strength has allowed Christ's strength to rush in.

> Concerning this I implored the Lord three times that it might leave me. And He has said to me, "My grace is sufficient for you, for power is perfected in weakness." (2 Cor. 12:8-9a)

I recently discovered Alexander Maclaren's use of the phrase "omnipotence of dependence."[1] Such concise phrasing of a powerful counter-intuitive truth. A three-word summation of the hope of Colossians 1:11. It is through my awareness of my complete weakness and inability, and in my urgent dependence upon Him, that I am strengthened with His omnipotence.

> Strengthened with all might, according to his glorious power, unto all patience and longsuffering with joyfulness (Col. 1:11 KJV)

The God of the universe is graciously offering all of His strength and power, His omnipotence, to us for the purpose of strengthening us to wait upon Him in patience and joyful long-suffering.

The gaping hole of Sarah's absence in my life is ever-present and unchanged. The crippling sorrow caused by Sarah's physical death and ongoing absence is my deepest wound, my most tender vulnerability, my greatest weakness.

Yet, it is through my greatest weakness that I most fully experience His great strength. But not only His great strength. It is also through my greatest weakness that I have most fully experienced His compassionate nearness, His long-suffering love, His daily new mercies, and the purest and truest understanding of the inexpressible joy of the hope He has set before us.

It is through my greatest weakness, the sorrow of my earthly loss of Sarah, that I know and love God more deeply than ever before.

It is impossible for me to adequately testify about Him apart from talking about it. And it would be supremely foolish of me to squander it by not talking about it. It is the costly setting of my priceless testimony of His love and faithfulness, and I am called to wisely steward both for His glory.

> And He has said to me, 'My grace is sufficient for you, for power is perfected in weakness.' Most gladly, therefore, I will rather boast about my weaknesses, so that the power of Christ may dwell in me. (2 Cor. 12:9)

Like Paul, I will continue talking about it, boasting about it even, so that the power of Christ may dwell in me, that I may increasingly experience the "omnipotence of dependence."

I will continue to talk about it to remind others and myself of His never-failing faithfulness. I talk about my weakness and His strength to encourage other weary sojourners traveling painful paths. But also because I've learned as I testify to His proven faithfulness in my life, I am reminded afresh of all He has done, and personally spurred to fruitfully press on in perseverance.

> But encourage one another day after day, as long as it is [still] called "Today," so that none of you will be hardened by the deceitfulness of sin. (Heb. 3:13)

I'm still talking about it because I'm still experiencing it, and I want to remind myself and others that it and all the other sorrows and weaknesses of this world are temporary. There is a coming day, in just a little while, when all will be made right, and every sin, sorrow, and weakness will eventually and finally be done away with.

> Therefore, do not throw away your confidence, which has a great reward. For you have need of endurance, so that when you have done the will of God, you may receive what was promised. FOR YET IN A VERY LITTLE WHILE, HE WHO IS COMING WILL COME, AND WILL NOT DELAY. (Heb. 10:35-37)

I'm still talking about it because my life is continuing to be transformed by God through it.

> Therefore we do not lose heart, but though our outer man is decaying, yet our inner man is being renewed day by day. For momentary, light affliction is producing for us an eternal weight of glory far beyond all comparison (2 Cor. 4:16-17)

With certainty, I will continue to talk about it for the remainder of my earthly days because my hope is fixed completely on the grace to be brought to me at the revelation of Jesus Christ and I am eagerly waiting with great anticipation for it.

> For the Lord Himself will descend from heaven with a shout, with the voice of [the] archangel and with the trumpet of God, and the dead in Christ will rise first. Then we who are alive and remain will be caught up together with them in the clouds to meet the Lord in the air, and so we shall always be with the Lord. Therefore comfort one another with these words. (1 Thess. 4:16-18)

And after that, praise God, as I continue to give thanks to Him—I will be joyfully and exuberantly singing about it for all of eternity.

> You have turned for me my mourning into dancing; You have loosed my sackcloth and girded me with gladness, That [my] soul may sing

praise to You and not be silent. O LORD my God, I will give thanks to You forever. (Ps. 30:11-12)

Come, Lord Jesus.

be brave.

---

1. Maclaren, Alexander. "Strengthened with Might (Ephesians 3:16)." *Blue Letter Bible*, blueletterbible.org/comm/maclaren_alexander/expositions-of-holy-scripture/ephesians/strengthened-with-might.cfm

SEVENTH YEAR SABBATH

MARCH 29, 2024

The moment we hear the incomprehensible words that our child has died we instantly recognize the devastation as catastrophic. But in the weeks, months, and years that follow we are involuntarily tasked with discovering the many detailed and varied points of impact. Each sharp pain or deep sorrow is another point in our mapping out the borders of the cavernous crater of our child's absence. In the process, we are not simply marking out the edges of destruction, we are also painfully reconciling the devastation with what remains. And for followers of Christ, we are reconciling both the devastation and what remains with our faith.

I did not knowingly recognize and accept this task as described but I almost immediately began performing the task because my family's and my meaningful survival necessitated it. Countless daunting questions, struggles, challenges, and experiences, each a treacherous jagged point along the edge of her absence. "What if?" and "If only" staggered my first steps, followed by a relentless onslaught of menacing questions about grief, joy, despair, peace, hope, relationships, forgiveness, loneliness, and healing, just to name a few.

There was a necessary and near-constant striving in my grief. I needed to prayerfully understand where and who I was personally, and where and who we were as a family in the aftermath—no simple task in such cataclysmic circumstances. And even more importantly, because my faith is central to who I am, I needed to reconcile everything that had happened and was happening with my faith. I needed to vigilantly test every question, feeling, thought, circumstance, and belief against Scripture to ensure I was clinging to truth.

Days of striving turned to weeks, weeks to months, and eventually, months turned to years of painstakingly navigating life around the perimeter of her absence. Year after year unavoidably circling the crater identifying, understanding, and reconciling each formidable point of impact. Each year painfully traversing points previously explored while discovering jagged new points interspersed along the way. But, thankfully, each successive year was marked by fewer and fewer discoveries of excruciating new points.

This past Christmas, our seventh without Sarah, I began pondering the biblical significance of "seven." Seven in Scripture is most often associated with completion or fullness, and in that vein often with a period of rest after completion: six days of work and sabbath rest, six years of working land followed by a sabbath year of rest for the land, and so on (Ex. 34:21; Lev. 25:4).

I began pondering this idea because as I was painfully missing Sarah in the midst of the holiday traditions it suddenly washed over me that there was a cessation of striving in my grief. Each previous year had been marked by an urgent striving to reconcile one or more painful new experiences or understandings with the truths of scripture, but this year there was an undeniable rest from reconciling. I recognized all the surrounding points of her absence, I intimately knew each of them from the previous six years. I was deeply and sorrowfully missing her as I always will, but there was a stillness in the missing this year, peace and a fullness of rest.

As the difficult days and dates of the seventh year have come and gone, they have further confirmed the striving of the past six years has gradually given way to a sabbath rest of sorts for me in this, the seventh year. Not a rest from missing her, longing for her presence, or feeling the many pains of her absence, but a rest from striving to reconcile the devastation with that which remains, and both with my faith.

As I cast my eyes across the countless points along the crater's edge, each painful point is a reminder of God's faithfulness to comfort, carry, teach, sustain, strengthen, guide, and redeem. I see the point where He taught me sorrow and joy coexist and I once again feel the refreshing flood of peace that lesson brought. I tearfully give thanks as I see the point where He taught me the sorrow of missing Sarah will last for the remainder of my earthly days, but that He will redemptively and powerfully use it to fix my eyes on the eternal, enabling me to live more urgently and fruitfully for Him. I gaze across the many other points and my heart is overwhelmed within me as I consider His faithfulness and long-suffering love.

I shift my focus back to that very first point of impact, the point where Scott told me Sarah was gone; that sacred point where God immediately whispered to my heart that Satan had asked to sift us, and most importantly, where He simultaneously reassured me if we would cling to Him He would carry us through. In His infinite faithfulness, compassion, mercy, and grace He has lovingly done just that. Upholding us by His righteous right hand, He has guided every step, caught every tear, and stilled every fear. And His Word promises He will continue to do so for the remainder of our journey home. Home, where *"in just a little while"* I will see Him face to face, and my sweet Sarah with Him (Heb. 10:37 NIV).

Resting by the edge of her absence this Good Friday morning, my soul is quieted by His love as sorrow and joy mingle once again. As I celebrate the reality of resurrection Sunday, gratitude and praise well within me. And as I consider that glorious resurrection dawning yet to come, I rejoice in Him and His hope set before me—greatly rejoice with joy rendered by sorrow so pure and precious that it is "inexpressible and full of glory" (1 Pet. 1:8).

Come, Lord Jesus.

So then, there remains a Sabbath rest for the people of God, for whoever has entered God's rest has also rested from his works as God did from his. Let us therefore strive to enter that rest, so that no one may fall by the same sort of disobedience. For the word of God is living and active, sharper than any two-edged sword, piercing to the division of soul and of spirit, of joints and of marrow, and discerning the thoughts and intentions of the heart. And no creature is hidden from his sight, but all are naked and exposed to the eyes of him to whom we must give account. Since then we have a great high priest who has passed through the heavens, Jesus, the Son of God, let us hold fast our confession. For we do not have a high priest who is unable to sympathize with our weaknesses, but one who in every respect has been tempted as we are, yet without sin. Let us then with confidence draw near to the throne of grace, that we may receive mercy and find grace to help in time of need. (Heb. 4:9-16 ESV)

there are far better things AHEAD than what we LEAVE BEHIND

— CS Lewis —

SARAH LAUREN HARMENING

DECEMBER 20, 1999 - JUNE 8, 2017

Sarah Lauren Harmening is her family's most extraordinary surprise Christmas gift, second only to Christ Jesus himself. She radiantly embodied innocence, purity, and joy. Her precious innocent spirit loved to frolic in the fictional stories of bygone eras, her very favorite being that of *Little Women* by Louisa May Alcott.

Her purity was exemplified on earth through her rich and pure love for her family and friends, but most of all her unpolluted, unwavering, and relentless love for Jesus Christ, her personal Lord and Savior. She lived and breathed to know Him and to make Him known. Her family is blessed by her prolific journaling, chronicling a heart in passionate pursuit of Him.

Sarah daily spent prolonged periods of time on the screened porch overlooking the trees, basking in His presence through His Word and prayer. She lifted her prayers and songs aloud to Him, mistakenly assuming those on the inside were unable to hear, thus blessing them with her sweet music to Him that now echoes in their broken hearts.

Sarah was on a mission to Botswana to share the love of Christ with whoever God assigned to her, but she was specifically looking forward to sharing Him with children. When others expressed concern about her going so very far from home, she quickly responded full of faith, "I have prayed and I know God has called me to it, so whatever happens is within His will."

At lunch the day before she went home to our Lord and Savior, she was discussing the faith of our persecuted brothers and sisters in Egypt after the most recent mass martyring. She recalled reading the entirety of *Jesus Freaks* by DC Talk, and how profoundly that impacted her. She said she used to worry that she would not have the courage to stand for Him like the martyrs in the book, but she finally understood it is Him who enabled them to stand, and He would do so for her as well.

Sweet Sarah took that final stand of fearless faith and surrender as she once again journaled out of the overflow of a heart surrendered to our heavenly Father and Lord Jesus Christ only moments before she stood in His presence. And she was, indeed, found faithful as she took her rank among those who previously inspired her so.

well done

"There are many Beths in the world, shy and quiet, sitting in corners till needed, and living for others so cheerfully that no one sees the sacrifices till the little cricket on the hearth stops chirping and the sweet, sunshiny presence vanishes, leaving silence and shadow behind."

—Louisa May Alcott

she had a LIVELY, PLAYFUL *disposition* WHICH DELIGHTED IN ANYTHING *ridiculous*

—Jane Austen

TOPICAL INDEX

UNDERSTANDING & NAVIGATING GRIEF

1. Sorrows Like Sea Billows (pp. 7-9)
2. Waves of Agony and Grace (pp. 15-18)
3. Layers of Grief and Love (pp. 23-25)
4. Heart, Soul, and Mind (pp. 79-81)
5. Broken Hallelujah (pp. 82-85)
6. The Sanitizing of Grief (pp. 86-89)
7. "Faking Fine" in the Midst of Grief? (pp. 141-144)
8. This Thorn of Mine (pp. 148-151)
9. Death's Sting is Right Here, Right Now (pp. 165-168)
10. The Hypocrisy of Grief (pp. 205-209)
11. Sorrow Looks Back (pp. 293-296)
12. Grieving Too Long (pp. 320-324)
13. Her Fifth Birthday (pp. 376-378)
14. Long and New Sorrow (pp. 387-389)
15. Her Present Absence (pp. 397-399)
16. Seventh Year Sabbath (pp. 405-408)

HARD QUESTIONS & DECISIONS

1. What If? (pp. 10-14)
2. Another Mission Trip (pp. 32-34)
3. Why Sarah? Why Us? (pp. 35-39)
4. Healing or Adapting? (pp. 48-51)
5. All to Jesus, I Surrender (pp. 76-78)
6. My Child Died. God is Good? (pp. 102-104)
7. When Deliverance Doesn't Come (pp. 158-161)
8. When God is Silent (pp. 162-164)
9. I'm Supposed to be Stoic? (pp. 169-172)
10. Do I Really Believe? (pp. 234-236)
11. Serve Like _____ (pp. 252-255)
12. Keep Crying Out and Testifying (pp. 297-302)
13. Pray Believing (pp. 316-319)
14. Facing Death (pp. 355-359)
15. Still Talking About It (pp. 400-404)

LONELINESS & ABANDONMENT

1. Shelter in the Storm (pp. 72-75)
2. Waiting in Solitude (pp. 90-95)
3. Extracting the Precious (pp. 118-121)
4. Alone, Yet Not Alone (pp. 145-147)
5. Abandonment in Grief (pp. 221-228)
6. Lonely and Afflicted (pp. 245-251)
7. Responding to Abandonment (pp. 273-276)
8. A Stranger With A Friend's Face (pp. 290-292)

SPIRITUAL WARFARE & PERSEVERANCE

1. Swallowed up by Life (pp. 29-31)
2. Waiting in the Pit (pp. 46-47)

TOPICAL INDEX

   3. "How Awesome Is That?" (pp. 56-59)
   4. The "Little Cricket" Martyr (pp. 60-64)
   5. Sowing in Tears (pp. 65-67)
   6. Learning to Walk (pp. 68-71)
   7. Rains of Refreshing (pp. 131-133)
   8. The God of the Valleys (pp. 152-154)
   9. "A Stranger With Thee" (pp. 173-176)
  10. Walking In Darkness (pp. 210-215)
  11. The Voice of the Lord in the Storm (pp. 216-220)
  12. Be of Good Courage (pp. 229-233)
  13. Guilt: Suicide Prevention or Awareness? (pp. 384-386)

HOPE

   1. New Mercy For Today (pp. 43-45)
   2. Longing to Die (pp. 105-109)
   3. Morning is Coming (pp. 134-136)
   4. Taking Hold of Hope (pp. 155-157)
   5. Soul Melting Sorrow (pp. 182-188)
   6. Hope Fixed Completely (pp. 194-198)
   7. Steadfast (pp. 237-241)
   8. Just Keep Trying (pp. 283-286)
   9. In Just a Little While (pp. 287-289)
  10. A Sword Pierced Soul (pp. 303-305)
  11. Worship in Affliction (pp. 325-327)
  12. Eagerly Waiting (pp. 331-334)
  13. Hope Against Hope (pp. 335-338)
  14. Peace Be With You (pp. 348-354)
  15. Hope Grieves (pp. 363-366)

REDEMPTION

   1. Suffering, Anguish and Redemption (pp. 1-6)
   2. The Hezekiah Years (pp. 19-22)

3. Death is Not Good (pp. 40-42)
4. The Stewardship of Pain (pp. 98-101)
5. Redeem My Pain, O God (pp. 137-140)
6. Fellow Partakers (pp. 277-282)
7. Comforted and Comforting (pp. 313-315)
8. Blessed Mourner (pp. 360-362)
9. Nestless (pp. 369-372)
10. A New Song (pp. 373-375)

UNDERSTANDING & FINDING JOY

1. "Restore To Me" (pp. 26-28)
2. Intermingled Joy and Suffering (pp. 52-55)
3. Sorrowful Yet Always Rejoicing (pp. 96-97)
4. Laughter in the Valley (pp. 126-130)
5. Why I Won't Say "Choose Joy" (pp. 199-204)
6. The Lines Have Fallen for Me (pp. 242-244)
7. Sunshine Christianity & Forbidden Lament (pp. 259-261)
8. Joy Inexpressible (pp. 345-347)
9. Five Years: Beauty For Ashes (pp. 379-383)
10. Seventh Year Sabbath (pp. 405-408)

HARD DAYS & DATES

Birthdays:

1. A Mother's Pain (pp. 115-117)
2. Steadfast (pp. 237-241)
3. Not a Happy Birthday (pp. 306-308)
4. Hope Grieves (pp. 363-366)
5. Her Fifth Birthday (pp. 376-378)
6. Long and New Sorrow (pp. 387-389)
7. Still Talking About It (pp. 400-404)

TOPICAL INDEX

Holidays:

1. Holidays: Moment by Moment (pp. 122-125)
2. Thanksgiving: Sorrowful Yet Always Rejoicing (pp. 96-97)
3. Christmas: Not so Merry Christmas (pp. 110-114)
4. Christmas: Steadfast (pp. 237-241)
5. Christmas: A Sword Pierced Soul (pp. 303-305)
6. Christmas: Fleeing for Refuge (pp. 309-312)
7. Christmas: Long and New Sorrow (pp. 387-389)
8. Easter: Taking Hold of Hope (pp. 155-157)
9. Easter: Easter in the Shadow (pp. 256-258)
10. Easter: Good Friday and Siblings Day (pp. 328-330)
11. Easter: Eagerly Waiting (pp. 331-334)
12. Easter: The Cup of Salvation (pp. 390-393)

Passing of Time:

1. Two Months: Intermingled Joy and Suffering (pp. 52-55)
2. Nine Months: The God of the Valleys (pp. 152-154)
3. One Year: The Second Year is Harder? (pp. 177-181)
4. Eighteen Months: Do I Really Believe? (pp. 234-236)
5. Two Years: Child Loss: The Second Year (pp. 262-272)
6. 951 Days: Comforted and Comforting (pp. 313-315)
7. Three Years: Three Years Ago Today (pp. 339-344)
8. Forty Months: Blessed Mourner (pp. 360-362)
9. Five Years: Beauty for Ashes (pp. 379-383)
10. Seven Years: Seventh Year Sabbath (pp. 405-408)

Other:

1. Wedding Anniversary: Remember My Chains (pp. 189-193)
2. Sibling Marriage: Joy Inexpressible (pp. 345-347)
3. Sibling Marriage: Grace Upon Grace (pp. 367-368)
4. Empty Nest: Nestless (pp. 369-372)
5. New Baby: Missing You Today Especially (pp. 394-396)

We read to know we're not alone

C. S. LEWIS

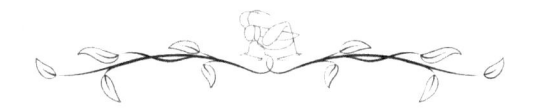

This book was
lovingly made available through

LITTLE CRICKET
— charity —

littlecricket.org